"With extraordinary rigour and imagination, Ba
questions at the intersection of politics and
perspective informed by both admirable philoso
a lively, direct concern with therapeutic practice. ᴜᴜᴜ…
liberal or conservative assumptions that weigh down so much
psychological theory, this is a significant contribution both to
therapeutic literature and to social and political thought."

Jeremy Gilbert, *Professor of Cultural and Political Theory at*
University of East London

"Manu Bazzano's book is a revelation – not revelation as the
therapeutic semblance of sanctimonious religiosity but as the tireless
production of what Walter Benjamin called 'profane illuminations' –
materialist epiphanies which are formed though his struggle with
current political, therapeutic and social injustices. Bazzano derives his
inspiration from orphans and exiles, authors without parents, poets
without patrons, artists and philosophers without 'tradition'. He
follows them in their attempt to challenge the political, social and
therapeutic fields by ruthlessly criticising and exposing all that is
corrupt, conservative, and decaying in our world. He demands nothing
less than our wholehearted commitment to the active, life-affirming
force of desire and its emancipatory potential. For Bazzano, this
commitment leads to the production of new (counter-) fantasies which
will reinvigorate the transformative power of radical imagination in
our fight against the forces of patriarchy, capitalism, and neoliberalism. If the battle cry of May '68 was to 'see the beach beneath
the street', today's battle cry should be to 'see the constellation of stars
beyond the clouds' of neoliberal apathy and despair."

Anastasios Gaitanidis, PhD, *Relational Psychoanalyst and Visiting*
Professor at Regent's University London

"In this stimulating and provocative work, we are invited to reject the
neo-liberal orthodoxies that dominate our lives and constrain understanding of what it means to be human. Bazzano's view – expressed
through thoughtful analysis of a variety of texts and perspectives from
Ovid through to modern critical thinkers such as Judith Butler – has
huge implications, including for psychology, here presented as bound
by a 'myopic' emphasis on subjectivity. This narrow focus distracts us

from direct engagement with the 'flow of neutral, inherently trans-formative desire' with which we rarely engage, preferring instead to give attention to the clamour of feelings and emotions that constitute the dominant terrain of modern psychotherapy."

Judy Moore, *Former Director of Counselling, University of East Anglia and Co-editor of* Senses of Focusing

"Manu Bazzano is fearlessly human and a brilliant mischief maker. His embrace of the outcast other, and what this act holds for what each of us can become, is both radical and loving. Spend time with even one page of his writing and you will be rewarded. However, a warning: If you don't want to think or be inspired to grow or connect more fully with your own humanity, don't buy this book."

Brian E. Levitt, *Author of* Questioning Psychology: Beyond Theory and Control

Subversion and Desire

This book presents the importance of subversion in psychotherapy and revaluates the positive role of desire as an integrating force in the individual and collective psyche.

The text provides a solid philosophical frame which helps to expand the scope of contemporary psychotherapy at a time when it is being curtailed by a reductionist neoliberal zeitgeist. The latter emphasizes cognition over motivation, behaviour over emotion, consciousness over the unconscious, the self over the organism, and tends to reframe psychotherapeutic practice as a reprogramming of individuals. In response, this book outlines concerted acts of "soft subversion" which can undermine the status quo and open new possibilities of individual and collective transformation. The author also retraces and reassesses some of the more inspiringly subversive legacies in psychoanalysis, with a view to sketching a life-affirming psychology wedded to broadminded political engagement.

Covering psychotherapy, politics, art and literature, and social and cultural theory, this book will appeal to anyone interested in understanding how psychotherapy and philosophy can be more radical and subversive endeavours.

Manu Bazzano, PhD, is a writer, psychotherapist/supervisor and visiting lecturer at various colleges and universities around the world. His background is philosophy and rock music. His work is informed by his lifelong practice of Zen and more recently Butoh, and by his love of art and literature. He holds a PhD in Philosophy from the University of Roehampton. Website: www.manubazzano.com

Subversion and Desire

Pathways to Transindividuation

Manu Bazzano

Routledge
Taylor & Francis Group

LONDON AND NEW YORK

Designed cover image: © Getty Images

First published 2023
by Routledge
4 Park Square, Milton Park, Abingdon, Oxon OX14 4RN

and by Routledge
605 Third Avenue, New York, NY 10158

*Routledge is an imprint of the Taylor & Francis Group, an informa
business*

British Library Cataloguing-in-Publication Data
A catalogue record for this book is available from the British
Library

ISBN: 978-1-032-24823-3 (hbk)
ISBN: 978-1-032-24822-6 (pbk)
ISBN: 978-1-003-28026-2 (ebk)

DOI: 10.4324/9781003280262

Typeset in Times New Roman
by MPS Limited, Dehradun

To Richard Pearce (1944–2021).

In Memoriam

Contents

Also by Manu Bazzano

Books

Zen Poems
Haiku for Lovers
Buddha Is Dead: Nietzsche and the Dawn of European Zen
The Speed of Angels
Spectre of the Stranger: Towards a Phenomenology of Hospitality
After Mindfulness: New Perspectives on Psychology and Meditation
Therapy and the Counter-Tradition (with Julie Webb)
Zen and Therapy: Heretical Perspectives
Re-visionining Person-Centred Therapy: Theory and Practice of a Radical Paradigm
Nietzsche and Psychotherapy
Re-visioning Existential Therapy: Counter-traditional Perspectives

Music Albums

Walk Inside the Painting (with Daedalo)
Naked Dance
Sex, Religion, and Cosmetics

Acknowledgements

I am greatly indebted to Julie Webb – friend, co-conspirator, tracing the arc of a passing thought crossing this heart-mind before I myself catch it, let alone commit it to paper. Her comments, suggestions, critique, and overall encouragement were vital, helping me bring this work to completion through hard times.

There are many friends, fellow travellers, and comrades whose love, support, and the willingness to indulge my fugues and forays make them truly precious to me. They remind me that philosophy is born in friendship: Susie May, Hugh Knopf, Toby Bull, John Davis, Anastasios Gaitanidis, Cristina Chicos, Dàniel Ványi, Brian Levitt, Georgeta Niculescu, Subhaga Gaetano Failla, Claudio Rud, Kerime Kadilar, Ivan Limas, Del Loewenthal, Richard House, Leonore Langner, and many others.

I am grateful to the participants of the independent courses I taught in London Waterloo over the last few years, and to the members of our London Zen community.

To those who created challenges over the last two years – whether out of enmity, spite, or pure misunderstanding: thank you.

To those institutions and professional bodies whose understanding of ethics aligns with the *malleus maleficarum*, and who foolishly believe they hold the monopoly on what constitutes psychotherapy theory and practice: thank you. You are my teachers, reminding me of what is to be avoided. Your narrow-minded and censorious ways spur me on to find new pathways outside the beaten tracks.

Sarita Doveton, artist, dancer, healer; lifelong companion who continues to inspire me with her unassuming, profound compassion and wisdom: thank you.

I am grateful to the editors of the Journals and magazines which published different versions of some of the chapters in the book, including Self & Society, European Journal of Psychotherapy and Counselling, Hermeneutic Circular, PCEP, Existential Analysis, and Articoli Liberi.

Introduction

The idea for this book emerged during a one-week holiday on the Greek island of Kefalonia in September 2018. It was to be about Ovid, transformation, and psychotherapy. That was the plan. The gods must be laughing at yet another failed human project. For I have failed, again, and if I failed better is for the reader to decide. I did manage *one* chapter on Ovid, and I'm glad about that. The book did take a life of its own, as the cliché has it, and I'm glad about that too. The book ends here, in a London flat where we lived for the past 13 years. It's a September day, and isn't that *uncanny* (that lovely word of now common use whose unsettling implications have been ejected from contemporary discourse)?

It is now, uncannily, a September day, four years after swimming in those cherished Mediterranean waters, and I find myself in a very different situation. One of the many things that happened is a cancer diagnosis. This meant the second half of the book was written while undergoing treatment. The gods are laughing again, and on a good day I join in. On a good day, tears, if they come up, become tears of joy. Life goes on, impelled by nonlife. Lifedeath/deathlife carries on, and in my arrogance I decided long ago to be its accomplice. I foolishly believe that at the tail end of every strong feeling or emotion there is joy. I remain incurably Spinozian. And Nietzschean too, out of the stirrings of an ancient love for tragedy – in the now interred meaning of joy as tragic joy, a joy disdainfully opposed to the desublimated glee of gourmand pleasure-seeking in air-conditioned lounges and dungeons.

The pain and joy and overwhelming desire to cut through the pretensions of established learning and those of my own hardly-earned

DOI: 10.4324/9781003280262-1

knowledge carried the work through. A reverse movement: from the Mediterranean to the mouth of a Greek river, *Maiandros*, giving name to meandering, a commitment to the gallant mission of getting lost, of losing my way as someone struck by love and grief. Wish I had it in me to write a field guide to getting lost, as others did, as others will. Wish I could quantify the value and valence of error and erring, and come out into the reassuring light of noon with an instructive tale of the sort one hears on popular podcasts. All the same, writing this book was a joy, even when the matter at hand at times evoked anger, sadness, and frustration. Even when the matter at hand made me despair for the future of psychotherapy and the humanities, plundered by the all-pervasive stupidity of neoliberal ideology. But even sad matters bring genuine pleasure when paired with the satisfaction of discovery and the excitement of exploration. I hope some readers will be affected by that joy and will feel encouraged to pursue further some of the ideas presented here.

*

I understand the practices of psychoanalysis and psychotherapy as being part of the same continuum and as such the two terms are used intermittently in the book.

Subversion implies questioning the canon in some of its unquestionable tenets, to challenge and problematize them. To actively doubt a canonical theme invariably means disrupting things with the aim of looking afresh at the foundations of a particular discipline. I confess to harbouring the rather naïve belief that there were and still are subversive aspects to psychotherapy. I admit to holding the view that anything deemed inconvenient and subversive has been duly ejected from psychotherapeutic practices. Given that these still hover in some shape or form, one of the intentions behind the present work is an attempt at retrieving and re-evaluating them. A starting point in this investigation may then be the way in which the therapist/analyst tends to respond to the complexity and ambivalence of the psyche. Normally, we find it hard to acknowledge (let alone learn from) the spontaneous suppleness of psychic life. Faced with its inherent multiplicity, we either elect the knee-jerk reaction of policing/pathologizing it, or choose instead the more sombre response of moulding psyche within a simplistic, unitary logic – for instance, by defining experience within the confines of an identity and/or character. At the same time, the very existence and persistence of our strange profession may indicate that things are not as clear-cut, nor as certain and solid as we would like them to be. Mainstream psychotherapy may be currently pursuing a positivist agenda of regulation and control of psychical life, yet not everyone is eager to be fixed so they can join the waiting-for-Godot queue in the shopping mall. Many continue to seek a space where ambivalence, deep uncertainty, and discomfort may be examined, and where one's life may be contested. Seen in this way, *subversion* ("turning from below") means questioning some of the tenets of the philosophical and psychotherapeutic tradition, particularly those held to be unassailable and which stultify theory and practice.

As for *desire*, this is understood as a generative, liberating force traversing individuals and collectivities, a political force able to produce new assemblages, dissemble stale clusters of power and prejudice, and create the future. In the life of an individual, desire manifests as an amalgamating force which does not wait for the wounds to be healed before one can begin to live, love, and participate in the collective life. As with Spinoza's *natura naturans* and Nietzsche's *will to power*, desire is not craving, nor is it based on lack. As for transindividuation, this was a new finding which – uncanningly – dictated itself to me in the last month of writing. It is discussed in the last chapter and in some way has come to represent the direction towards which the entire exploration is heading. This exploration has only just begun. I hope it will continue. And if it won't be me doing it, I am certain others will.

London, 30 September 2022

Chapter 1

Player of Tender Loves

Like many of us, Ovid too feels obliged to ascribe causes and origins to life and the world and to pay homage to the metaphysics of his time. But the subject in the opening sentence of his magnum opus *Metamorphoses* – written between 2 BC and 17 CE – is *animus*, often piously translated as "soul", but whose meaning is closer to "fancy" or "inspiration": my fancy, he says, makes me tell of bodies changed into new shapes. Poetic fancy creates.

He too bows to some degree of order and to the internal injunction to measure and quantify, though he never does so as doggedly as Robert McNamara or your average dealer in neoliberal academic psychology. Ovid yields to the gods all the same, plaiting a metaphysical crossword, borrowing right, left, and centre from other poets/philosophers, starting with the heathen Homeric trinity of the sea, earth, and sky, then glancing back, by blending Hesiod's *void* with Lucretius' *space*, at what most cosmogonies sneeringly call "chaos", the alleged amorphous whirl before the cartoonish fiat of manly light, preamble to law, order, and all things patrolled.

The conventional view, embraced by Ovid, places chaos at the "beginning": everything fluctuates, there is no discernible form; there is (horror of horrors!) no ground for any one *thing* to stand on; no light in the sky, no swimmable sea. Everything is but an unvarying mass of matter with no distinction between hard and soft, hot and cold, wet and dry. Then, lo and behold, *natus homo est*: humanity is born, and with humanity the *pathos* (i.e., the suffering and grief) of love, for which there may be no cure. Medea is a case in point. Tragic heroine, foreigner, sorceress, and filicide in Euripides' tragedy,

DOI: 10.4324/9781003280262-2

in Ovid's account (*Metamorphoses*, VII) this native of Colchis, a town on the same Black Sea where Ovid is exiled, she is above all a lovesick young woman whose own reaction towards a bewildering emotion becomes the prototype for the poet's many examples of women (and men) in love. It is hard to resist the insinuation that love may well be the root cause of all those magnificent monsters which threaten and enrich our life. It chimes with Proust, for whom sexual love constitutes the very ground on which all the powerful feelings and emotions – these geological upheavals of thought – tend to breed. I do not know whether the inherent intelligence of emotions is the pathway to greater insight. That may be so, but in Ovid at least it seems the road of excess does not lead to the palace of wisdom – at least not the timid, moralizing wisdom-while-u-wait found in current psychotherapy culture. In the case of Orpheus, in Book X of *Metamorphoses*, what may be generically construed as "wisdom" emerges as the victuals of sorrow, troubled thought and tears, with the Ur-poet sitting by the river Styx, having lost his beloved Eurydice twice and the ferryman fending him off.

There are many reasons for liking Ovid. He had fallen out of favour with the emperor because his widely popular erotic poems were not attuned to Augustus' moralizing task. What's more, his disinclination to be the laureate of compliance, versifier and epic bearer of the Roman Empire's grandiose edifying mission did not amuse the emperor who in 8 AD relegated him from Rome to Tomis (now Constanţa, a Romanian city on the Black Sea). Ovid is the poet of love and exile, the two spiritual engines forever dislodging the self from metastable homeland and belonging.

Interpretations differ. Contemporary readers Jia Tolentino, Mary Beard, and others[1] see power, violence, and rape at the very centre of the *Metamorphoses*, possibly implying masculinist connivance. While it is true that violence and intensity tend to crowd Ovid's tales, a reading which took these themes at face value without looking at the central and most remarkable aspect of the *Metamorphoses* would be partial at best and at worst sensationalist. The most remarkable aspect of the *Metamorphoses* is Ovid's unusual view of what we commonly call "madness". I am no classicist or literary critic. My "field" happens to be psychotherapy. I am therefore fated to speak from a place where fear of madness hovers in more overt and concerted guise than it habitually does in other human interactions. And whenever Ovid writes of humans and demigods alike edging close to the treacherous point of no return, the threshold of an immanent beyond, to me his verses ring (painfully, delightfully) true. What do I mean by "point of no return?" And how carefully must I tread? Firstly, because I know I may be coming to that threshold myself at times. How can I or anyone be immune to the danger of madness unless we streamline our inherent fragility? True, the real and present danger that practitioners of the *psych arts* may be at times prone to "losing it" has been suitably, even officially, recognized: the formal acknowledgement bears an attractive label: the "wounded healer", a phenomenon duly examined in endless books, articles and seminars and diligently recycled by regiments of therapy trainees. It has, in other words, become canonized and, as such, its subversive valence is largely neutered.

Secondly, Levinas alerts us to the violence implicit in notions of mystical rupture, divine revelation, and possession by a numinous force.[2] Like readers of the *Metamorphoses* schooled in the good manners of the tradition or influenced by Disney, Pixar, Dickens, and other moralizing narratives, client and therapist alike wish for some form of redemption or a happy ending to their psychical meandering. But Ovid does not resort to easy redemption, as the tradition before him did: consider Achilles' encounter with Priam in the *Iliad* or Juno's reconciliatory meeting with Jupiter in the *Aeneid*. Instead, at the end of the *Metamorphoses*, the reader is still left with the feeling that chaos will resurface unheeded. Similarly, unless we understand therapy as the task of sending clients back to their reserved seats in the traffic jam or to a narcotic and compliant mindset within a thoroughly unjust world, there won't be happy endings in therapy either, but instead the opening onto a crisis that may bring about transformation.

Everything is subject to change, Ovid tells us, except change itself. Unlike his own contemporaries and the Greeks before him, Ovid did not see madness as belonging to a separate domain from the everyday (whether banished outside the city walls or, mythically, allotted to a particular deity – Lyssa, for instance, goddess of blind fury – or to a particular hero/demigod such as Achilles, whose wrath was as legendary as it was infamous). Instead, Ovid presents madness as pervasive, integral to the universe.[3] It pervades his words; it invites the reader to contemplate that point of no return, the dangerous threshold beyond which, possessed by passion, we self-combust, hovering, gliding, and shape-shifting: passion – described not with clinical neutrality but from the viewpoint of convulsion. In Ovid, every lover falls prey to Narcissus's error, Laplanche reminds us. There is a "narcissistic element in every love relation", a Platonist undercurrent to daydream the "self-sufficiency of perfect love".[4]

Ovid sees a direct link between passion and what we commonly call madness. Implied by the root word *pathos*, origin of both passion and pathology, this link ought to be of interest to those who are said to explore the vagaries and vicissitudes of human experience – when they are not caught up, that is, within the tentacles of neoliberal stupidity. In that sense too Ovid is an inspiration, for he dared resist what was expected of him. He did not succumb, like Virgil before him (despite the poignant beauty of the latter's poetry), to becoming a court poet, obedient to the dominant ideology of his time.

His erotic/elegiac poems – collected in *Amores* and *Ars Amatoria*[5] – are as far removed from the official Roman poetry of Empire as one can imagine. With their preference of *otium* over *negotium* – of leisure and ingenious idleness over self-improvement, striving and military conquest – they ring a quietly subversive tone, daintily mocking the loud-mouthed coarseness of pursuing wealth and power. With their witty, shrewd advice to men and women alike on pursuing love and pleasure from other men's wives, husbands, and concubines alike, they graciously deride the imperial anti-adultery laws and the moral tenets on the rightful conduct of the Roman citizen, husband, and father. It is no coincidence that both Boccaccio and Chaucer turned to Ovid for inspiration.

It is remarkable that Ovid succeeds in weaving his imaginative erotic landscapes against this backdrop of prudery and coercion, and in celebrating Cupid's enticing, whimsical, and insistent powers. The latter are all the stronger when measured not only against imperial law, but against the mock-mastery of a narrator self-styled as *magister amoris* who tries to enforce a rational system of control (*ratio*) over passion (*impetus*), only to have his introjected name-of-the-Father routinely thrashed by the boy-god. In a stance that presents parallels with the cosmogony later depicted in his *Metamorphoses*, Ovid seems to suggest, without quite endorsing the view, that in eternal battle between chaos and order, chaos wins in the end. As the latest and greatest of all elegists, he resists the moralizing imperatives of standard epic poetry and the servile deference of official political philosophy, refusing to bow to the anthropomorphic ideal of a fully rationalized and beautified human being who has narcissistically convinced himself to have conquered the daimonic. Then as now, a genuine artist or poet is a friend of the devil, and cannot be contented with singing the praises of the dull and dreary ideal of a fully ther-apized, fully-functioning and fully-compliant human being. Ovid's instinctive allegiance is with the natural forces that traverse as well as constitute the human, those forces disparagingly referred to as "chaos" out of fear and inability to exert mastery over them. What is conveniently forgotten or bypassed in bimillennial religious and philosophical dominant narratives (including Judaeo-Christianity) is the *self-generative* and creative attributes of chaos which do not require the fiat of creation or the ordering activity of light.[6]

In *Remedia Amoris* (Cures for Love), the sequel to his *Ars Amatoria*, the poet/*magister amoris* does his best to deal with the unpredictable fire of passion. He is not waging war against Cupid, he tells the boy-god, but only trying to save a few lost souls from utter despair and self-destruction. Sounding at times as overconfident as a contemporary cognitive-behavioural therapist or as zealously super-ficial as an advocate of positive psychology, he swears to have crafted an infallible method for healing the love malady. Soon, however, he concedes that the *impetus* cannot be controlled: we must learn to deal with it. It is pointless, he tells us, to even try to extinguish the fire while it is raging.

There is an intriguing ambivalence in the apparently linear shift from Ovid's erotic poems to his most ambitious work of the *Metamorphoses*. He no longer writes in elegiac couplets but uses instead the hexameter verse of epic poetry. But this is no ordinary epic; it does not follow the vicissitudes of a hero, nor is it constructed around a well-known romance or a teleological narrative of redemption. Here the protago-nists are both multiple and polymorphous: there are many subjects, and each of them undergoing a most radical transformation. The real protagonists of this unusual epic are change and multiplicity. Metamorphosis is of course part of nature – from egg to caterpillar to chrysalis to butterfly and, in humans, from child to adult through old age and death, a process that would be both wondrous and unsettling if we could see it unfolding at a fast pace.

This perspective on death may be tracking a fiercer, more polyvalent stance, more actively accepting of death than Virgil's renowned *pietas*. To sensibilities sedimented during two thousand years of Christianity, this stance is understandably remote. The lyrical melancholy of Virgilian pietas is more readily accessible, not solely because of its poetic beauty but more importantly because we have never *not* been engaged in a dialogue with Virgil, his work heralding the birth of Christian piety. But even Virgil's stance would be problematic to a facile consolatory religiosity. Take for instance the muted splendour found earlier in Aeneid's Book IV: 305–314. Aeneas is in the underworld, and by the river Styx he sees the huddled crowd of the newly dead – mothers, men, sons, and unwed girls among them. There are as many of them as the leaves that fall with the first cold winds in autumn, or the birds who land on southern sunny shores from the sea in winter. Like them, the dead begged to cross the Styx, longingly stretching their hands to the further shore. They do not long for life; they want to become fully dead.[7] Extinction, oblivion and everlasting peace are in stark contrast with the need to be forever preserved in the cocoon of an atomistic soul. But neither peace nor preservation is granted in Ovid's perspective. Instead, constant, unremitting change involving seemingly wanton alterations into an altogether different order of things, from human to flower, animal, lake, tree, or snake. We are already moving away from the edifying wonder of myth or genteel teleological fairy tale to a dimension that borders on horror. But then horror (alongside the monstrous – *monstra* literally meaning "abnormal portents") hints at latent, immanent actualizations present in nature but unavailable to empirical analysis. They are assignable, I suggest, within that dimension which Deleuze calls the *virtual* and Nietzsche the *Dionysian*: the delicate flux of pre-subjective, impersonal natural forces that both prefigure and surpass what we normally call individuality. Seen from the perspective of the atomistic subject, at a hypothetical high speed and high resolution, this dimension is horrific. From the point of view of the atomistic self, transformation belongs to the domain of horror, which coincides, incidentally, with the dimension of *power*, not the miserable craving for domination over others, but as deep trust in the actuality and directionality of natural forces. Fear of transformation is fear of true power, understood with Nietzsche as the desire of a living thing to express its strength and venture beyond self-preservation.

Resistance to transformation, endemic in the political and psychological culture of the last humans, is essentially one's inability to keep to the advance of active forces. We prefer instead genteel positive change and invariably choose therapeutic practices which recoil from transformation and provide instead palliative, narcotic consolation to our alienated existence.

The classic world did of course cast a probing glance at tales of transformation before; my understanding is that, unlike Ovid, it rarely did so without supplying a ready-made teleology of redemption and/or moral narratives of reward and punishment which sedated somewhat their unsettling power. Even the ancient horror story of Medea's cousin, Circe, expert illusionist, goddess of sorcery (*pharmakeia*), transmutation, and necromancy, has often been read as a cautionary tale against drunkenness and as one more exemplary instance of Odysseus' probity and prowess, prototype of the objective scientist/explorer who was to rule the waves in centuries to come. This is the essentially ascetic ideal of the man who is above the vagaries of passion and a risky sensuous perception of the world – able to denigrate life and get handsomely rewarded for it. My own personal reading of Circe, parallel to some interpretations found in contemporary fiction,[8] is of awe and admiration of her extraordinary powers. I marvel at the sheer panache in venting her craft and at her ability to use as self-protection against intruders.

Tales of transformations are few and far between in Greek literature from the days of Homer onwards. They are mainly portrayed as godly deeds performed for human advantage. Ovid chooses a different angle, suspending the popular compulsion to construct moralizing tales.

Ovid is an exiled poet who continues to appeal to exiled poets or writers/artists whose homeland is not a spiritual home. Joyce's epigraph of his *Portrait of the Artist* is taken from Book VIII of *Metamorphoses*, praising the writers mind's application to unknown arts. Pound mentions him too from his confused and controversial exile from the US, and so does Osip Mandelstam, "a Jew in an anti-Semitic Russia, a non-practicing Jew among the observant, a Russian born in Warsaw … and later an exile who spent much of his life abroad".[9] All three saw themselves in Ovid, the exile par excellence, the victim of a brutal, narrow-minded and ignorant imperial power. At the time of the rise of fascism in Europe in the 1930s, others saw him as an anti-nationalist who could provide a more inspiring historical and literary paradigm than Virgil's, irremediably consigned, despite his lyricism and poignant awareness of the tears of things, to be forever associated with empire. In Ovid, the "private" life of the passions, searched in countless manifestations, takes on an uncanningly subversive character, as if in its more dramatic expression as factual metamorphoses, affirmation of flux alone destabilizes a static version of being on which institutional power is found. Free-spirited and unmeasured at first, then in turn vivacious, mournful, drunken, reflective, and finally enraptured in serene contemplation of beauty, each of Benjamin Britten's *Six Metamorphoses after Ovid* conveys a naturalistic movement as unshackled by the demands of convention as Ovid's poetry itself.

Ovid died an exile in an area whose present name is Dobruja, Romania. It is touching to see him occupying a special place – "the country's tutelary genius" and even "its first national poet"[10] – in a country which is currently stigmatized by fatuous leaders busy protecting the borders of their own ignorance and prejudice against migrants. It is equally poignant to find that there exists an entire tradition of Romanian Ovidianism going back three centuries. From a place of exile, the homeland looks like a sweet melodious place of love and joy, but an unbroken literary tradition across the centuries speculates on Ovid's fictional and calamitous return to Rome, where he finds much greater misfortune than what he experienced during his life in Tumis. For dominant narratives within the philosophical and religious traditions before and after Ovid, exile, like nomadism, is a curse and a punishment. In Latin literature, from Virgil to Ennius, exile (*exilium*) is often explicitly likened to death (referred to as *exitium*), the two words linked by a notion of *ex*clusion and *ex*it that is also related to the thrownness and existential solitude of *ex*istence present in existentialism as a counter-philosophy. Ovid himself refers to his banishment from Rome as a living death and to the day of departure as a funeral.

According to traditional narratives, allegiance to a notion of identity and its usual props (integration, belonging, as well as loyalty to a particular deity and/or governing worldview, whether religious or secular, alone deemed to be true) is the sole assurance for attaining prosperity, happiness and the bourgeois ideal of mental health. It is only by accident or fate that we are at all allowed an admittedly difficult foray into some unknown, peopled with monsters and sorcerers, and on condition that we eventually return to the Ithaca of identity and sing along to the anthems of our home turf. This is not only sold as a desirable condition; it is the only one permitted. High-minded notions of universalism, relatedness and harmonious interdependence, normally summoned to counterbalance the innate provincialism of identity, do not constitute credible alternatives because they are part and parcel of the very same insidious dominant narrative. Universalism is the main export product of the imperialist's self-same identity.

The ancestral home looks idyllic when contemplated from afar. Factual homecoming may turn out to be disastrous. In his own oneiric variation on the apocryphal medieval theme of Ovid's return to Rome, Antonio Tabucchi[11] imagines the exile poet dreaming on a winter night of having become Augustus' favourite poet. A twist of fate (or a miracle of the gods) meant that the poet of metamorphoses has himself turned into a different being, a giant butterfly with yellow and blue wings and enormous eyes. He arrives triumphantly on a golden chariot pulled by six white horses. But he can't stand up, for his legs are too thin under the weight of his enormous wings. He is forced to recline on cushions, his feet kicking in the air, in a picture reminiscent of Kafka's own famous tale of transformation. The cheering crowds mistake him for an Asian deity. When he desperately tries to tell them that he is Ovid, the poet of love and exile, his voice is but a faint shrill. He finally makes it to the palace where Augustus invites him to read the smart and witty verses composed for the occasion. Fearing that only a screech will come out of him, Ovid decides to convey his poetry through movement, gently fluttering his majestic wings in a graceful dance. The emperor, a bundle of uncouth and defensive manliness, is visibly offended by the effeminate display and as insulted by the tender sexuality emanating by the butterfly/ poet's dance as he once had been by Ovid's writings on the art of love. He claps his hands and commands the praetorian guards to cut off his wings which fall on the ground like light feathers. Defiantly, with a sudden movement the poet/butterfly turns around and on unsteady legs makes it to the palace terrace from where he sees a vicious crowd below demanding to rip him to pieces. The dream ends with the vulnerable poet/butterfly's final act of freedom: a spontaneous, defiant dance step down the stairway which reasserts that very same gentleness that so insulted Augustus. Not only is poetry of his kind stronger than might; it also grants immortality, he tells us, more than the vulgar, pompous monuments and tombs of rulers or the statues of slave-traders and colonial rulers ever will.

John F. Miller[12] details the medieval legend, adopted by Boccaccio among others, according to which Ovid did eventually return to Rome and was crushed to death by an adoring crowd eager to see closely the literary celebrity. In Tabucchi's version, his death is no accident, for both emperor and crowd deliberately join forces in destroying the Empire's double enemy, a poet *and* a butterfly. Not only does he fall short of being the manly epic poet of military virtues and imperial officialdom, choosing instead to sing of the pleasures and pains of love, sex, and seduction, of humans going through anguished transmutations. He also dares to show up as a butterfly – *psyche* in Greek, incarnation of an "inner life" whose intricacy alone displaces the merits of political conquest, unveiling them as pointless.

Psyche is also the night moth singed by the candle of desire, eternally in love with Eros, catching sight of him half-asleep in an alcove, tender in his humanity and forgetful of his wings. Both become absorbed in their mutual gaze. Time slows down. They step into a charmed idleness, mother of all things nice – from lyrical poetry to music to philosophy, to attributing intrinsic unadorned value to human life. It was Ovid's talent for honouring playfulness and tenderness in sexual love that made him an enemy of Augustus and it is that very talent he celebrates in his epitaph where he refers to himself as *tenerorum lusor amorum*, the playful poet of tender loves. The exile poet for whom exile is a living death chooses a line of flight that restores him to life through art. It would be a mistake (the great and only error, as Deleuze would say) to think of a line of flight as escapism. Quite the opposite: "to flee is to produce the real, to create life, to find a weapon".[13] In the process, a new language is created.

*

Even though the tender playful loves of *Ars Amatoria* are often replaced in *Metamorphosis* by the deeper pathos of human love, humour and comedy remain present, especially the comedy of the gods in love. This creates a singular alchemy in whose fire a new poetry (and possibly a new language and a new perspective) is forged. To remain alive, every form of art – be it poetry, dance, psychotherapy, philosophy or progressive politics – needs renewal through a new language. This is not entirely dissimilar, I would suggest, from the need to fashion an egalitarian imaginary for an emancipatory politics. The notion of global interdependence and ethical obligation towards all sentient beings may sound naive to a cynical neoliberal ideology dominating public discourse today.[14] This is why the creation of a counter-fantasy is vital in shaping a way of dwelling on earth that is, with Hölderlin, *poetic*.[15] Without counter-fantasies, we may be bound to recycling old stuff, which is what arguably has been happening not only in politics but in the world of psychology, with hardly a shred of a single emancipatory idea percolating through a jungle of metrics, coercive regulations, an ecstasy of obedience to the dictates of ignorant policymakers, and what Sennett calls "the baleful influence of accountants felt everywhere in modern life".[16]

A new language needs strong poets; it needs creators of new concepts and metaphors – in literature as in psychology, religion, and politics. Strong poets often begin by using, even cherishing, old languages and imagery. While finding ourselves enlivened and entertained, seduced by the argumentations, we begin, however, to sense that old forms and contents, old structures and processes are slipping away, subverted, and substituted by a new vision. This is as true for the teachings of the historical Buddha as it is for the writings of Gramsci or Nietzsche. The same applies to Ovid.

Virgil had succeeded in adapting Homeric scenarios into a series of intricate representations that breathed "new life and purposes into an obsolete form and content"[17]. It is debatable whether this astonishing work of revision dented Augustan ideology or left it unscathed. What is more, the epic feat was performed in the service of imperial ideology. With *Metamorphoses*, Ovid, a generation younger than Virgil (who was 27 when Ovid was born) walked a different, uneven terrain. Appearing to be following the epic style, he instead subverted it. Summoning many of the tragic, infamous, and implausible humans, gods, and demigods of the old mythology (and, in the process, the entire Roman-Alexandrian canon), Ovid not only made the old bones live, as it was said of Virgil. He made them dance to the wondrous and terrifying tune of transformation. He also brought to their utmost conclusions the ambitions of the new poets of the late Republic (Cinna, Calvus and the more well-known Catullus five decades before) who had parted ways with the deep-rooted classicism of their predecessors and had both encouraged and practiced a new style. As often with the appearance of the work of a strong poet, it represents the flowering of a trans-generational movement at work for some time. It went as far back as the Alexandrian poets of 280–260 BC: Philetas, Callimachus and Theocritus among them, who rejected the grand epic style in support of non-classical, "small scale" content and form. Callimachus' poetry favoured a spicy moment instead of valiant deeds. It favoured concision, quickness, and innovation. It celebrated the accidental, what happens between the lines. It went against the moralizing and imperial ideologies of its time, eerily similar in their attempt to impose a master discourse, to the much later positivist historiographies of progress of the nineteenth and twentieth century, still rife today, and against which Walter Benjamin (via Bergson and Proust) mounted and eloquent and convincing critique.[18] Against "scientific" Marxism, vulgar empiricism and the Social Democrats of his time – against the banality of the idea of progress itself, Benjamin did not see the advent of justice and the classless society as the culmination of a steady advance through the stages of vacant, analogous time (his 13th thesis of history) but as breach in the continuum of history.

> Marx says that revolutions are the locomotive of world history. But perhaps it is quite otherwise. Perhaps revolutions are an attempt by the passengers on this train – namely, the human race – to activate the emergency brake.[19]

Does psychical or political transformation take place solely as the culmination of a linear narrative process? Does the patient/client in therapy experience change as the culmination of a gradual process signposted by interpretation, insight, and healing, corroborated by the application of the right theory, technique or interpretation? Or is therapy instead an "accident waiting to happen"?[20]

As with any trailblazer, in the eyes of the authorities Ovid was culpable of candidly presenting the mores of his times by glorifying illicit love affairs. No one in his society was particularly shocked by either gay life or adulterous liaisons. But to make them an object of poetry and to even elevate them as the zenith of Roman culture and civilization by portraying, for instance, the deeds of refined and promiscuous adulteresses as the very expression of a more urbane way of living was another matter. To bend poetry (an art customarily associated with the epic and moral domains, an art which praised the virtuous lives of war heroes and outstanding citizens) to the ironic exaltation of the boudoir was an affront to August's moralizing task and to his own person too. It is easy to chastise the young, precociously bright Ovid, man about town stretching nonchalantly the poetic form beyond the innovations introduced by Catullus and Propertius. For if love poetry in these two writers was already unromantically marked by irony and level-headedness, with Ovid it's as if Cupid himself stole a foot from the second hexameter line, turning it into a twisted form of the elegiac. In terms of content, this scorns the alleged authenticity of rustic life and praises a sophisticated promiscuity and *multiplicity* in a relaxed and provocative style.

Chastising may come not only from the more obvious standpoint of the moralist but also from a "romantic" perspective which in valuing the redemptive function of passion and suffering in love, would be appalled in seeing sexual love depicted with cleverness and irony as a marvellous sport propelled by flightiness, vanity, and light-heartedness. But even avowed love of surfaces cannot escape the tears of things; even predilection for self-driven pleasure as opposed to transformative and even tragic desire cannot evade attachments. Perhaps to contemporary sensibilities the declared frivolity of Ovid's *Amores* shockingly reveals the side of the coin overlooked by the accepted idiom of love: we are not only compassionate beings but also angels of pornography. In his deliberate aim to provoke, Ovid is insolently modern. Were he a therapist, he'd certainly break the ethical code of the profession out of a more rigorous allegiance with the ambiguity of life itself. Let others delight in the things of old, he tells us in *Ars Amatoria*. I exalt in my modernity.[21] This partly explains the regularity with which Ovidian revivals occur. The light-footedness of his early verse morphs into an ambience sustained by a mythical keynote of intensity. All the extreme passions hovering on the threshold of human experience are present in the *Metamorphoses*.

To modern sensibilities, Ovid's transition from early erotica to his mature tales of transfiguration represents an important shift from pleasure to desire. While pleasure is inextricably related to subjectivity, desire describes a constant flow momentarily traversing body-subjects but not bound by it. Overall, psychology is restricted in its endeavour by its myopic focus on subjectivity (and its attendant feelings and emotions) rather than on the flow of neutral, inherently transformative desire *before* it gets broken down and catalogued into subjective feelings and emotions.

*

If his early poetry, suave and sardonic, courts foolhardiness by dancing on the brink of human playfulness and daring, the *Metamorphoses* offer a counterpoint of pathos (suffering, elation, power-as-intensity) which brings something other than the proverbial wisdom of maturity: wisdom not as a claim of mastery but as active acceptance of greater natural forces at work – not archetypes in the Jungian/Platonist sense but as natural archetypes[22]. The events and areas of experience humans contend with in Ovid's tales of transformation are the very same which psychoanalysis and psychotherapy are eager to work with and often keen to segregate and pathologize. They verge from the personal to the collective. From suicide to sex-change to intoxication and depression to holocausts, plagues, rape, incest, and sexual harassment. The *Metamorphoses* move at a brisk, cinematic pace. Change happens at high speed; it jolts the imagination, the next picture superimposed on the previous one, all actions happening in the present tense. The five major tales (Tereus-Philomela, Scylla, Byblis, Myrrha, Ceyx-Alcyone) share both mood and content. All of them contend with fierce erotic passion climaxing in tragedy and then metamorphosis as rescue remedy. In Book VII, Ovid brings in Medea to perform the dual role of preluding the key refrain of intense sexual love – modesty overawed by eros, *pudor* defeated by *amor* – and the subordinate refrain of counter-metamorphosis – the normal course of nature turned around, the old becoming young; animals becoming human; the image, becoming the reality it replicates. Medea's soliloquy is a variation of the classic *suasoria,* an exercise in rhetoric, usually the soliloquy of a historical figure deciding what step to take at a crucial moment in their life. In this case, Medea, burning for a stranger who has stirred her heart, battles between reason and passion, persuading herself to follow the latter. However, with reason failing to indicate a course of action outside the necessary constraints of logos, of allegiances to family and homeland, decision is indeed the moment of madness. It is also the moment of betrayal. "Shall I betray my father's country?" Medea asks herself. "Carried by the winds, shall I leave my native country, my sister, my brother, my father, and my gods?" She will do all of the above and become a stranger in a strange land and will commit these and more awful transgressions still. The therapy room is often crowded with tales of decisions deferred, of decisions taken, or taken prematurely.

The classic conflict between love and reason, so starkly depicted in Medea's soliloquy, also appears in Book IX, through Ovid's sober and sympathetic account of Byblis' yearning for her twin brother Caunus. She does not know what she is doing in wanting to love her brother in a way that a sister should not. Her tragedy is a tragedy of self-delusion[23] or, if seen less charitably, a tragedy induced by sophistry, a perversion of reason. Ovid invites us to follow her self-delusion closely, as she writes a love letter to her brother, and that closeness is what makes it possible to respond sympathetically. Ovid does not chastise or condemn. The Augustan moral imperative or more generally formal obeisance to a code of conduct does not appeal to him. Sympathy gestures towards a greater, perhaps more rigorous ethics than the Hegelian morality of *Sittlichkeit*. Byblis' lust is not consummated, but that does not dim Byblis' anguish, an anguish so inconsolable that is only resolved in her metamorphosis into a fountain. Thought alone (and the shame that comes with her expressing it to her brother) is enough to bring ruin if not the full horror of incestuous love, deferred to Myrrha's tale in Book X.

The tragic story of Myrrha, whose beauty was said to surpass that of Venus, tells us of a crime greater than that of hating one's father: loving him. Paradoxically, Myrrha's incestuous love for her father Cinyras takes to its logical conclusions a narrative of endogamy which arguably dominated some of the more orthodox narratives in antiquity. Exaggerated defence of kinship in the Bible (often a true *ideology* of kinship) constituted, for instance, a necessary adjunct to vehement hatred of foreigners and worshippers of the wrong god(s).[24]

Myrrha's story also stresses the dangers implied in the metamorphoses of transition – in this case, into adulthood. The passage into adulthood is marked in antiquity by the legal institution of *manus* marriage. Even though this practice was no longer popular under Augustus, the expectation persisted that a young woman would be handed over by her father to an older husband *in loco filiae* (in the place of a daughter).[25] The bride was in the hand (*manus*) of her spouse. She was no longer the property of her father but became like a daughter to her husband, with legal effects not unlike those of adoption. No idealization of the quasi-paternal relationship between husband and young wife manages to hide the grim reality. Viewed from one perspective, Myrrha's violation is a stark representation of the compelling attraction the abyss holds for some. Falling, trespassing, transgressing; in some cases, reaching the heights of abjection. Strangely, as Nietzsche knew, the abyss emanates light. Myrrha loved her father to the point of vertigo. Even when it is not overtly sexual, the closeness of a parent can feel to a son/daughter as being permeated by a powerful pressure. Seen from a different angle, the scandal of her infringement is not entirely outside the harsh patriarchal frame of the mores of antiquity. In her 1939 *Memoir*, Virginia Woolf relates the attachment between her half-sister Stella and her father Leslie Stephen, and in particular her father's jealousy towards Stella's future husband. "How the family system tortures and exacerbates", she writes in a passage which at odds with the familialism of contemporary psychotherapy, adding:

> I feel that if father could have been induced to say, 'I am jealous', not 'You are selfish', the whole family atmosphere would have been cleared and brightened[26].

Commenting on the gruesome case of Josef Fritzl, the 73-year-old man who had imprisoned his 18-year-old daughter Elizabeth in a cellar under his family home in Amstetten, Austria, for 24 years, repeatedly raping her and fathering seven children on her, Elfriede Jelinek wrote in her essay *The Forsaken Place*:

> Here counts the word of the Father, who's actually already Grandfather, nothing special, Fathers and Grandfathers exist in

one person, the Holy Trinity does also exist, one in three persons, here we have the Grandfather, who is all persons and executes all speaking [...]

No one should grow beyond one's limitations, everything should stay between ourselves, we don't want to let anything come out so that they can't talk about us abroad. We like to disseminate the word of the Fathers in the channels of the fatherland, and we channel it back after we've enjoyed it adequately. Abroad, please listen to our word, to the Opera Ball and the New Year's Concert, listen to it all!, but not to our screaming![27]

Jelinek's excoriating piece exposes the inherent arbitrariness of the family and its ideological patriarchal function. Fritzl is the flipside of the sanctified and sensitive nappy-changing new man in the same way as the boorish tinpot dictator is the flipside of the sharing-and-caring Silicon Valley entrepreneurial dude. Both exist and are reared within the very same ideological frame. Jelinek, a Nobel prize winner for literature, has often been vilified by reviewers and the public and the main reason appears to be that she depicts normality as monstrous.

After his arrest, Fritzl said he *had to* lock his daughter up. She kept going out on her own and she was, after all, his possession. Possession is the keyword here. In a capitalist society, Marx wrote, "the only bond between people is natural necessity, need, and private interest, the preservation of their property and their egoistic persons".[28] Similarly, the good life in liberal and neoliberal theory is closely wedded to private property. The nuclear family continues to perform, as in the days of Marx, a very useful ideological task. It continues to impart toleration of hierarchy and through it the wealthy perpetuate inequality by bequeathing their private property to their offspring.

The original title of Jelinek's essay, *Im Verlassenen*, literally translates as "In abandon-ness", highlighting both the words *Verlassen*, to abandon, or desert as well as *Verlies*, dungeon. Family may be a place of love and nurture where secure attachments are created; it can also be a bedrock of raving insanity and stultifying patriarchal violence.

In either case, becoming free from the family is crucial to becoming a citizen. The very etymology of the word emancipation, from *e* (out) *mancipium* (slave), going back to the Roman law is the freeing of a son or wife from the legal authority of the father, to make his or her own way in the world.

Work represents for women and men alike, but especially for women, a promise of true freedom. But this belief is for several reasons an illusion. Upward social mobility, individual freedom and responsibility are myths in a world where "a mere eight men control ... more wealth than half the inhabitants of the planet". What's more, by exposing sexual harassment in privileged industries, woke capitalism has fully expressed the extent of "middle-class disillusions with the emancipatory promise of work".[29]

In Myrrha's story, Cupid denies all responsibility. It was one of the Furies who possessed her, Ovid tells us, and precipitated the catastrophe. As with contemporary accounts of love in psychology literature and elsewhere, which tend to lyricize agape over eros and conveniently dispense with a more three-dimensional account of love, the untamed, consuming passion is forgotten in favour of more genteel manifestations. Myrrha's passion, we are led to understand by Ovid, is not suitably steeped in love. It belongs to a different register of intensity and pathology. At the mercy of a Fury, her die is cast. The moon and the stars leave the darkened sky in horror. She flees in anguish and asks the gods to help her so that she can no longer pollute the living and the dead. One thing only can solve her unrelenting anguish: metamorphosis. She mutates into a tree and from her bark Adonis is born, who will continue the trans-generational legacy of love disasters. Tragedy and ruin are the hallmarks of most tales of passion in Ovid – Thereus-Philomela, Scylla, Myrrha, Ceyx-Alcyone, and Byblis. When metamorphosis finally comes, it is as a liberation from the human frame and the suffering it entails. Only a mature Ovid, enduring the anguish of exile from his beloved city and a far cry from his youthful exuberant frivolity, could depict human experience in these terms.

Notes

1   Mary Beard, 'No Competitive Martyrdom' *Times Literary Supplement,* https://www.the-tls.co.uk/articles/no-competitive-martyrdom, retrieved 10 April 2020; Jia Tolentino, 'How a Woman becomes a Lake, *New Yorker,* https://www.newyorker.com/culture/cultural-comment/how-a-woman-becomes-a-lake, retrieved 10 April 2020

2   Emmanuel Levinas, *Entre Nous: On Thinking-of-the-Other*. New York: Columbia University Press.
3   Lee Fratantuono, *Madness Transformed: A Reading of Ovid's Metamorphoses*. Lanham, Maryland: Lexington Books, 2011.
4   Jean Laplanche, *Life and Death in Psychoanalysis*. Trans. J. Mehlman, Baltimore, MA: John Hopkins University Press.
5   Ovid's Erotic Poems: *Amores and Ars Amatoria*, trans L. Krisak. Philadelphia, PA: University of Pennsylvania Press, 2014.
6   See Manu Bazzano, *Nietzsche and Psychotherapy*. Abingdon, OX: Routledge, 2019, pp. 140–141.
7   Virgil, *The Aeneid*. Translated with an Introduction by Shadi Bartsch. London: Profile, 2020, p. xv.
8   For example, Madeline Miller, *Circe*. London, Bloomsbury, 2018.
9   T. Ziolkowski, 'Ovid in the Twentieth Century', In Knox, P.E. (Ed.), *A Companion to Ovid*. Hoboken, NJ: John Wiley & Sons, 2020.
10 A. Mitescu, 'Ovid's presence in Romanian culture', *Romanian Review*, 26, 54–57. London: Blackwell, 2009, pp. 454–468; p. 456.
11 Antonio Tabucchi, *Dreams of Dreams and the Last Days of Fernando Pessoa*. San Francisco, CA: City Lights, 2001.
12 John F. Miller's 'Tabucchi's Dream of Ovid', *Literary Imagination: The Review of the Association of Literary Scholars and Critics*, 3.2 (2001), pp. 237–247.
13 Gilles Deleuze with C. Parnet, *Dialogues II*, London: Continuum, 2002, p. 49.
14 "The idea of global obligations that serve all inhabitants of the world, human and animal, is about as far from the neoliberal consecration of individualism as it could be, and yet it is regularly dismissed as naive. So I am summoning my courage to expose my naiveté, my fantasy – my counter-fantasy, if you will". Judith Butler, *The Force of Non-violence*, London and New York, Verso, 2020, p. 44.
15 Discuss this topic at length in Manu Bazzano, *Spectre of the Stranger: Towards a Phenomenology of Hospitality*. Eastbourne: Sussex Academic Press, 2012.
16 Richard Sennett, *Together: The Rituals, Pleasures and Politics of Cooperation*. London, Penguin, 2012, pp. 72–73.
17 Brooks Otis, *Ovid as an Epic Poet*, London: Cambridge University Press, 1966, p. 1.
18 Walter Benjamin, *On the Concept of History*, trans. Harry Zohn, in *Selected Writings*, Volume 4: *1938–1940*, Harvard University Press, Cambridge MA and London, 2003, pp. 389–400. See also Andrew McGettigan, 'As Flowers Turn towards the Sun: Walter Benjamin's Bergsonian Image of the Past', Radical Philosophy 158, November-December 2009, https://www.radicalphilosophy.com/article/as-flowers-turn-towards-the-sun 19
19 Walter Benjamin, *Selected Writings*, 4, 1938–1940, p. 402.
20 Julie Webb, 'Therapy as an Accident Waiting to Happen', In Manu Bazzano (Ed.) *Re-Visioning Person-centred Therapy: the Theory and Practice of a Radical Paradigm*. Abingdon: Routledge, 2018, pp. 3–16.
21 Ovid, *Ars Amatoria* vv, pp. 121–122. https://www.sacred-texts.com/cla/ovid/lboo/
22 Manu Bazzano, *Nietzsche and Psychotherapy*. Abingdon, OX: Routledge, pp. 150–153.
23 Betty Rose Nagle, 'Byblis and Myrrha: Two Incest Narratives in the Metamorphoses', *The Classical Journal*, 78. 4, April–May 1983, pp. 301–315.
24 Manu Bazzano, *Spectre of the Stranger: Towards a Phenomenology of Hospitality*, op. cit.

25 Susan E. Looper-Friedman, *The Decline of Manus Marriage in Rome* HeinOnline, 1987. https://heinonline.org/HOL/LandingPage?handle=hein.journals/tijvrec55& div=24&id=&page=, retrieved 21 August 2021.
26 Katherine Angel, *Daddy Issues*. London: Peninsula Press, 2019, https://granta.com/daddy-issues/
27 Elfriede Jelinek, *The Forsaken Place*, 2018, https://www.elfriedejelinek.com/famstete.htm, retrieved 22 August 2021.
28 Karl Marx, 'On the Jewish Question', *The Marx-Engels Reader*, ed. R. C. Tucker, trans. R. Rogowski, New York, Norton, 1978, p. 42.
29 Katherine Angel, *Daddy Issues*, op. cit.

Chapter 2

Counter-Fantasies

*

Once during a street performance by the *Living Theatre,* a bystander (later identified as a lecturer in our campus) suddenly jumped into action by punching one of the actors, who promptly hit him back. The accident caused a stir; lively discussions ensued. At that particular point in the performance, the actors were advocating non-violence. "You see? – the lecturer gleefully remonstrated – non-violence may be a nice idea, but it's clearly impracticable". For all my love of the *Living Theatre* (an experimental New York ensemble inspired by Artaud and motivated by an anarchist/pacifist ethos), I sympathized with the lecturer. I thought his stance expressed a fairly established argument within the Left which claims (or used to claim) that we live and breathe within a pre-existing force field of violence, and that to believe one can freely adopt a morally superior nonviolent stance is near delusional. Judith Butler, a contemporary gadfly in a lineage of indispensable philosophers, begs to differ. In *The Force of Non-Violence,*[1] her own version of non-violence is thankfully removed from the abstract, saintly stance normally associated with the term; it is wedded instead to unambiguous political commitment to a notion of equality grounded in interdependence. For Butler, non-violence is not an absolute principle but an ongoing tussle with the tangible presence of violence in society. It is not passivity, but an admirable way to channel our innate aggressive instinct. Non-violence means accepting aggression and then choosing *not* to act violently.

DOI: 10.4324/9781003280262-3

*

Clearly, there is more to violence than the physical blow, the rape, the verbal assault. Social structures are themselves violent, engendering and supporting discrimination and injustice, including systemic racism. The book's subtitle is *an Ethico-Political Bind*: when assembling her more avowedly *political* argument, Butler converses in a compelling manner with the likes of Walter Benjamin, Foucault, Frantz Fanon, and Etienne Balibar, building on their important legacies, rectifying, often persuasively, some of their stances. When bringing in psychoanalysis in order to discuss the more unconscious aspects of *ethics*, she relies (excessively, in my view) on Melanie Klein's hermetically sealed description of the psyche.

The "force" in the book's title may well be included in the meaning of *Gewalt* in German (e.g., *Naturgewalt*, "force of nature"), a term used by Walter Benjamin in his seminal essay *On the Critique of Violence*[2] and normally translated as "violence". In that sense, the *force* of non-violence also indicates the necessary violence (aggression) of non-violence. True, this very same definition has been used manipulatively by authoritarian governments since the times of Max Weber to chastise peaceful demonstrators and, historically, to condemn creatively disruptive actions such as work strikes, hunger strikes, sanctions, cultural boycotts, petitions, and all the different ways of refuting unjust, inhuman, homophobic and racist authority – *Black Lives Matter* being a case in point. "Force" is a term pregnant with meaning: a Nietzschean/Deleuzian slant, not mentioned by Butler, would differentiate between the *reactive force* of state, government and police aimed at defending tooth and nail institutional injustice, and the *active force* of progressive movements, aimed at instating equality and justice.[3]

Non-violence cannot be reductively defined as a ban against killing, nor can it be exclusively claimed by dubious political stances which favour an abstract notion of "life" while deeming expendable the very real and concrete life of others. Consider the *Pro-Life* movement: the existential condition of the woman is ignored in the name of a merely notional defence of life.

There are several interesting parallels here with Walter Benjamin; in the aforementioned essay, he confronts Kurt Hiller, for whom "higher still than the happiness and justice of a particular existence is existence as such", seeing Heller's view as "wrong, even dishonourable".[4] Privileging abstract existence (*Dasein*) over existents, i.e., the concrete life of sentient beings is, incidentally, Heidegger's dishonourable blunder at the core of his thought.

"Self-defence" is a case in point: *who* or *what* is the self being evoked here? Who or what is defending itself against the alleged threat of desperate migrants dying at sea, against black people choked to death or shot in the back by police officers? It would appear that the net of relatedness this "self" is embedded in is confined to the lives of those who are proximate and similar, whose lives are deemed more valuable and more grievable than others.

This brings us to the question of interdependence itself, a key concept in Butler's current argument, one that is, however, insufficiently articulated. This is where a brief foray into Buddhist thought may be of help. Central to the Buddha's teaching is *dependent origination* (if this exists, that exists; if this ceases to exist, that also ceases to exist), a notion that percolated into western culture via the American transcendentalists and was (badly) rendered as inter-connectedness. In the process of translation, what was meant to be a far-reaching deconstruction of the self, a "seeing-through" its ephemeral, painfully non-autonomous (i.e., non self-existing) nature, morphed into a Romantic paean to the unity among all things and of harmony between humans and "Mother Nature." The first stirrings of two profoundly naive stances pervasive today – namely, contemporary psychotherapy's "relatedness" and our thoroughly anthropocentric romance with the wilderness – may be traced here.

What is missing in Butler's notion of interdependence? The important reminder of the absence of an abiding self in all living things. Grievability, a key Butlerian notion, begins here: in life, or deathlife (*shōji* in Zen). My suggestion to base nonviolence in impermanence makes Butler's notion all the more potent: all lives are equally grievable because each life is unique and all the more precious because impermanent in an impermanent world. And each death, Derrida would say, is the end of the world as such since each human being is the remarkable and unrepeatable origin of the world itself.

*

Butler's stance remains unique, her work building on poststructuralism and Critical Theory, injecting them with the urgency and passion of feminism, gender politics and identity, renewing and revising the often-stale political discourse of the traditional Left. Among other things, her work over the years has been useful, I believe, in helping us realize that despite psychoanalysis' many constitutively normative biases (for instance, the elevation of the Oedipus complex to a transcendent structure essential in the making of the self), it may be possible to make use of its language, insights, and methodologies and turn psychoanalysis against its own cherished doctrines and hopefully (I am being optimistic) into an arsenal for psychical subversion. All the same, the fact remains that Butler agrees completely to psychoanalysis' structural premises and does not see them as intrinsically normalizing.[5] Fortunately, for some of us practicing therapists, Deleuze and Guattari[6] helped us see clearly that Freud's psychoanalysis is *intrinsically* normative and that its tenets need to be taken with a deconstructive pinch of salt. Claire Colebrook explains:

> For Deleuze and Guattari ... it is that negative notion of desire and anxiety—the very structure of psychoanalysis *as a theory*—which remains tied to normalizing notions of 'man'. For Freud it is anxiety that effects repression: the subject, faced with a world of intensity and affect, must delimit and organize the libido into a state of equilibrium or constancy.[7]

At times, psychoanalytic theory proves too binding even for Butler, as demonstrated by her critique of psychoanalytic intersubjectivity she offered years ago in relation to the work of Jessica Benjamin.[8] It built up an argument which contemporary psychotherapy would learn a great deal from – if, that is, the latter were ever open to question the now normative ideal of relatedness.[9] Briefly, at the heart of Butler's argument was the notion that the therapeutic dyad is "an achievement, not a presupposition".[10] Rupture and destruction are ever-present in the inevitably asymmetrical encounter and constitute the foundation for psychical transformation. Hegel's notion of recognition (*Anerkennung*, also rendered as "acknowledgement") in the "I and You" encounter between the Master and the Slave (crucial in laying down the first concrete foundations for a historically concrete *self* beyond the solipsistic perception of "me" inherited by liberal and later neoliberal individualism) never overlooks struggle and conflict, nor gives in to humanistic sentimentality. Tersely reinstated by Butler in her postscript to her book is also a central argument found in Hegel's *Phenomenology*: the dyadic encounter is only a small if important part of the story. Yes, I need you and you need me in order to endure and thrive. But you and I need the tangible presence of a supporting world of social relations. What we do *not* need is a monstrous technostructure, an anthropomorphised market economy whose demands we're obliged to feed day in and day out with our own precarious lives of flesh and blood.

*

There is *phantasy* and *fantasy*, Judith Butler says paraphrasing Melanie Klein's view of the psyche. *Phantasy* is unconscious, often setting the scenery for the frenzied phantasms of racism, homophobia, hatred of the poor and the migrants. *Fantasy* is, on the other hand, understood as conscious aspiration, crucial both in fashioning a vision of origins (as in the so-called state of nature, whether the dog-eats-dog Hobbesian version or the noble wildness of Rousseau) and in *forging a new imaginary for the future*. This is no mere academic disquisition; without adequate (counter)-fantasy, there's no future for justice, equality, or for an ethics of solidarity.

Counter-fantasy is sorely missing in the contemporary political Left, a lacuna expressively addressed in Butler's work.. The Left is bound to lose again and again if it relies solely on old narratives and worldviews, especially when it is up against, for instance, the deeply entrenched conservatism of English civic society. Jeremy Corbyn was subjected to a carefully and cynically orchestrated campaign of political assassination at the hands of a unanimous chorus of mercenary hacks, distinguished raconteurs of centrist hogwash *à la* Jonathan Freedland, and the abysmally dull management consultancy project headed by Keir Starmer. With hindsight, the tricky question is whether the core of the project of profound and much-needed renewal behind Corbyn, for all its tremendous courage, ethical rigour and commitment, lacked a coherent counter-fantasy.

*

Melanie Klein's stress on the inevitable tangle of love/hate in intimate relationships certainly rings true and it may be helpful in motivating one of the "applications" of psychotherapy outside the clinic, namely an emancipatory ethico-political project unburdened by credulity. Equally useful is her reminder that you and I are to one another defective replacements for our irrevocable past. Klein's discovery of partial objects was a stroke of genius, a very perceptive insight into the structure and workings of the psyche, but hopelessly devoted to so-called "integration", with fatal consequences for psychotherapy to this day. Integration is a prescriptive and ludicrous imposition: "parts" are *not* destined to be included within a prearranged "whole" as Melanie Klein believes, nor do they necessarily consti- tute the disastrous origin of the paranoid-schizoid position, one that is going to be fixed through re-incorporation of the various splinters within a multifaceted psyche. From Nietzsche we learned that ascribing unity to phenomena is precisely one of the meanings of *nihilism*, caused by our having "lost the faith in [our own and the world's intrinsic] value".[11] Believing that we need to ascribe our own cute notion of unity to an unfathomable, excessive world is nihilistic: as if the world would be nothing (*nihil*) without our normative fantasies. Equally, envisaging a form of intrapsychic unity and a consolatory holistic inter-relatedness that were once lost ignores that there is another, altogether different unifying link which also constitutes a valid, *emancipatory* alternative to the integrated "whole" dreamed up by Klein and by virtually most contemporary psychotherapists after her. Its name is *desire*; its work is *desiring-production*,[12] a future-oriented (rather than archaeological), liberative practice that understands psyche not as a theatre but as a factory. We are not here to repeat, redress or refurbish an Oedipal, Hamletian, or Antigonian scenography. Nor are we here to itemize and embalm the silver river of experience within the precincts of some insipid Dasein, a set of smothering Jungian archetypes or some farcical Wachowskian matrix. What prevents us each time from conceiving of desire as a generative, active force rather than a reactive force based on lack is *fear*. And what prompts us to supinely accept each time the sinister surrogate of unity available, i.e., an autocratic and controlling technostructure that governs our existence is, once again, fear: not the Kierkegaardian anxiety, precursor of independence or the intrinsic existential dread born out of wisdom, but the reactive panic at the magnitude of lifedeath, the fleeting sight of which makes us reach for the closest bargain on offer in the metaphysical jumble sale.

*

Drawing sizeable inspiration from Melanie Klein, as Butler does, is a problematic move. Klein's emphasis on the process of "projection" cannot be seriously situated at the origin of psychical formation unless your name is Bishop George Berkeley. Not everything comes from the so-called inner life, "like rabbits or doves from the magic box of tricks."[13] This (literally) *self-centred*, "Ptolemaic" view of human experience conveniently forgets that *others are no mere projections*; their presence is real, thoroughly external, concrete, and compelling. We cannot simply conjure up the other out of the hat of the same as all idealist thinkers have done, from Berkeley to Fichte to (late) Hegel. I cannot conveniently manufacture the alien simply in order to better recognize and acknowledge myself and my existence. The external, real existence of the other cannot be re-appropriated for myself and my life project.

The other's real presence is mysterious, painful – *seductive* even, to use Laplanche's (and early Freud's) unequivocal, untimely terminology – and it is precisely this factor that constitutes the basis for the creation of a radical ethics. Even more important is the other's *enigmatic message* to the self, a message the other is not fully conscious of, a message subtly working within us, opening our experience to the domain of *culture*. It is by working, more or less consciously, with the other's enigmatic message within us that we come to compose our songs, dance our dance, and paint our canvas and in the process learn the lessons of solidarity and transformation. Our dance (our cultural message) to the world is bound to be political even if we happen to live, as we all are, within gated and imagined communities. It is in the nature of the cultural message to fly over those gates and reach receptacles, be they contemporary or future. The Paris commune continues with the October revolution, with May '68 and with every new contemporary and future insurgence. The song of our cultural message may be set to avant-garde music or a popular ballad or to the rhythms of chanting and shouting of outrage at the White House, at 10 Downing Street and wherever privilege and conceit huddle and squeeze oozing their scented stink onto the streets of our cities. The above are precisely the sort of subversive insights and implications lying dormant and inexplicably unseen within the psychoanalytic/ psychotherapeutic cultural legacy. Inexplicably, that is, as long as one passes over the embarrassingly sycophantic stance contemporary psychotherapy on the whole has assumed towards the (neopositivist, neoliberal) powers.

*

Given how indispensable the cultural domain is to revolutionary politics, it is baffling that it should be missing entirely from Butler's ethico-political project. To Antonio Gramsci we owe the often-quoted, rarely applied insight about the importance of *cultural hegemony*, crucial especially for any emancipatory political project operating within the manipulative democracies of the developed world. No plausible examination of violence can afford to bypass predominance by consent, the smuggling of ideology as common sense, the manufacturing of false consciousness, the cultural manipulation with which ruling classes and elites historically hold sway, before they resort to coercion, mass incarceration and police brutality. A counter-hegemonic cultural struggle is crucial to a political project of emancipation; without new visions outside the narrow parameters of neoliberalism, the Left does not stand a chance in the world. The other important facet of hegemony (one that looks, with progressive forces on the defensive on a global scale, disconsolately remote) is for Gramsci the persistent effort to maintain cultural hegemony even when progressive forces are in power. The set of loyalties on which that hegemony is founded is in constant need of re-adjustment and re-negotiation.[14] This is diametrically opposed to projects such as New Labour and others across the world, for whom gaining and remaining in power invariably means abandoning progressive cultural values and adhering to the coarse ideologies of nationalism, social climbing, motivational codswallop and supine obeisance to the dictates of an anthropomorphized market. True, the Gramscian notion of hegemony rarely features in socialist Anglophone literature and discourse. But there are remarkable exceptions: the work of Stuart Hall[15] and that of Ernesto Laclau and Chantal Mouffe.[16] There are unsettling parallels between Gramsci's 1920s and more recent dark ages when (with Thatcher and Reagan in power) the sinister wailing was first heard as from the cradle of Rosemary's baby of what became the new neoliberal norm, the rule of the 1% over the compliant and often therapized 99%. Paraphrasing and reframing Gramsci for our times, Stuart Hall relived and reflected on Gramsci's painful disappointment when, after the October revolution, the tide turned, all over Europe, in the opposite direction. When a *conjuncture* unrolls, there is no turning back. In Stuart Hall's own words:

> What I have called 'Gramsci's question' in the *Notebooks* emerges in the aftermath of that moment, with the recognition that history was not going to go that way, especially in the advanced industrial capitalist societies of Western Europe. Gramsci had to confront the turning back, the failure, of that moment: the fact that such a moment, having passed, would never return in its old form. Gramsci, here, came face to face with the revolutionary character of history itself. When a conjuncture unrolls, there is no 'going back'. History shifts gears. The terrain changes. You are in a new moment. You have to attend, 'violently', with all the 'pessimism of the intellect' at your command, to the 'discipline of the conjuncture'.[17]

We must attend, "violently" (that is, urgently, forcefully) – Hall says paraphrasing Gramsci – to the discipline required by the seemingly intractable and concerted challenges of cultural, economic, and political dominance by the dark forces of ignorance and conceit. In Butler's terms, we must attend to the challenge we now face with the full *force* of non-violence. What she does *not* say is that, despite obvious differences with the 1920s, the Right dominates the present conjuncture culturally as well as politically, and that without addressing the issue of cultural hegemony, the Left is forever doomed. It is my belief that the *ethics* in the ethico-political project promoted by Butler may be better assisted by utilizing the *subversive* insights present in psychotherapy rather than settling with the psychical conservatism present in those aspects of the Freudian/Kleinian upon which Butler seemingly relies.

There *are* parallels between the 1920s and the current conjuncture – not only in terms of the observable likeness between historical fascists and the sinister characters now pacing the international leadership catwalk of horrors, but more in terms of the nature of the *crisis*. Stuart Hall's insights are invaluable here. The crisis in question – in the 1920s as in the late 1980s when Hall was reflecting on this, *as* in our current circumstances, is a *monumental crisis of the Left*. Not the very same crisis, but one that is recognizable now, as I write this, on a September day in 2020, in the *now of recognisability*. The Right has morphed and shifted with incredible cunning, getting people strolling in Hungry Ghosts Boulevard with the promise of financial freedom in the dark years of Thatcher's reign, and now wearing jeans and T-shirts, sharing and caring on social media while shouting for "liberty" in shrill homo-social rallies in support of Trump while in little England we call incompetent and opportunistic prime ministers by their first name. The Left has conceived of the Right as "always exactly the same: the same people, with the same interests, thinking the same thoughts".[18] In moments of profound political crisis, the discourse on the Left also becomes oversimplified and defensive, clutching for respectable and puritanical allegiances in the vain hope of gaining the attention of a chattering majority kept in the dark and fed on *Fox News*. This may explain Butler's perplexingly defensive choice of clutching for support from Klein's conservative view of the psychical domain as well as in the ethico-political stance of Gandhi.

The latter choice is untenable. Gandhi was a man whose ontological absolutism, hatred of the body, divinely-inspired, eloquent defence of the brutal, unjust and racist caste system *and* of racial segregation against black people in Africa – justly denounced over the years by the likes of the luminous Dalit leader B.R. Ambedkar,[19] Perry Anderson,[20] Arundhati Roy,[21,22] Ashwin Desai and Goolam Vahed[23] among others – have begun to discolour somewhat Gandhi's genteel aura imprinted on the minds and T-shirts of conservative middle-class yogis and yoginis gazing at their precious navels on expensive yoga mats and healing the Earth one spoonful of muesli at a time between one asana and another.

*

The Greek and Latin origins of the term *crisis* suggest a decisive moment when things can get better or worse in a disease. When faced with a client's/patient's individual crisis, the psychotherapist's task is to help rebuild (or build from scratch) the transitional space eroded by an environment bent on pursuing unsavoury goals – in our neo-liberal age, *profit* for the 1% and the maintenance of an alienated existence for all involved – rather than *culture*. But there is a twist, as Julia Kristeva made abundantly clear.[24] Dangerous and uncertain it may be, but a crisis also represents an atypical moment of departure from the enclosure of our alienated existence; the psychotherapist's ethico-political task is to make sure that therapy acts as "the instrument of a departure from that enclosure, not as its warden".[25] The question is "Are we to build [through the creation of] a psychic space a certain mastery?" Or would we be better off pursuing a different course of action, namely, to "follow, impel, favour break-aways, drifting?".[26] Merely attempting to stitch together the old psychic patchwork of identifications and projections that rests on the reassuringly dull and claustrophobic bedrock of family sagas recycled *ad infinitum* by a narcotic pseudo-culture: this is the task for a psychic constabulary, not for a psychotherapist. Under the guise of crisis, a different way of being may be struggling to emerge. In this domain of *undecidability* the therapist's/analyst's task is to help others speak, write, and mould an uncertain language through *free association* – a lost art in our barren psychic landscape. For there are no words (yet) for the cluster of emergent phenomena we often call a crisis. The eccentric, polyvalent nature of this new discourse is a breakthrough, a threshold outside the old mummy–daddy scenarios, something that cannot be achieved via that tired existential trope, "meaning".

> It is not a matter of filling John's 'crisis' – his emptiness – with meaning, or of assigning a sure place to Juliet's erotic wander-ings. But to trigger a discourse where his own 'emptiness' and her own 'out-of-placeness' become essential elements, indispensable 'characters' … of a work in progress. What is at stake is turning the crisis into a *work in progress*.[27]

*

Overt, unpunished violence (as in the killing of George Floyd and Chris Kaba) is often the exhibitionistic display of an unchecked autocratic *id* run amok and becoming personified in high office as ogre (Trump, Bolsonaro), buffoon (Johnson, Berlusconi) or a combination of the two (Mussolini) – each era in turn producing its own variation on a hideous assembly line of flashers and bullies. Historically, as in the 1930s, overt violence is the frenzied last resort from a ruling class terrified of the looming spectres of democratic socialism or libertarian communism. Extreme forms of coercion are only occasionally implemented in civic societies narcotized by social media and the so-called news dished out by the corporations. In his astoundingly prescient essay *Postscript on the Societies of Control*, Deleuze[28] traces the development of forms of domination exercised by different societies through history: *societies of sovereignty* gave way in the Napoleonic era to *disciplinary societies* (described by Foucault), in turn ousted by our contemporary *societies of control* where corporate "healthy" competition between employees and the all-pervading "motivation" pits one individual against the other while simultaneously dividing each individual within. Focusing on the shift from discipline to control, he notes that "if the most idiotic television … shows are so successful, it's because they express the corporate situation with great precision".[29] It could be that money marks the difference between the two forms of society, from minted money "that locks gold in as numerical standard … to floating rates of exchange".[30] If the animal symbol for disciplinary society was the mole, a creature living in enclosed spaces, societies of control are represented by the serpent, undulating, "in orbit, in a continuous network"[31] forever surfing, inhabiting a shiftier and more difficult world.

*

Stating one of the reasons for her disagreement with Deleuze, Butler wrote a few years back:

> Psychoanalysis seems centered on the problem of lack for Deleuze, but I tend to center on the problem of negativity. One reason I have opposed Deleuze is that I find no registration of the

negative in his work, and I feared he was proposing a *manic defence* against negativity. [32]

Somewhat encouragingly, Butler more recently revisited mania, framing it in a more positive light and without fear of being accused of bypassing negativity as she has done so sternly against Deleuze. She does so in her discussion of Freud's political thought in relation to the necessary moral restrictions imposed by the super-ego on the instinctual desire to unleash destructive tendencies, especially when these are encouraged by current leaders who endorse misogyny and racism on a large scale. The recognizable problem with the super-ego is that it can itself become a lethal force when held hostage by "a pure culture of the death drive [which] often enough succeeds in driving the ego into death".[33] What is the antidote? Many within the humanistic tradition would say "love", and analysts too, I suspect, would say something of the sort. After all, if the super-ego tends to be hijacked by Thanatos, the neutralizing force is bound to be Eros. That is at least what (a dualistic) logic would suggest. Self-preservation, *amor proprio, conatus essendi,* love of thy neighbour as yourself, evolutionary survival: from every corner, the tradition reminds us of this "instinctual" need. Except that from Sappho onwards we also know that Eros is *glukupikron,* sweetbitter, for many of us have tested the sweetness before the inevitable chagrin. Even though we forget, and in the blessed realm of forgetfulness keep cynicism at bay. We tend to ascribe to love (agape as much as eros, seizure by the numinous as much as craving for the glutinous) the positive terminal in the life force's battery. But love can also be the name ascribed to the "ambivalent constellation of love and hate"[34] or of self-preservation/self-destruction.

There is another possible alternative to self-destruction: *mania.* Dictionaries tend to describe mania as mental and physical hyperactivity, disorganization of behaviour and mood, as well as excessive, unreasonable enthusiasm. But it may also be conceived of as an effective *antidote to self-destruction.*

> 'Mania is ... the protest of the living organism against the prospect of its destruction by an unchecked super-ego. So, if the super-ego is the continuation of the death drive, mania is the protest against destructive action directed toward the world and toward the self.

Mania asks: 'Is there any way out of this vicious circle in which destructiveness is countered by self-destructiveness?'[35].

It would appear that a Deleuzian/Nietzschean appreciation of the active, life-affirming forces which in a body-subject defies organismic holistic synthesis as much as repressive interpellation has some place after all in an emancipatory psycho-political project.

*

Becoming aware of my phantasmatic projections onto the other is only one-third of the story. I must also realize and fully take on board the concrete presence and otherness of the other, and then attempt to respond adequately through ethico-political action.

Butler's parallel of the Kleinian view of the child–parent bond and the one between society (institutions) and the individual comes close to inadvertently replicating the paternalism of patriarchal and capitalist institutions she rightly decries. Where is the place for the inevitable, necessarily disruptive subversion of institutions if all we demand of them is to take care of us like children to their parents?

At the cusp of phantasy and fantasy is the daydream, the place where we can envisage either the *beach* underneath the street, as revolutionaries did in May 1968, or the *sewers*, as our cynical age arguably tends to do. Laplanche presents a far more nuanced view than Klein's and one that sits effortlessly alongside emancipatory politics and may go some way, if pursued, in developing a consistent counter-fantasy. In Laplanche's view, paraphrased by Butler, we are not dealing with a division between fantasy and reality but are operating at all times within an organizing psychic modality through which reality itself is consistently being interpreted. Paying close attention to the fantasies we create is crucial, and even more crucial is cultivating counter-fantasies outside the discriminatory, racist and unjust psycho-political structures we inhabit today.

Notes

1 Judith Butler, *The Force of Non-Violence: An Ethico-Political Bind*. London and New York: Verso, 2020.
2 Walter Benjamin, *One-Way Street and Other Writings*. London: Penguin, 2009.
3 Manu Bazzano, *Nietzsche and Psychotherapy*. Abingdon, OX: Routledge, 2019.
4 *One-Way Street and Other Writings*, op.cit., p. 26.

5 Claire Colebrook, *Sex After Life: Essays on Extinction*. Vol. 2. Ann Arbour, MI: Open Humanities Press, 2014, https://quod.lib.umich.edu/o/ohp/12329363.0001. 001, retrieved 25 August 2020.
6 Gilles Deleuze and Felix Guattari, *Anti-Oedipus: Capitalism and Schizophrenia*. Minneapolis, MN: University of Minnesota Press, 1972.
7 *Sex After Life*, op.cit.
8 Judith Butler, *Undoing Gender*. Abingdon, OX: Routledge, 2004.
9 John Mackessy and Manu Bazzano, 'Is Relatedness a Normative Ideal?' In Bazzano, M. (Ed.), *Re-Visioning Existential Therapy: Counter-traditional Perspectives*. Abingdon, OX: Routledge, 2020.
10 *Undoing Gender,* op.cit., p. 146.
11 Friedrich Nietzsche, *The Will to Power*. New York: Vintage Books, 1968, p. 12.
12 *Anti-Oedipus*, op. cit.
13 Jean Laplanche, *Essays on Otherness*. London and New York: Routledge, 1999, p. 133.
14 Antonio Gramsci, *Selections from the Prison Notebooks of Antonio Gramsci*. New York: International Publishers, 1971.
15 Stuart Hall, *The Hard Road to Renewal: Thatcherism and the Crisis of the Left*. London and New York: Verso, 1998.
16 Ernesto Laclau and Chantal Mouffe, *Hegemony and Socialist Strategy: Towards a Radical Democratic Politics*. London and New York: Verso, 2001.
17 The Hard Road to Renewal, op. cit., p. 162.
18 Ibid., p. 162.
19 Bhimrao Ramji Ambedkar, *The Annihilation of Caste. The Annotated Critical Edition*. London and New York: Verso, 2016.
20 Perry Anderson, *The Indian Ideology*. London & New York: Verso, 2013.
21 Arundhati Roy, *The Doctor and the Saint: Caste, Race, and the Annihilation of Caste: the Debate between B.R. Ambedkar and M.K. Gandhi*. Chicago, IL: Haymarket Books, 2017.
22 Arundhati Roy, 'Debunking the Gandhi Myth', Interview, The Laura Flanders Show, 2014, https://www.youtube.com/watch?v=4-yMiBGBOe0&app=desktop, retrieved 5 September 2020
23 Ashwin Desai and Goolem Vahed, *The South-African Gandhi: Stretcher-Bearer of Empire*. Stanford, CA: Stanford University Press, 2015.
24 Julia Kristeva, *Tales of Love*. New York: Columbia University Press, 1987.
25 Ibid., p. 379.
26 Ibid., p. 379.
27 Ibid., p. 380.
28 Gilles Deleuze, 'Postscript on the Societies of Control', *JSTOR Archive, October* 1992, Vol. 59, pp. 3–7, http://links.jstor.org/sici?sici=01622870%28199224%2959% 3C3%3APOTSOC%3E2.0.CO%3B2-T, retrieved 24 August 2020.
29 *Postscript on the Societies of Control*, op. cit., p. 4.
30 Ibid., p. 5.
31 Ibid., p. 6.
32 Judith Butler, *Undoing Gender*, op. cit., 2004, p. 198.
33 Sigmund Freud, 'Mourning and Melancholia', *SE* vol. 14, 1917, pp. 248–252; p. 251.
34 *The Force of Non-Violence*, op. cit., p. 162.
35 Ibid., p. 167.

Chapter 3

Where It Was, the Other Shall Be

Four events (from myth, literature, astronomy, and psychoanalysis) are worth mentioning as a prelude to the theme examined here.

The first event: in the Odyssey's twelfth Canto, Circe warns Ulysses of the dangers ahead, including the encounter with the Sirens. Her suggestions are plain: his men should plug their ears with beeswax and tie him to the mast of the ship, and when he pleads to be untied, to bind him even tighter. For anyone who goes too close, she cautions, there will be no sailing home, no wife will ever come to meet him, no happy children will smile at him.[1] Ulysses hears the Sirens' song; he "defeats" them. There was only one other man, Butes, one of the Argonauts, who heard the song, Apollonius tells us. His soul melted when hearing it, and the poor wretch swam through the dark surge to mount the beach, and was saved *in extremis* by the goddess Cypris, who snatched him away from certain death. Despite mentions of a song everywhere, there has never been an answer to the emperor Tiberius' question *Quid Sirenes cantare sint solitæ*? (What are the Sirens inclined to sing?). Interpretations vary, and the beauty of this and other myths is that they generate multiple interpretations. Some say, Blanchot among them,[2] that there is no song as such, but silence – the silence of distance which orients sailors' navigation, functioning as expedient mirage, the temporary destiny/destination of a fictional goal. There is the implied misogyny of interpreting the Sirens' song as a call to ruin and more poignantly the fear that by hearing the song, one may discover a song within oneself, a song whose nature is nonhuman.

In further development of the Sirens' myth, these winged creatures, half bird/half women (the fish came later) become custodians of the

DOI: 10.4324/9781003280262-4

threshold. There are funereal versions of Sirens, and in Neapolitan iconography images of Sirens became one with images of female saints. One episode in particular in the historical elaboration of the myth is indicative as a turning point in Christianity's rejection of paganism. St Ambrose, bishop of Milan from 374 to 397 AD, sermonized that in the same way as Ulysses was tied to the mast and resisted the Sirens' call, Christ was nailed to the cross to encourage us to withstand the call of the flesh. Ambrose became famous for other things too. A synagogue had been burned under his jurisdiction, and when the local authority wanted it rebuilt, Ambrose objected on the grounds that the beliefs of the Jews were inimical to Christianity.

In the history of the myth, the demonization of Sirens became one of the many features of Christianity's hegemony, and it trampled on the views of eminent philosophers such as Pythagoras and Plato and of poets such as Ovid, who respected the Sirens and called them wise.

The second event is the publication in 1543 of Copernicus' *De revolutionibus orbium caelestium* (On the revolution of the celestial spheres), a work inscribed in a (counter)-tradition within astronomy going back to Aristarchus in the third century BC and which in turn became the inspiration to an eminent lineage comprising Galileo, Kepler, Newton, and Einstein. The heliocentric perspective promoted by Copernicus went against the geocentric view of Ptolemy who in the second century AD brought to fruition the strands of a dominant tradition going back to Plato, Aristotle, and Hipparchus and whose model of the universe dominated astronomy. Copernicus' counter-traditional stance *decentred* the cosmic perspective, opening it up to the dizzy prospect of infinite possibilities and the absence of a centre in the universe. The heliocentric view was anathema to the tradition. Aristarchus was accused of impiety and the threat of being deemed a heretic was very real, as the well-known example of Galileo testifies. This violent, dogmatic resistance to a radically new perspective is understandable; it upsets the order of things. Contemplating even for a moment the movement of various wandering drifting stars in a vast universe without a centre contravenes all basic descriptions of an orderly system revolving around planet Earth. The very word "planets", Laplanche reminds us, come from the verb *planáo* meaning "to lead astray, to seduce", a term used in the Bible to describe "'seduction' by God or by Christ".[3]

Copernicus's perspective had wide implications also outside the field of astronomy, including philosophy and psychotherapy. These implications still reverberate today as does the animosity against it.

The first implication is *infinity*. Being able to conceive immensity, to feel with Giacomo Leopardi the sweet shipwreck of drowning in the immensity of the world is one of the consequences of the helio-centric perspective. We owe it to Aristarchus of Samos, and to his courage for withstanding the bien-pensants' accusation of impiety.

The second implication is *decentring*. "If the centre of the world can be everywhere", then "its circumference is nowhere".[4]

An infinite, decentred world: an exhilarating or terrifying perspec-tive, depending on one's view. Those in power who found it terrifying invariably accused scientists of wickedness. A decentred Earth implies a decentred human being, as well as a devalorization and relativization of all systems and cosmogonies constructed by humans. There are valuable and deep-seated reasons why the Ptolemaic vision had and continues to have a strong hold on humanity. It protects us from the humiliation of realizing that we are next to insignificant in the universe. It also protects us – slightly, fleetingly – from the sense that we are not the main point of reference of what we know or what we think we know. This epistemological decentring is very hard to accept as is our enduring resistance to take on board the theory of relativity and quantum theory. As a result of this resistance, our default tendency is to resort to re-centring, as Kant did when (after proposing a Copernican investigation in order to bring metaphysics on the path of science) he reasserted the Ptolemaic view by establishing a close link between his notion of the transcendental subject and Ptolemy's per-spective. What Kant calls *schematism*, i.e., the sensuous condition under which "pure concepts" can be understood, is an art centred and originating in the human soul.[5]

A similar move is present in Husserl, in a 1934 paper; the literal translation of the descriptive title Husserl wrote on the envelope of his manuscript sent to the publisher spells it out: *Subversion of Copernican doctrine: the Earth, as Primal Ark, does not move.*[6] Ark, as in Noah's ark, is a term closely linked to *arché* – first principle, origin, cause. The Earth becomes first principle. This is certainly an organizing principle

for the phenomenology to come, one echoed by Merleau-Ponty's subsequent parallel emphasis on human enfleshment (the body-subject) as
constitutive ground of experience. The "Ego" of Husserlian terminology
is *apodictic*, that is, beyond dispute, the very ground and source of
human experience – in Laplanche's commentary, a "constitutive subject
[as well as] the contingent subject of flesh and blood whose feet are on
that Earth".[7]

What Laplanche does not take into account is the possibility that
the body-subject can become, with Nietzsche's help, a threshold towards multiplicity and ambiguity hence, potentially, towards infinity
and decentring – admittedly a difficult task from within the "self-
centred" phenomenological perspective.

The third event: in chapter eleven of Joyce's *Ulysses*, published in
1920, the Sirens show up as two barmaids, Mina Kennedy with
golden hair and Lydia Douce with bronze hair. At 3:38 pm of 16 June
1904, they are watching through the windows of the Ormond Hotel a
procession go by the north bank of the Liffey, laughing at a man who is
craning his neck to have a better look at them. Many things happen in
the chapter which have the feel of a musical carousel and of an elaborate musical arrangement. Leopold Bloom is carrying the erotic
novel *The Sweets of Sin* as a present for Molly. Bloom's wife is going to
have sex that very day with Blazes Boylan. A piano tuner has just left,
and when Simon Dedalus comes in, he starts improvising on the piano
a tune called *Martha*, the story of a noblewoman called Lady Harriet
who disguising herself as Martha, meanders to the rough side of town,
ends up having a liaison with a man and is not seen for a few days. She
then returns to her life as an aristocrat and one day meets the man and
rejects him. The man is affronted by this but eventually things are
pacified and there is a happy ending. The whole chapter is musical,
even operatic. It adheres to an ontology of its own – *melos* instead of
logos, a musical ontology which bypasses the abstractions of being.
There is a linearity of sorts: introduction, duets, the tenor, the trio,
the quintet, but above all there is the *fugue*, one of the most
important forms of polyphonic writing. Polyphony may suggest an
assimilation of cultural/musical tropes so thorough that these take
flight and breed nature from the folds of culture. This is akin to a
line of flight. The entire edifice of cultural discipline, rules, and
conventions may be designed for the decisive moment of departure

and fleeing. At an organismic level – in etiology and the related field of human experience – a line of flight creates reality. Originating in moments of danger, it helps the human and the animal "regain its associated milieu".[8] Reality then, is not pre-existent; it is created. Like truth, it is generated rather than being something unveiled.

The unavoidable question is whether Ulysses, man of knowledge and science, is in fact a coward, even though his desire to go back to Ithaca is humanly understandable: after all, "he is trying to get home; it's a homecoming he wants" (John Mackessy, 2021, personal communication). The fact remains that he did not truly absorb the transformative power of the Sirens' song but from this and other encounters with otherness, sailed back to the Ithaca of the self-same. His forays into the unconscious are made with the purpose of mining it. The danger is real of course, and when he comes back from the encounter with the Sirens, his existence becomes more stable and secure – and more dull.

The fourth event: in a letter to his colleague Wilhelm Fliess, written on the autumn equinox of 1897, Freud abandons his general theory of seduction, an occurrence which will need backtracking. From its inception, psychoanalysis had (unwittingly) a subversive agenda: the decentring of the human subject. Giving primacy to the unconscious and fashioning a method "for the investigation of mental processes which are almost inaccessible in any other way",[9] went against both the aims and the principles of the tradition. Intellectual trends may have shifted since then, but positivist pressures persist, strengthened by the ever-recurring ambition to construct a semblance of mastery over the complexity of experience and the obscure motives for our actions.

It was not long before that very ambition began to hijack psychoanalysis itself. Freud's disowning of his own tentative formulation of the theory of seduction in his letter to Fliess represents a turning point. Freud had come to doubt his own hypothesis on the neuroses, attributing this change of heart to a host of reasons, including his own displeasure at not finding credible conclusions to his line of inquiry. The very idea that hysteria may be connected to sexual abuse enacted by the father suddenly felt outrageous. He had found, he wrote to Fliess, no clear correlation between frequent instances of hysteria and the rarer examples of sexual abuse. He was troubled by the implication that his theory had almost irresistibly leaned towards the conflation of neurosis with the father's perversion and what was summarily put away was a more generalized form of seduction.[10]

There are significant clinical implications attached to this change of heart. Before examining these, it is important to note that on a broader level the abandonment of seduction theory meant a change of direction for the entire psychoanalytic enterprise, in turn setting the tone for the route taken by various forms of psychotherapy that followed. As a result, the decentring of the human subject became virtually unthinkable. This was always the case with psychology, but now it became true also for psychoanalysis and consequently psychotherapy. One would need to look elsewhere – to art, literature, and poststructuralism in philosophy – to find compelling cases in favour of the decentring of the self. As for psychoanalysis, the move from decentring to substantiating the human subject announced by the abandonment of the theory of seduction nearly invalidated the age-old claim that Freud's enterprise constituted, alongside Marx's and Nietzsche's, one of the key components of the hermeneutics of suspicion. It put on hold indefinitely the Copernican revolution initiated by Freud,[11] neutering the claim that like Copernicus and Darwin before him (the former with respect to the cosmos, the latter in relation to natural evolution) Freud too ministered a considerable jolt to anthropocentrism and to our species' metaphysical narcissism. Much has been written on the link between Freud and Darwin. Here I will discuss briefly, after Laplanche, the link with Copernicus, partly because, unlike Darwin, he is much less prone to rely on implicit metaphysical biases. Within the field of astronomical theory, I understand Copernicus' thought to be the nearest equivalent to the philosophical counter-tradition of which poststructuralism is an integral part.

It is tempting at this point to want to advocate a theory and a practice focused almost exclusively on a decentred perspective, taking issue with any "changeling", be it a biological unit (the organism), a ghostly entity (transcendental ego), or a near Gnostic faculty (the felt sense) which has usurped the open space, claiming substantiality and centrality. It will be impossible to resist that temptation. It is worth pausing for a moment, however, on the revealing correlation found by Laplanche, according to which Freud is both Copernicus *and* Ptolemy. Potentially at least, from the persistent swaying between a Copernican decentring of the human subject and a Ptolemaic reviving of the latter, a braid may be woven which may add richness and complexity to psychical exploration. Privileging one over the other is only a partial conclusion. As it happens, one tendency took over in psychoanalysis and psychotherapy, possibly as a reflection of a generalized cultural and political sway in favour of mastery and, more recently, with the added compulsions to measure and quantify: the tendency to substantiate the human subject and promote cultures of control.

In his effort to uncover validating grand narratives at the heart of psychoanalysis, there is in Freud a constant tendency to go off track and unwittingly mislead the psychoanalytic exploration, allowing his original insights to be shackled by three major strands, each of them reflected in three major distracting "departures" in post-Freudian analysis as well as in psychotherapy. John Fletcher explains:

> The first involves the biologizing of sexuality and finds its direct descendants in Melanie Klein and her followers. The second, which finds its heir in the structuralism of Lacan, consists in situating structure or the structural in the heart of the unconscious. A third going-astray is indicated by the theme of the Ptolemaic reconstruction or recentering of the human being on itself (the legacy of which one might see at work in classical psychology).[12]

These departures bypass otherness, effectively ignoring the tangible presence and concrete influence of the other in the life of the self, making it difficult to realize *heteronomy* at the heart of what we normally understand as autonomy. In order to retrieve this realization, we need to go back, with Laplanche, to re-examine and perhaps develop anew the theory of general seduction.

"Seduction" in this context does *not* refer to abusive incidents suffered by children at the hands of their parents but instead to that ordinary and necessary *induction* to socialization taking place via the enigmatic, relatively unconscious communication transmitted from parents to children. Laplanche writes:

> The attentions of a mother or the aggression of a father are seductive only because they are not transparent ... because they convey something enigmatic.[13]

Necessarily grounded in nurture and care (the "good breast"), the scene of primal seduction has at its centre the "internalized object that results from the exciting implantation of the other".[14] The latter is not so much the bad breast of Kleinian lore, threatening to destroy the child, but the *sexual* breast, conveying an excitation whose overwhelming intensity resembles an attack. The message implanted is unknown and unknowable, but it is only by pursuing its depth that the nascent human subject potentially finds the new. Having come so close to this unruly and fertile revelation, Freud performed a round-about turn, deciding to submit to a different authority and laying down the foundations for a different kind of endeavour. At this crucial juncture, psychoanalysis ceased to be the unique, open-ended investigation – through free association – of hitherto inaccessible mental and organismic processes, and turned instead into another form of hermeneutics. It became yet another quest for "hidden meanings". It joined the ranks of most other psychotherapeutic and psychological orientations, all overtly or covertly animated by positivist agendas, no matter how different their individual lingo – whether the aim is aligning self-concept with organism, making the unconscious conscious, fostering psychological "growth", uncovering an alleged "real self", becoming fully embodied, becoming authentic, and so forth. What these notional itineraries have in common is a *reduction* of the infinity of meanings to a unitary meaning, the translation of multiplicity into unity. The outcome of this process of translation amounts to *repression*. It is not the task of the therapist to interpret, to be "a hermeneut, whether or not by means of the psychoanalytic ideologies which are at everybody's fingertips". In its more subversive, that is, thoroughgoing form, psychoanalytic/psychotherapeutic enterprise "runs counter" to the universal human tendency to interpret and apprehend, and it is in this sense that psychoanalysis and psychotherapy may be considered as "anti-hermeneutics".[15]

There are two prevalent misleading tendencies in the practice of psychotherapy today: *phenomenology* and *metaphysics*.

The phenomenological tendency endeavours to reinstate at the centre of psychical exploration the first-person Cartesian subject, a person who is believed to be the prime motor of her deeds and intentions. Examples of this are ego-psychology and conventional existential therapy. Even when they might draw on sources outside the Cartesian frame, these approaches invariably emphasize the "intentionality of a subject at the heart of all psychical acts"[16] and the integral accountability of the subject in relation to these acts. This tendency restricts and anthropomorphises psychical exploration. What these approaches fail to take into account is the presence of otherness within us. In so doing, they curtail the route to the possible origin of this internal *alien*ation, concrete others external to us, which is in turn "the residue of a fundamental decentring whose center for the child is the other adult, and whose force of gravitation is designated by the enigmatic message".[17]

The second misleading tendency is metaphysics, understood in Auguste Comte's sense of a domain replacing supernatural (theological) principles and causes with reified abstract forces, by turning dynamic and enigmatic processes into static entities – grammatically, turning adjectives and verbs into (often capitalized) nouns: "Being", the Unconscious, the Formative Tendency, etc. Dynamic tendencies in the psyche and in experience become metaphysical entities and shadows of God.

A thorough reframing of Freud's general theory of seduction, as mapped out by Laplanche, offers a different route. We must remember that in this context seduction is a foundational occurrence in the life of a human being. Against the dominant Cartesianism of most psychoanalytic/psychotherapeutic endeavours, seduction decentres the subject and affirms the *primacy* and *agency* of the other. This also goes counter to Freud's own understanding of the theory of seduction, where the subject is fully constituted and "has" an unconscious. Even though instinctual/biological reflexes in the child are "innate" (suckling, crying, excreting), they are met by the adult in a crucially asymmetrical fashion: "the infant's passivity and openness" meets the powerful, influential "actions, gestures, and words of the other".[18] What is missing in most psychoanalytic accounts of the primal scene is the *implantation* of enigmatic signifiers from the parent/caregiver into the skin or skin-ego of the infant. This implantation is not entirely translatable; it remains outside the confines of explained memories and fantasies. Taking from Lacan the crucial differentiation between signifier *of* and signifier *to*, Laplanche focuses on the latter. It is not a relation to a particular meaning that is central to this investigation, but the fact that it is directed at a particular subject, one (the infant) who is unable to assign a specific meaning to it but who nevertheless is aware that it is communicated to them. The enigmatic nature of the message is not only due to the fact that the infant cannot "read" it. Parents/ caregivers are themselves unaware of the message which traverses them and is implanted on the child. Placing the enigmatic message at the centre changes the primal scene and gives primacy to the other. The other becomes the origin of psychical life in the self. This move clarifies, expands on, and radicalizes Freud's theory of seduction. It deems insufficient Freud's reliance of the arousal of a pre-given instinct in relation to which the presence of the mother is only fleetingly perceived as sexual. Reorienting the centre of psychical life in the parent's message is a fertile and intelligent way to begin an investigation outside the self-boundedness of inner life, that "closing-in-on-itself of the Freudian psychical system, its *monadological* character".[19] Freud's famous maxim *Wo Es War, soll Ich werden* (where it was, there I shall be) marks a return to the self after forays into the unconscious. It affirms the central role of the self (even if admittedly understood as something more than the narcissistic ego). The shift in emphasis suggested by Laplanche paints a different scenario: "*Wo Es war, wird (soll? muss?) immer noch Anderes sein*",[20] he writes, modifying Freud's dictum: Where it was there will (should? must?) still be the other. To which I would add: not the other but others, for the id is not the unitary Schopenhauerian "will" but multiplicity – others "within" and "without" the psyche: where it was, *others* shall be. It is the therapist's duty to bear this in mind, and pay more attention to the primacy of the other and the primacy of the enigmatic message.

The role of seduction as foundational induction into life has been denied in psychoanalysis and psychotherapy (along with its close counterpart, other-centredness) despite academic gesticulations signalling its presence, and then almost exclusively in relation to child mistreatment and abuse. Everything denied finds other conduits and this is no exception. Already in the 1920s Georg Groddeck[21] wrote of the id as a force which moves us rather than one we "utilize". The idea became influential yet was incorporated within a monadic psyche, as a presence within us rather than an ambiguous manifestation of otherness. The unbroken if ambiguous presence of seduction in psychotherapy enables a dialectical movement of innovations, testy reactions and detours which together weave "a sort of braid". At times, "one strand of the plait lies uppermost, at times the other".[22] The presence of seduction and otherness in the mix allows for expansion of the experiential field outside the self-boundedness of the ego-self. The countermovement is then an attempt to integrate, resystematize, and *save appearances*. The notion of "saving the appearances" has a fascinating history closely linked to the Copernican/ Ptolemaic dispute discussed above. It first emerged in the commentary on Aristotle's *On the Heavens* by the sixth century Neoplatonist philosopher Simplicius for whom hypotheses which explain appearances are not necessarily true. Two differing hypotheses can in his view both explain (or "save") appearances, as in the case of Copernican and Ptolemaic explanations.

There is an interesting correlation: in Book 8 of Milton's *Paradise Lost*, Adam asks the angel Raphael about the motions of the stars, sun, and planets. He had assumed the Ptolemaic view, that other planets orbit the earth. But Raphael is noncommittal and even conveys ironic distance from all elaborate human construction, replying: *This to attain, whether Heaven move or Earth, imports not.* Humans build, unbuild, he says, contriving to save appearances.[23] In ancient astronomy, this need to save appearances and assimilate unexpected detours and deviations from a unitary view of the cosmos is manifested in the formulation of *epicycles*. The main equivalent of an epicycle in psychoanalysis, after the rejection of seduction theory, is the *death drive*, which reinstated "the balance of the Freudian system [reaffirming] something of the order of sexuality in its most savage dimension".[24] Freud will call this dimension *demonic*, ascribing it to the domain of biology while at the same time unwittingly offsetting a thoroughly domesticated psychical landscape.[25]

*

Subversive elements present at the heart of psychoanalysis and psychotherapy have not been completely obliterated, despite zealous attempts to do so. The Copernican revolution initiated by Freud remains unattained but the dream of subversion works quietly underground – in the psyche as in the polis – waiting for the right moment to re-emerge in the light of day. Despite strenuous efforts by its maker and devotees to domesticate it and turn it into a new science of policing the psyche, at its inception the Freudian project harboured two revolutionary seeds: (a) the formulation of an unconscious – of something eccentric or rather ex-centric, "alien", ex-ternal, other, at the heart of the subject; (b) the theory of seduction, which locates the origin of this alien-ness into the parents' enigmatic message to the infant.

Then there is the question of method. Pre-Freudian and post-Freudian formulations of the unconscious presume that "it" can be translated, made conscious, apprehended and redeemed through the known methodologies which are conventionally useful for other investigations: hermeneutics, linguistics, quantitative research, reliance on intersubjective conscious dialogue, etc., all geared towards more or less secularist modes of divination.

The ground-breaking discovery, however, had more to do with the formulation of a method able to dissolve all methodologies. *Lösung* or dis-solution is at the heart of *analysis*, to loosen, a term first appearing in Homer's account of Penelope unravelling at night her day's weaving, which may also be taken to mean that she unweaves so that she can weave a new cloth, the tapestry of mourning for Ulysses.

It is encouraging to see, incidentally, the slow but significant emergence in the field of research of *post-qualitative* methods aimed precisely at the dissolution of positivist methodologies.[26]

Why do we need a method which dissolves all methodologies when studying experience? From within the psychoanalytic frame the answer is: because there is "no point-for-point correspondence", ... no analogy or resemblance between "the behavioural or conscious discursive sequence from which the associations start" and the splinter of an unconscious sequence which can be "outlined through cross-reference".[27] The best model of this non-method so far is *free association*.

This notion can and should be extended to other theoretical approaches and to investigations outside the clinic. It is not possible to know the dark by bringing a light. To become acquainted with the dark, we must go dark.[28] It is not possible to transpose one language into another. Every time we do so, no matter how sophisticated, shrewd, or ethically sound the language in question may be – whether Freudian, Kleinian, Jungian, Rogerian, Heideggerian, Merleau-Pontian, etc. – the thread is lost and we enter an ideological terrain – a terrain of repression and betrayal despite all our good intentions. Symbolism stifles association. Dialogical hyper-rational discourse curbs the intensity and the transformative potential of affect. Pre-fabricated, didactic notions of "authenticity" and "truth" prevent new phenomena from emerging. Without a direct or even indirect link to the actual practice and/or ethos of free association, the psychotherapeutic endeavour merely turns into another kind of hermeneutics.

Laplanche is Freud's closest interpreter and translator. Admittedly, the fact that his painstaking emphasis on *other-centredness* in psychotherapy goes hand in hand with ascribing *primacy to sexuality* problematize things in our neo-puritanical age. Many will fret that wanting to look closely at a mistrusted theory of seduction skirts perilously close to insinuating tinges of impingement and exploitation in an area where, as we are told, the only certifiable affects are care, love, and sustenance. Sadly, the price we pay is very high when we choose to ignore the tactile and verbal interactions which are integral to adult care and "without which the child cannot survive and cannot emerge as a subject of desire".[29] By sanitizing and de-eroticizing these exchanges, by attacking the theory of infantile sexuality and the theory of the drives, by fumigating the unconscious, conventional attachment theorists have kissed goodbye to any possibility of psychical transformation. The immolation of sexuality in the name of a mislaid morality has also meant bypassing otherness, for affirming the primacy of sexuality welcomes the question of the other – in the child's case, an opening "onto the adult other in his or her alien-ness".[30] The current understanding of trauma touted by a lucrative trauma industry, feeding on a crude mix of neuroscience and attachment theory, is misguided. In the case of trauma, or rather the *memory* of trauma, the other "acts like a foreign body which long after its entry must continue to be regarded as an *agens* that is still at work". The unconscious itself is "an alien inside me, and even put inside me by an alien".[31] In his most daring and visionary moments, Freud called it *possession*.

It may be impossible, and even undesirable, to ground one's perspective solely on the primacy of otherness. Persistent emphasis on other-centredness throughout the present work is an attempt to re-balance the excessive self-centredness of the entire psychotherapeutic endeavour. The extra-vagance or "outer-wondering" of these reflections deliberately resist the magnetic pull of the tradition, but it is an uphill struggle. The attempt to reduce, translate, and colonize the fundamental alien-ness implanted onto our psyche is unrelenting and pervades our culture. First of all, psychiatry: through feeble claims, it translated alien-ness as "degeneracy, hereditary dispositions, constitutional inferiority".[32] Then psychoanalysis, bulling us into accepting that the unconscious is something deep within the heart of our so-called being, and thirsting to recover "repressed memories". On the back of psychoanalysis, all other therapeutic approaches followed suit, despite protestations to the contrary, by endorsing the repressive notion of integration: I have to re-absorb something which has been "split off", so that so-called divided self reacquires its place as master, manager, and chief accountant of experience. Please listen doc, the self was divided from the start, division and multiplicity are its essential nature. The unconscious is not pathological, and it is doubtful whether the right course of action is to fight the client/patient's alleged irresolution and defences so that they may restore a modicum of normality. What's more, to think all of the unconscious can be made conscious (that the truth of being can be finally unveiled, that the memory of trauma that makes one sick can be assimilated) is the greatest falsehood peddled by our profession. In a nutshell, the question is: "how is it that the unconscious can consist of that which is repressed, and yet despite this be inexhaustible – be capable ... of endlessly slipping away from our grasp?"[33]

Concerted attempts to neutralize the unconscious go hand in hand with neutering sexuality and deactivating otherness – modes of actions turbocharged by neoliberal psychology to which all orientations now subscribe despite their various jargons of authenticity and misguided radicalism. The set of underlying delusions animating this repressive and normative project is staggering. At its origin lies the *incorporation and distortion of alterity* – the alterity of the unconscious, the alterity of sexuality, and the alterity of concrete others. As a result, all talk of learning from the creative unconscious, from sexuality and from relatedness sounds hollow. The other remains exiled from the psychotherapeutic enterprise – its presence reduced to a trace when obliquely acknowledged via the transference, patchworked within a "world", its simulacrum a jack-in-the-box scarecrow anxiously waved about in order to bolster moralizing codes of ethics bent on exercising the letter of the law while annihilating its heart. No amount of self-centred, sermonizing altruism can replace the viscerally felt presence of the other through the primary seduction. Equally, no amount of emphasis on the transindividual role of language, as in Lacan, can adequately account for the otherness of the other. Emphasis on language – a structuralist move par excellence – diffuses or even obliterates the other. The primary caregiver's implanted enigmatic message may be, and often is, primarily nonverbal. The infant receiving it (*infans* in Latin = unable to speak) receives it nonverbally and/or without understanding it on a cognitive level.

What is advocated here is the decentring revolution advocated by Laplanche for whom "internal alien-ness [is] maintained by external alien-ness; external alien-ness, in turn, [is] held in place by the enigmatic relation of the other to his own internal alien".[34] Why did the psychoanalytic/psychotherapeutic enterprise fall short of this crucial step, thus remaining shackled to a self-bound view of psyche and experience? Laplanche attributes this historical-cultural blunder to a host of factors, including overstated focus on the unconscious as pathological, the patent disregard of the enigmatic message implanted onto the child, as well as the crucial mistake of invoking (via Darwin's influence) phylogenesis, i.e., the evolutionary history of a species or group of related species.

Once the initial dismay Darwinism spawned among the righteous and the religiose began to abate, it became a given, especially among Freudians,[35] that re-joining humans to their animal and biological heredity deflates their misguided sense of mastery. But that can only happen if Darwinism is reframed within a counter-traditional critique which places humans on the same plane of immanence with other sentient beings and strips it clean of its totalizing and christianizing arborescence (the family tree now becoming the tree of life). It can only happen, in other words, if Darwinism is washed clean of Darwinism – anathema to secularist societies thriving on the persistent influence of God's many shadows. One of Laplanche's great merits is to have smuggled post-structuralism into the very heart of psychoanalysis. He never mentions rhizomatic philosophy or arborescence, yet his critique of phylogenetic thought bears the same counter-traditional punch:

> The family tree ... now goes back beyond Abraham ... beyond
> Adam, to take in the history of all life to the point where the term
> "phylogenesis", once restricted to the origin of a single species,
> ends up encompassing the entire evolution of life, of which the
> human species is the last link in the chain. Solidly in place, firmly
> centered on the animal pyramid, man does not fail to consider
> himself its culmination, the blossom of the family tree.[36]

Spiritualist and neo-traditionalist doctrines such as the ones expounded
by Teilhard de Chardin and more recently by Ken Wilber firmly reinstated humans and "cosmic consciousness" at the peak of evolution.[37]
The doctrine of evolution does not decentre humans; it reinstates them
as the darlings of creation. Similarly, Freud's reliance on the genetic
nature of drives and fantasies enfeebled the subversive valence of psychoanalysis, and helped place it within other hermeneutical disciplines
where the Cartesian self is firmly back on the saddle. Go within, the
recentring of the human subject implies, meditate and/or examine
yourself in the therapy room. You will one day discover that all
those troubling feelings and emotion are nothing strange, nothing
alien. Fears, repressed desires, crippling anxieties? Don't worry.
They are merely somatic manifestations of the origins of life, ways
to readjust *your* worldview to worlding. Indivisible monads are
back on the driving seat of evolution, in the diving bell of their
soul's apparatus. Closed in on itself, there is only one hope for the
monad: becoming a *nomad*, from the Greek *nemein*, roaming in
search of new pastures, exploring the far reaches of experience and
psyche without the compulsion to make it back to the Ithaca of
ipseity, to the living room of the self-same where the trophies of
psychical exploration are exhibited for friends and visitors.

   A rich and creative tension would ensue if the natural undecided
oscillation between a Ptolemaic and Copernican view of the psyche
were permitted in our culture, but mainstream psychoanalysis/psy-
chotherapy has repressed most Copernican motion, feeding instead
on perpetual Ptolemaic setbacks, "taking the point of view of the
subject in interpersonal matters and of the ego in intrapersonal
ones",[38] essentially promoting narcissistic closure. Attempts to evade
the claustrophobia of an enclosed psyche, whether through the
intersubjectivity between two monads, the given relatedness of

Dasein, or Jungian anagogic interpretation, only succeed in giving it a diverting new décor and do not come anywhere near in addressing the alien-ness in the familiar, the other in the self.

It sounds outrageous to contemporary sensibilities to affirm with Laplanche that psychoanalysis and psychotherapy are not forms of hermeneutics (whether realistic or creative hermeneutics), which very nearly cover the entire spectrum of what psychotherapy has become. It may be useful to briefly register two positions in relation to trauma. *Realistic* hermeneutics sees it as a sort of disorder of memory; recovering the person's "real story" will allow them to disengage from the blockages, repetition compulsions, and defences, and restore them to greater autonomy. This is in many ways an archaeological endeavour (with its ambivalent ancestral links to art lovers, travellers, and grave or monument robbers). Its modern version commands that the precious object in question – the suppressed memory retrieved at last – will be in some way or other made instructive and edifying for the present and in such a way that the past no longer inhibits the present. *Creative* hermeneutics (in true constructivist fashion, and harking back to Ricoeur, Heidegger, and Jung) admits to the relativism of facts and focuses instead on experience, defined as that which is being inquired in the present, which includes the way the past is currently constructed.

To the impasse created by the alternation between the two opposing views described above, Laplanche poses "a third category, that of the message whose meaning is immanent, in particular taking the form of the mostly nonverbal messages conveyed by the adult to the small child".[39] This opens a new route to psychotherapeutic investigation: how can the ambivalent, intrinsically traumatizing message be transposed and alchemically transformed into the person's path, encouraging them to create their own ambivalent message to the world? For this kind of investigation to take place, however, we need to bypass the distancing brought about by years of training and practice and look at some phenomena at face value, or "phenomenologically". This implies being ready to look at *seduction* rather than seduction *fantasy*, at *persecution* (in the psychotic) rather than *delusion* of persecution, at *revelation* (in the religious person) rather than revelation *myth*. It implies looking at active forces at work in relation to which the subject in some way or other has to respond.

The system of psychotherapeutic knowledge becomes a reassuring armour that shields us from the affective intensity of the above phenomena and from the underlying suspicion that the clients/patients expressing them may be on to something. It also *re-centres* the investigation and incorporates otherness. Without respectful acknowledgement of the alien-ness and intrinsic multiplicity within the person, however, the whole enterprise is doomed to serving a cosmetic role of superficial psychological adaptation. Without a concerted effort to refrain from effecting a psycho-*synthesis* of the multiple aspects that constitute the subject (now, that would be real nondirectivity!), the whole enterprise ends up serving the agendas of our societies of control. Without refraining from conjuring the other out of the hat of the same, we miss the constitutive presence of otherness, and allow psychotherapy to become yet another form of colonialization. We miss the crucial, subversive insight present at the dawn of psychoanalysis, namely that the "I" does not generate psychical reality, that the latter is inherently intrusive.

It is only in a very indirect way that the notion of transference acknowledges the presence of the other, even when coated in the language and practice of intersubjective psychoanalysis and relational existential/humanistic therapy. In Freud, the subject is a fully furnished person, endowed and burdened, that is, with a constellations of neuroses, conflicts, and occasional piercing insights. In Melanie Klein, the subject is a fully insulated person – a heightened version of the above to the point where concrete others are reduced to internal objects. Things open out somewhat with Ferenczi and Lacan, the former introducing a notion of mutuality – very similar to the relatedness championed by conventional existential therapy, i.e., that is the connectedness between two fully insulated, fully self-preserved monads, the latter sacrificing the other to the altar of language in a way not wholly dissimilar to Heidegger sacrificing existents for existence. Both modes of thinking privilege the impersonal over and above the nitty-gritty. As with the other modes of thinking sketched above, they also largely ignore the enigmatic message.

It has become counterintuitive to affirm that the work of the therapist needs to focus on guarding the enigma and reopening the pathways of psyche to the dimension of alterity so brazenly exiled by the psychological and philosophical traditions.

We have come at a crossroad in our investigation. It may be possible after all for the subservient and thoroughly colonized practice of psychotherapy to take flight and be put in the service of emancipation. To this purpose some particular insights from Laplanche become invaluable, insights which unquestionably reveal his brilliance and foresight. As with astronomy before, this time too associations come from far afield – from astronautics. There is a specific interval in the launch of a spaceship – a "window" – when it can either go "into orbit from the earth or allow for a departure from a satellite already in orbit, of a vessel aiming to leave the earth's gravitational system".[40] Similarly in therapy there are advantageous moments or windows where the work can take flight – or else remain in the gravitational pull and continue to go round in the familiar orbit. Laplanche does not mention this, but the "windows" in question and their relation to the earth's orbit are reminiscent of Nietzsche's notion of the eternal recurrence and its link to the liberating insight or opening that may occur to bold explorers.

There is no certainty that the work can take off and leave the gravitational pull or whether it will instead revolve in endless repetition. What is crucial is that *external* intervention is as (or perhaps more) important than mere internal dynamics, internal changes and readaptations in personality structure or "worldview". The aspect of en*counter* becomes crucial. The therapist as *other*, undermining the monadological emphasis of most theoretical approaches. The therapist as a subversive agent going against the dogmas and dictates of neoliberal therapy.

*

Notes

1 Homer, *Odyssey*. Books I-XII, With Introduction and Notes, by W. W. Merry. Oxford: Clarendon Press, 2018.
2 Maurice Blanchot, *The Sirens' Song: Selected Essays*. Edited by Gabriel Josipivici. Bloomington, IN: Indiana University Press, 1982.
3 Jean Laplanche, *Essays on Otherness*. London and New York: Routledge, 1999, p. 54.
4 *Essays on Otherness,* op. cit., p. 56.
5 Immanuel Kant, *Critique of Pure Reason*, trans. N. Kemp-Smith. London: Macmillan, 1978.
6 Husserl's text is to be found in English as 'Foundational Investigations of the Phenomenological Origins of the Spatiality of Nature', in Edmund Husserl:

Shorter Works, ed. Peter McCormick and Fredrik Elliston. Indianapolis, IND: University of Notre Dame Press, 1981.

7   Laplanche, *Essays on Otherness*, op. cit., p. 58.
8   Gilles Deleuze and Felix Guattari, *A Thousand Plateaus: Capitalism and Schizophrenia*, trans. Massumi B. New York: Continuum, 1980, p. 61.
9   Sigmund Freud, *Standard Edition of the Complete Psychological Works (SE)*, Vol XVIII, the Hogarth Press, 1974, p. 235.
10 Sigmund Freud, *The Complete Letters of Sigmund Freud to Wilhelm Fliess: 188–1904.* Cambridge, MA: Harvard University Press, 1985.
11 Sigmund Freud, 'A Difficulty in the Path of Psycho-analysis', *SE* XVII, pp. 137–144.
12 John Fletcher, *Psychoanalysis and the question of the other*, in Jean Laplanche, Essays on Otherness, op. cit., pp. 1–51; p. 4.
13 Cited in John Fletcher, Psychoanalysis and the question of the other, op. cit., p. 13.
14 Ibid, p. 14.
15 Jean Laplanche, *Essays on Otherness*, op. cit., p. 112.
16 Ibid, p. 113, emphasis added.
17 ibid, p. 114.
18 *Psychoanalysis and the question of the other*, op. cit., p. 11.
19 *Essays on Otherness*, op. cit., p. 81.
20 Ibid, p. 83.
21 Georg Groddeck, *The Book of the It*. Eastford, CT: Martino Fine Books, 2015.
22 *Essays on Otherness*, op. cit., p. 61.
23 John Milton, *Paradise Lost*. Oxford, OX: Oxford University Press, 2008.
24 *Essays on Otherness*, p. 61.
25 For a discussion of the demonic (and daimonic) see chapter 8, *Of the Devil's Party* in this book.
26 Manu Bazzano, 'Making Love to Your Data', *Therapy Today*, March 2021, pp. 42–45, http://manubazzano.com/wp-content/uploads/2021/02/PostQualitative TTmarch.pdf
27 *Essays on Otherness*, op. cit., p. 62.
28 I am paraphrasing a passage from Wendel Berry's poem, To know the dark: "To go in the dark with a light is to know the light. / To know the dark, go dark. Go without sight, / and find that the dark, too, blooms and sings, / and is travelled by dark feet and dark wings". Wendell Berry, *The Selected Poems of Wendell Berry.* Berkeley, CA: Counterpoint, 1998, p. 68.
29 Judith Butler, 'Seduction, Gender and the Drive', in John Fletcher and Nicholas Ray (eds), *Seductions and Enigmas*, London: Lawrence & Wishart, 2014, pp. 118–133, p. 121.
30 *Essays on Otherness*, op. cit., p. 64.
31 Ibid, p. 65.
32 Ibid, p. 67.
33 Ibid, p. 70.
34 Ibid, p. 80.
35 For instance, Adam Phillips, *Darwin's Worms*, London: Faber, 1999.
36 *Essays on Otherness*, op. cit., pp. 80–81.
37 Manu Bazzano, 'House of Cards: on Ken Wilber's Neo-traditionalism'. *Self & Society*, 44: 2, 145–156, DOI: 10.1080/03060497.2016.1147666.
38 *Essays on Otherness*, op. cit., p. 82.
39 Ibid, p. 165.
40 Ibid, pp. 231–232.

Chapter 4

After Attachment Theory

Once I publicized a lecture titled "Against Attachment Theory". Someone asked indignantly, "How can *anyone* be against attachment theory?" Another wanted to know, "How can there be anything *critical* to say about a theory on which there is widespread consensus?" I have come across similar reactions any time I questioned the tenets of attachment theory (AT). I question them because I see them as a set of hypotheses rather than articles of faith within a belief system. Inquiry, perplexity, and constructive doubt are normally deemed useful for study and research, and the strong resistance I encounter when wanting to discuss this topic beyond supine acceptance of its tenets seems to confirm that AT has become a belief system. There appears to be a widespread consensus across theoretical orientations on the validity of AT alongside a championing of its presumed universality. This might suggest the presence of *ideology* at work. Considering that sociologists, feminists, and queer theorists have been saying for decades that AT constitutes an attack on working mothers, that it is a consecration of essentialism and the patriarchal system, as well as a defence of familialism, one could also ask: "Why didn't the psychotherapy world even notice that there is a wider discussion happening on this topic?" One might equally want to stress that excessive emphasis on the importance of a secure base has meant the bypassing of the equally central aspects of exploration, adventure, and lines of flight *from* the celebrated secure base. The one-sided, universally accepted view in relation to AT has contributed to the neutering of more subversive and innovative insights present in psychoanalytic/psychotherapeutic theory and practice, and to the reinforcement of a

DOI: 10.4324/9781003280262-5

reductive understanding of mental distress and its potential "cure". It is high time for the articulation of a different view and a different praxis.

*

Would it be right to call AT an *illusion*? Freud was credited with being one of the representatives, alongside Marx and Nietzsche, of the hermeneutics of suspicion, and in *The Future of an Illusion*,[1] he tackles religious beliefs, which he broadly defined as *illusions*. For Freud (in a manner that is reminiscent of Pyrrho, the sceptic philosopher of antiquity to whom we owe *epoché*, now banalized as "bracketing"), a religious belief is made up of "teachings and assertions about facts and conditions of external (or internal) reality which tell one something one has not discovered for oneself and which lay claim to one's beliefs".[2] Crucially, he added, "illusions need not necessarily be false – that is to say, unrealizable or in contradiction to reality".[3] Illusions are not delusions. "We call a belief – he wrote – an illusion when a wish-fulfilment is a prominent factor in its motivation, and in doing so we disregards its relations to reality, just as the illusion itself sets no store by verification".[4]

Freud differentiated between illusion, error, and delusion: Illusion is neither true nor false. To be at variance with reality is not illusion's main characteristic. An illusion may come true, which is not the case with either error or delusion. An error is factually false; a delusion is in contradiction with reality whilst being factually false. Above all, an illusion fulfils a wish; it can be seen as an error that can satisfy a wish. For instance, Christopher Columbus died a happy man, believing he had discovered a new route to the East Indies. He didn't, but such is the power of personal illusion. He was also celebrated as a great explorer, even though as a brutal viceroy and governor of the Caribbean islands on which he landed, he carried out the mass killings of native peoples.[5] Such is the power of collective illusion. Illusion is deceptive, and oddly persuasive. Marx used a similar term, *phantasmagoria*, a sequence of artificial imaginings, to describe commodity fetishism – i.e., the propensity to assign to commodities (including money) a power that resides solely to the labour applied to create commodities. He also used the term when describing the monetary system. A similar, blatant example of illusion is the widely held belief in free markets, a belief dating back to eighteenth-century France and the Physiocrats, economists who believed that the wealth of nations was derived solely from agriculture. Why is the free market an illusion through and through? Bernard Harcourt explains:

> All free markets ... are artificial, constructed, regulated, and administered by often complex mechanisms that necessarily distribute wealth in large and small ways. ... [I]n a purportedly free market, the state is just as present, enforcing private contract; preventing and punishing trespass on private property; over-seeing, regulating, policing, and enforcing through criminal, administrative, and civil sanctions ... distributing wealth through the tax code, military spending, bureaucratic governance.[6]

Given the above definitions and examples, one could confidently say that AT is an illusion; that despite its foundational and universalizing claims, it is not ultimately "true"; and that, as its wide appeal may suggest, it appears to fulfil a wish. If so, what kind of wish does AT fulfil?

*

AT has been described as "the most important developmental construct ever investigated".[7] It has been influential in many areas of research, particularly in Anglophone countries, and has been popular in describing parent-child interactions. It is among the most significant discourses in shaping perceptions of child development and parenting across and beyond Anglophone countries. It is a key notion in intervention programmes for underprivileged children and those suffering from neglect. More recently, it has supplied the main theoretical underpinnings – albeit in a simplified version – for the ever-flourishing trauma industry. It has also been accepted by the majority of therapeutic orientations as the necessary framework for understanding relatedness, a prevalent theme in counselling and psychotherapy practice today.

In short, AT has been accepted as *foundational truth*. The philosophical counter-tradition teaches us that imposing a foundation and presenting truth claims are power moves and that a judicious researcher/practitioner will at the very least try to avert them. Unless of course a researcher becomes unwittingly invested in perpetuating the status quo while lip-praising science. Feminist scholars and sociologists alike voiced fierce criticism of AT. They claimed that it amounts to a powerful pretext for apportioning sole responsibility to mothers for the care of children and then blaming them for not doing it adequately. Similar criticisms point out that AT is weighed down by Western values and meanings presented as universal.[8] Other scholars examined the cultural *relativity* (rather than the alleged *universality*) of what they see as three core hypotheses of AT, namely: (a) that caregiver's kindness leads to secure attachment; (b) that secure attachment leads to greater social adaptation; (c) that securely attached children see the primal caregiver as a secure base for exploration of the outside world. Could theories of attachment be articulated in more culturally specific ways? This is a sensible question when considering minority groups or the fact that different cultures have different histories, values, ethnicities, philosophies, and politics, and that what may be valid in the Anglosphere may not apply to the rest of the world.

Consider the following statement:

> When most investigators [have] ... a common cultural perspective or ideological position, the effect may be to retard or to corrupt the search for scientific knowledge by collectively blinding them to alternative conceptions.[9]

It may be surprising to find that the above passage is not from some subversive group's manifesto bent on destroying the system but is from Janet Spence's 1985 American Psychological Association's presidential address. After nearly four decades, her statement could be applied to AT, to its ethnocentrism and foundational claims of universality, and more importantly perhaps to the uncritical acceptance it has received in the world of counselling and psychotherapy.

While virtually every psychological tenet and approach has been routinely scrutinized, AT has remained untouched. Family systems theory has been taken apart for emphasizing differentiation. Despite their wide ideological differences, both client-centred therapy and psychoanalysis were broadly criticized for their alleged individualism. Daniel Stern's work has been critiqued for its depiction of a "masterful, feeling, continuous infant"[10] that matches Western notions of human experience. Why then did psychotherapy culture fail to properly address AT's shortcomings? One explanation would be that psycho-therapy and critical thought are not great bedfellows. A more specific response would argue that proponents of AT have, at least conjec-turally, acknowledged specific cultural influences which temper claims of universality.[11] All the same, the fact remains that attachment the-orist's emphasis "on the evolutionary roots of attachment" meant that they systematically understated "the role of culture".[12]

*

The word "attachment" first appeared in psychoanalysis as the English word used to translate Freud's *Anlehnung* ("depending-on"), adopted in the *Three Essays on the Theory of Sexuality* to denote a kind of love arising out of the child's need for their self-preservation and directed at their caregiver.[13] Later on, John Bowlby, drawing on his psychoanalytic training in Object Relations, on Darwinism, and on his own studies in animal behaviour, introduced the notions of *attachment* and the *attachment system.*[14] He noticed the tendency in primate infants, whenever they experienced anxiety or separation, to seek closeness to an adult attachment figure through actions such as crawling and weeping. In doing so, Bowlby observed, primate infants predict a reaction by the adult which will soothe their distress. Something similar happens with human infants, he argued, who have an innate ability, whenever they experience panic or disconnection, to look for the accessibility of a caregiver. This tendency is made up of many aspects: social, physical, as well as hormonal. For Bowlby, the attachment system is like a *machine* which emerges and develops in relation to the experience of caregiving. When caregiving is not, ac-cording to his view, "integrated", as with children growing up in institutional settings, the attachment system is not suitably activated. In order to operate, the attachment system needs an active response from the caregiver (invariably, in Bowlby's account, the mother) to the child's distress. "Can we doubt that the more and better an infant smiles – Bowlby writes – the better is he loved and cared for?" He memorably adds: "It is fortunate for their survival that babies are so designed by Nature that they beguile and enslave mothers".[15] The mother remains central for Bowlby. What about the father? "Little will be said of the father–child relation – he wrote – his value as the economic and emotional support of the mother will be assumed".[16]

*

In the 1970s Bowlby's colleague Mary Ainsworth devised a standardized method for evaluating disparities in child attachment. She called it the *Strange Situation Procedure*. Attentive to the levels of anxiety which may come up in children in relation to the caregiver's accessibility, she devised a series of episodes each lasting about 3 minutes: Mother and baby are alone at first. They are then joined by a stranger. The mother leaves baby and stranger alone. Mother returns and stranger leaves. Mother leaves and the baby is alone. Stranger returns. Mother returns and stranger leaves. These various occurrences of union, separation, and reunion, utilize elements of novelty so as to activate and then observe the child's instinctive expectations. The child's response also depended on the caregiver's expression when returning and, crucially, on how regular or prolonged instances of separation are within different societies and cultures.[17] From these observations, Ainsworth drew three classifications of child's behaviour. These are (1) *Secure*, when the child shows signs of distress and wants closeness when the caregiver returns and is comforted, with the caregiver becoming a safe base from which the child can set out to play. (2) *Insecure-avoidant*, when the child shows no noticeable response during either separation or reunion but is then found to have unseen signs of distress such as faster heartbeat. In these cases, it was discovered that caregivers would tend to respond *conditionally* to the child, i.e., by being welcoming when the child did not show distress. (3) *Insecure-resistant-ambivalent*, when the child would be distressed before separation and would not be soothed at the moment of reunion. In these cases, it was discovered that caregivers were not consistent in their responses to the child. Mary Main and Judith Solomon later added a *fourth* grouping, *disorganized/disoriented*,[18] one where there is disruption caused by conflicting actions and feelings. All four classifications have been influential in how the well-being of an adult will be assessed in later life. For instance, some research shows that disorganized/disoriented attachment in early life had strong links to of dissociation in adolescence.[19]

*

Given that for centuries calls to "nature" and "biology" have been used against women and in favour of the patriarchal family and of gender conservatism, suspicion of AT from feminists and sociologists is more than justifiable. So is the "legitimate scepticism" towards forms of research attempting to bring together "biological, social and political assemblages".[20] What's more, overenthusiastic appeals to the allegedly unassailable objectivity of neuroscience in the last two decades have strengthened conservative policies which have made wide use of AT.

Despite the undivided opinion in favour of AT in the world of psychology, other fields beg to differ. Sociologist, anthropologists, feminists, and queer theorists mounted persuasive criticisms of AT. Their main point is that it is a "profoundly conservative"[21] view bolstering heteronormativity and defending the traditional family, enhancing the biopolitical disciplining of parents, and engendering "mother-blaming scenarios"[22] with women deemed responsible for the future of the nation. Even though AT has been over the last few decades "upgraded" through a neuroscientific twist, it is also true, as Erica Burman has made clear, that the "neuro" turn has not been subjected to adequate critical reflection. Moreover, there is a social investment in the child which has little to do with the child's nascent subjectivity and a lot to do with seeing in the child the future labourer/consumer. Parallel to this, there has been a widespread return to antiquated ideas of character and resilience, both notions tending to forget the socio-political context and blaming the parent instead – usually the mother. For Burman, the way in which AT conceives distress in the child is inconsistent: "If the child will not settle to play some distance from her mother while she is there – Burman writes – the attachment is considered insecure. Conversely, this conclusion is also drawn if the child fails to protest at his or her mother's departure".[23]

When the consensus on a particular area of research is so widespread that no dissent nor different views are really allowed, the question arises whether we are, as suggested above, in the presence of an *ideology*.

In their influential report *Early Intervention: Good Parents, Great Kids, Better Citizens*, former Government Minister Graham Allen and former Conservative leader Iain Duncan Smith underlined how important it is to make sure that children's attachment relationship with their mother is organized in a way that will produce obedient and self-reliant citizens.[24] Allen and Duncan Smith's simplistic understanding of AT was marshalled to support their insistence that the State should play a negligible role in supporting its citizens and for blaming mothers. They did not take into account the fact that research on attachment since the 1990s[25] has shown that the individual caregiver's sensitivity to the child has less effect on that child's attachment the more the caregiver is *deprived* of economic, health, and social resources. The perverse merit of such biased and psychologically illiterate piece of "research" is that it reveals inadvertently the classism AT encourages and is prone to. The nurture and care evoked by AT is terminally W.A.S.P. and middle-class, a rarefied post-war scenery in the light, with a sense of a future, meaning, and inherited wealth. For those in the dark pit of poverty, petty crime, malnutrition, and the inevitable "mental health issues", AT provides perfect pseudo-erudite padding to a veritable programme of authoritarian re-education dressed up in caring jargon.

Most psychotherapy trainings have now effectively become transmission belts for the dissemination of middle-class ideology and modes of living. To this sophisticated process of indoctrination, AT – universally accepted across all orientations – has provided a coherent theoretical base and support.

*

Could there be, biases on the other side of the argument? Must preference towards biology rather than culture necessarily imply a dyed-in-the-wool, politically conservative viewpoint?

In my own experience, and in the experience of several trainee counsellors and psychotherapists I talk to, part of the problem lies with the fact that the four attachment styles tend to be taught and learned as a rigid taxonomy rather than a set of hypotheses attempting to describe fluid phenomena. To understand attachment behaviour as a static set of categories that comes *before* the dynamic interplay of biological, social, and political energies is a mistake. The value of AT lies in providing us with a psychology of primary dynamic processes and relationships. What are, for instance, the subtle *processes* and *relational phenomena* operating below the layer of the classifications? Unfortunately, the study of these processes is ignored in favour of a mechanical learning of classifications within whose labels clients find themselves at times pigeonholed.

Inspired by the ground-breaking work of Gilbert Simondon,[26] Gilles Deleuze invited us to consider how the classificatory systems partly hide important generative processes within attachment phenomena. He invited us to look at "spatio-temporal dynamisms [that] are the actualizing, differentiating agencies". These must be examined, "even though they are hidden".[27] In a sense, the promise of AT has yet to be fulfilled. Its foundation in *ethology* (i.e., the close study of human behaviour and social organization from a biological perspective) has yet to be realized. Appeal to biology can go two ways: it can be, and often is, reductive. Or it can expand towards a stimulating observation of biological, social, political assemblages which function beneath and beyond the level of the "person". The person does not come before these layers but is *composed* of them. What would it mean to apply in a positive way the call to biology present in AT in relation to the life of an adolescent? "In the life of an adolescent – psychiatrist and social activist Félix Guattari writes – the intrusion of the biological components of puberty is inseparable from the micro-social context within which they appear".[28] Similarly, in relation to childhood, Guattari points out that an ethological perspective would be able to identify that "the child, as an individuated organic totality, only constitutes one intersection among the multiple material, biological, socio-economic and semiotic components which traverse it".[29]

Whether in relation to the child, the adolescent, or indeed the adult whose current experience is affected by early attachment styles, the crucial thing for the therapist to bear in mind is that the person does *not* come *before* the environment but is codetermined with it. Similarly, the attachment system (and its classifications) does *not* exist *before* the exchanges and processes through which it takes place.

It is crucial to differentiate between the taxonomy of attachment styles (and their subsequent reification into unmovable tenets) and attachment *phenomena*. A rather nuanced and minoritarian viewpoint in humanistic psychology in relation to transference and countertransference may be valuable here: instead of blanket denial of their emergence, this stance invites us to closely study transferential and countertransferential *phenomena*. Similarly, when critiquing AT, it may be good to pay attention to valuable – and even affirm – the meaning of attachment phenomena. For Deleuze and Guattari,

> it is not a question of denying the vital importance of parents or the love attachment of children to their mothers and fathers. It is a question of knowing what the place and the function of parents are within desiring-production, rather than doing the opposite and forcing the entire interplay of desiring-machines to fit within the restricted code of Oedipus.[30]

Attachment phenomena are real, and child-parent relationships are important. But greater attention is needed to understand in what ways complex and intertwined social, biological, and political assemblages are at work *prior to* and, as it were, underneath the individual selves. Unlike phenomenology, which often refers back to the individual (the Cartesian subject to whom phenomena appear), the study of phenomena – and of attachment phenomena in particular – is here emphasized on a *pre-individual* level. Studying phenomena means just that: maintaining their autonomous occurrence without assigning them to the human subjects. Reifying the latter – turning them into "things", and self-existing units is the first step towards turning AT into an expedient weapon to justify the normalization of society and the proliferation of systems of mental surveillance. The jury is out as to whether surveillance and normalization are intrinsic to AT or whether they are a by-product of its over-simplification.

*

One of the foundations for AT, especially according to Bowlby and Main, is the study of human and animal behaviour. This is stimulating insofar as it makes AT an ethological rather than anthropocentric perspective: it looks at the environment, at animal/human behaviour first; it does not place the human at the centre. AT came out of dialogue with ethologists such as Tinbergen and Hinde, who were friends of Bowlby. A very important aspect of ethology is that, as both Bowlby and Main explain, every child has to maintain a line of potential movement from and to the caregiver in order to explore the world.[31,32] "Whereas other mammals might have burrows or other associated spatial milieus to which they return, primates have determinate figures, living milieus, to whom they always wish to know their line of flight".[33] A safe environment fosters exploration – for the child as much as for the adult. The aim of establishing of a secure base is to allow exploration, what Deleuze and Guattari call line of flight.

A line of flight is important for two reasons: (a) as a way out when danger appears within the familiar milieu; (b) as a route of exploration outside the familiar milieu. Children confronted with separation and reunion in the "strange situation" encounter the possibility of experiencing what Deleuze and Guattari call "becoming-orphan", a state of isolation and abandonment cut away from supporting bonds. The jury is out as to whether this experience is limited to neglected children or whether, as some research seems to imply, children are inclined by evolution to hold universal fantasies of survival and abandonment.[34,35,36] What is beyond dispute is that toddlers "crawling about exploring the various rooms of the house [they live] in"[37] are natural-born-explorers. They map their surroundings, drawing connections between the bodies and the energies they encounter in their search. An important part of the exploration is coming face to face – for the child as for the adult in our consulting room – with the very real feeling of abandonment, an experience which has a potentially positive outcome: it may help the adult's individualization, becoming freer and less dependent on the parent figure and parents' substitutes.

*

John Bowlby wedded ideas from Melanie Klein's Object Relations school of psychoanalysis (within whose confines he trained), to ethological research and Darwinism. These various currents of thoughts share a particular understanding of biology and evolution which emphasizes nurture and self-preservation and bypasses risk and evolutionary leaps. In Object Relations in particular we find a fundamental detour from classic psychoanalysis which will prove detrimental to psychotherapy as a whole, namely the wholesale *biologization of sexuality*. With the elaboration of his theory, Bowlby will then later deliver the final blow by placing the emphasis on the survival *instinct* and ignoring the drive.

With its emphasis on the nurturing quality of the bond between the primary caregiver and the child and on the importance of a secure base, recreated by the nurturing relationship between therapist and client, AT has almost exclusively focused on one aspect of human experience whilst ignoring another, equally crucial aspect. In classical psychoanalytic terms, it has privileged *instinct* at the expense of the *drive*. While there is no obvious disconnection between the two, the drive builds, as it were, on the surf of the instinct wave, breaking through a new curve beyond instinctual self-preservation and the biological need to reproduce. While the two are not separate, there is rupture. The drive generates a qualitatively new terrain, which is the domain of sexuality, no longer realized in terms of reproduction of the species but in terms of culture, i.e., in terms of the fertile terrain inaugurated by the primary scene of seduction, through the transubstantiation of the enigmatic message into one's own cultural message. It is also a sexuality no longer confined to the genitals but also pre- or para-genital. "What is most important is that it is a sexuality that has its source in fantasy, where fantasy is not self-generated, but, rather, follows the experience of being impinged upon and incited".[38] Gaining access to a life of fantasy is, arguably, the beginning of culture, that is, of a creative development of biological instincts. Focusing exclusively on the latter, understanding the communication and interaction between caregiver and child solely in terms of nurture, implies seriously restricting the development of the child into an emerging cultural subject and a subject of desire.

Current consensus in psychotherapy and counselling on the question of early attachment amounts to a "moralisation of childcare", understood as a "radically de-eroticised and de-eroticising activity" which represents "an assault on the theory of infantile sexuality, the theory of the drives, and any account of the unconscious". How much of the invaluable insights from psychoanalysis and psychotherapy has been sacrificed "in the name of a self-serving and delusional morality?" The difficulty when studying attachment phenomena consists in having to accept the very same actions that "help to sustain the infant are those which will be, of necessity, overwhelming and enigmatic, will communicate an adult sexuality that cannot be fathomed".[39] What are the consequences of accepting a view that understands attachment solely in terms of nurture and leaves out the unconscious communication of adult sexuality? Could this be the reason why contemporary therapy has arguably become so terrified of eros, of erotic transference and countertransference?

AT, important and in many ways valuable to our understanding of human development, is not a universally valid construct – especially in the way it seems to be taught and learned in most therapy and psychology trainings. It is culturally determined, grounded in Western values.

Critiquing AT does not mean denying that children *do* form an attachment to their primary caregiver(s) and that this affective connection constitutes a crucial step to the life of the adult and citizen. The question is what kind of adult and citizen one has a mind – whether an obedient, immature subject complying to an unjust social order, or a compassionate, empathic citizen who can think, act, and contribute creatively to society.

Notes

1 Sigmund Freud, *The Future of an Illusion*. Trans James Strachey. New York: W.W. Norton, 1961.
2 Ibid., p. 25.
3 Ibid., p. 31.
4 Ibid., p. 31.
5 Laurence Bergreen, *Columbus: The Four Voyages, 1492–1504*. London: Penguin, 2011.
6 Bernard Harcourt, *Critique and Praxis*. New York: Columbia University Press, p. 204.
7 Robbie Duschinsky, Monica Greco, Judith Solomon, 'The Politics of Attachment: Lines of Flight with Bowlby, Deleuze and Guattari' *Theory, Culture, and Society*, 2015 Vol. 32(7–8), pp. 173–195; p. 174.
8 A. Sroufe, B. Egeland, E. Carlson, A. Collins, 'Placing early experiences in developmental context'. In: Klaus E. Grossman K, Karin Grossman, Everett Waters (eds) *Attachment from Infancy to Adulthood*, New York: Guilford Press, 2005, pp. 48–70; p. 51.
9 Janet T. Spence, 'Achievement American style: The rewards and costs of individualism'. *American Psychologist*, 40, 1985, pp. 1285–1295.
10 P. Cushman, 'Ideology obscured: Political uses of the self in Daniel Stem's infant'. *American Psychologist*, 1991, (46), pp. 206–219; p. 211.
11 For instance, John Bowlby, *Attachment and loss: Vol. 2. Separation: Anxiety and anger*. New York: Basic Books Bowlby, 1973; M. Main, 'Cross-cultural studies of attachment organization: Recent studies, changing methodologies, and the concept of conditional strategies' in *Human Development*, 33, 48–611990; M. H van A. IJzendnorn & A. Sagi, 'Cross-cultural patterns of attachment: Universal and

contextual dimensions'. In J. Cassidy & P. R. Shaver (Eds.), *Handbook of attachment: Theory, research, and clinical applications* (pp. 713–734). New York: Guilford Press, 1999.

12 Fred Rothbaum, John Weisz, Martha Pott, Kazuo Miyake, Gilda Morelli 'Attachment and Culture', *American Psychologist, American Psychological Association,* October 2000, pp. 1093–1104. https://weiszlab.fas.harvard.edu/files/jweisz/files/rothbaum_et_al_2000_j_ch_fam_studies.pdf, retrieved 6 October 2021.

13 Sigmund Freud, *Three Essays on the Theory of Sexuality,* London, Verso, 2017.

14 John Bowlby, *Attachment,* London: Penguin, 1969.

15 John Bowlby, 'The nature of the child's tie to his mother', *International Journal of Psycho-Analysis,* 1958, 39, pp. 350–373.

16 John Bowlby, *Child Care and the Growth of Love,* 1953, London: Penguin, p. 13.

17 Naomi Quinn and Jeannette Marie Mageo (eds) *Attachment Reconsidered: Cultural Perspectives on a Western Theory.* London: Palgrave, 2013.

18 Mary Main and Judith Solomon, 'Discovery of a new, insecure-disorganized/disoriented attachment pattern'. In: Michael W. Yogman, T. Berry Brazelton (eds) *Affective Development in Infancy,* Norwood, NJ: Ablex, 1986 pp. 95–124.

19 E.A. Carlson, 'A prospective longitudinal study of attachment disorganization/disorientation'. *Child Development,* 1998 69(4), pp. 1107–1128.

20 Robbie Duschinsky, Monica Greco, Judith Solomon 'The Politics of Attachment' *op.cit.*

21 S. Contratto, 'A feminist critique of attachment theory'. In: Mary Ballou, Laura Brown (eds) *Rethinking Mental Health and Disorder: Feminist Perspectives,* New York: Guilford Press, 2002, pp. 29–47; p. 29.

22 Ibid., p. 34.

23 Erica Burman, *Deconstructing Developmental Psychology,* Abingdon, OX: Routledge, 2007, p. 136.

24 Graham Allen and Iain Duncan Smith, 'Early Intervention: Good Parents, Great Kids, Better Citizens', *The Smith Institute,* 2008, https://www.smith-institute.org.uk/book/early-intervention-good-parents-great-kids-better-citizens/, Retrieved 1 June 2022.

25 M. De Wolff and M. van IJzendoorn, 'Sensitivity and attachment: a meta-analysis on parental antecedents of infant attachment'. *Child Development.* 1997 (68), pp. 571–591.

26 Gilbert Simondon, *Individuation in Light of Notions of Form and Information,* translated by Taylor Atkins. University of Minnesota Press, 2022.

27 Gilles Deleuze, *Difference and Repetition,* trans. P. Patton. New York: Continuum 2001, p. 226.

28 Felix Guattari *Machinic Unconscious,* trans. Taylor Adkins, Cambridge, MA: MIT Press, 2011, p. 160.

29 Ibid., p. 160.

30 Gilles Deleuze and Felix Guattari, *Anti-Oedipus: Capitalism and Schizophrenia.* Minneapolis, MN: University of Minnesota Press, p. 51.

31 John Bowlby, *Attachment.* London: Penguin, 1969.

32 Mary Main, The 'ultimate' causation of some infant attachment phenomena. *Behavioural and Brain Sciences* 1979 (2), pp. 640–643.

33 'The Politics of Attachment', op.cit.

34 Morris N. Eagle, *Attachment and Psychoanalysis,* New York: Guilford Press, 2013.

35 Peter Fonagy, *Attachment Theory and Psychoanalysis,* London: Karnac, 2001.

36 Arietta Slade, The place of fear in attachment theory and psychoanalysis. In: Judy, Yellin, Orit Badouk Epstein, Kate White (eds), *Terror Within and Without: Attachment and Disintegration*, London: Karnac, 2013, pp. 39–58.
37 *Anti-Oedipus,* op.cit., pp. 46–47.
38 Judith Butler, 'Seduction, Gender and the Drive', in John Fletcher and Nicholas Ray (eds) *Seductions and Enigmas*, London: Lawrence & Wishart, 2014, pp. 118–133; p. 121.
39 Ibid., p. 121.

Chapter 5

What Is the Body?

We are sick because we are badly constructed. We think we know what the body is – whether we say, "I *have* a body" or "I *am* a body". Body of biology and organs. Medical body, an assemblage of data recited with dulcet tones by doctors in the National Health Service. The inert body on a hospital bed, under the neon light, behind green and blue plastic curtains. Mortal case for the immortal soul. Gnostic body: the know-it-all body who keeps the score, scores points on the *ressentiment* scale, the body that must be listened to. Or else. Body-subject: through the wonder of perception momentarily escaping the Cartesian bind – but not for long. To the exhilarating double-act Deleuze/Guattari we owe a thorough re-examination of the body. Did anyone pay attention? Not in the least. We are back to the dawn of the modern era: "I have a body"; "I am a body", swaying between romanticism and biologism. We have ignored the vibrant lineage Deleuze and Guattari brought back to vivid life, especially Spinoza and Nietzsche who had so much to tell us about the body. We learn from Spinoza that the body does not have to turn into either a subject or an object. We learn that the crucial question is *What is the body capable of?* For Spinoza, this is a question of how intense the amount of joy or sadness a body can sustain in its connections with other bodies. Inevitably, questions about the body imply questions about desire. On this score, the tradition – religious, philosophical, psychological – has thoroughly failed us. It has anticipated or followed Platonism in conceiving desire as need, craving, *tanha*. It understood desire as thirst, covetousness, and lack, as an ontological black hole in the heart of being. In the words of Julie Webb: "Craving is a kind

DOI: 10.4324/9781003280262-6

of inertia; all remains unchanged while desire is alive in movement/ action. Desire does not bring us alive; it *is* life" (2022, personal communication).

In resurrecting the counter-traditional views on the body present in Nietzsche and Spinoza, Deleuze and Guattari showed a different perspective. Desire is not yearning, but a movement that creates vital connections. It is something more: it produces reality by being sovereignly aimless, by seeking nothing but greater development and multiplication; by gathering singularities; by breaking down so-called objectivities.

Out of this process of reconceptualization of the body and desire comes a different attunement to ethics that is active and positive rather than negative and reactive, one that is conceived less "in terms of morality, a code of conduct or set or principles to regulate conduct from the outside" and more "in terms of the exploration of becoming".[1] What may also emerge is greater appreciation of multiplicities paired with a reluctance to degrade the understanding of ethics to an imaginary metaphysical unity. Multiplicities are *substantive*; they are not traits ascribable to an imaginary unity, an origin, an arboreal *root*. They are *rhizomatic*.[2] A rhizome is a circular, horizontal system of ramification made up of underground stems such as bulbs and tubers and which, unlike roots and radicles, does not grow by means of binary divisions. This mode of perception would require a "new ontology – an ontogenesis – ... in order to understand the becomings that underlie and make being possible".[3] It presents us with a counter-traditional understanding of ethics: neither static nor based on moral imperatives but dynamic, grounded on actual practices – a necessarily political form of ethics propelled by the key questions: (a) *What is a body capable of?* (b) *What can desire generate?*

This conception disbands the so-called rational/autonomous subject alongside that other favourite trope of the tradition, the liberal contract which connects the subject to a social community of other atomized subjects.

Is this a form of social anarchism? Yes, if one can think of a "spiritual" anarchism in the wake of Spinoza, a perspective that sees good and bad no longer as moral codes but in relation to a capability for engagement and passion and mutual affect – of bodies with other bodies, of minds with other minds. The latter is a form of rhizomatic connection wholly independent from those notions of unity and holism so ubiquitous in contemporary accounts of relatedness, intersubjectivity, and interconnectedness. Rhizomatic links are at variance with both Buber *and* Levinas, with "I-Thou" as much as "Thou-I". This is because no privilege is ever given to an autonomous and sovereign human subject, revered by the religious, philosophical, and psychological traditions as the crown of creation. What matters are *processes* and *flows*. Rigorously applied, rhizomatic philosophy would for instance elevate current ecological discourse outside its naïve anthropocentrism and conservatism:

> All individuals exist in Nature as on a *plane of consistence* whose entire figure, variable at each moment, they go to compose. They affect one another insofar as the relation that constitutes each individual forms a degree of power, a power of being affected. Everything in the universe is encounters, happy or unhappy encounters.[4]

Deleuze's rhizomatic philosophy paved the way for this new ontology and for an innovative way of understanding ethics by depicting the body as a sum of intensities and velocities, as an assemblage of luxuriant currents of energies which cannot be simplistically reduced to unity, organization, and hierarchy.

For Elizabeth Grosz, rhizomatics and feminism share this new understanding, their common aim being a dismantling of Platonism. Rhizomatics could and should inspire men's work at a moment in its history where an abysmal spiritual vacuum is being filled to the brim by moronic essentialism.

Rhizomatic thinking becomes crucial when trying to truly honour difference, that is, without reducing it to an arbitrary and authoritarian notion of "the One" and to equally misleading and dominant binary logic. It is simply not true that difference can only be understood, as the tradition would have it, in terms of a variation or a negation of identity.[5]

In *Difference and Repetition*, Deleuze spells out the way in which the philosophical tradition has controlled and manipulated difference: it did so by promoting four misconceptions inherent to representation: *analogy*, *identity*, *opposition*, and *resemblance*. "Perhaps – he writes – the majority of philosophers had subordinated difference to identity or to the Same, to the Similar, to the Opposed or to the Analogous".[6] As a result, "we do not think difference in itself".[7]

When difference is considered in its own terms, that is, without being made dependent on the identity of the self-same, two crucial traits appear: *becoming* and *multiplicity*. The first is outside the tropes, ideas, and restrictions of being; the second is outside the mere reproduction of identity. Deleuze and Guattari write:

> It is only when the multiple is ... treated as a substantive, "multiplicity", that it ceases to have a relation to the One as subject or object, natural or spiritual reality, image and world. A multiplicity has neither subject nor object, only determinations.[8]

What this implies in relation to how we understand the body is that the latter cannot be subservient to arbitrary notions of unity and consistency, whether these are derived from the unitary notion of organism or the continuum of consciousness. The body is no longer seen as the place inhabited by consciousness, psyche, or the soul – a conventional notion prevalent in psychoanalytic, psychodynamic, and transpersonal approaches. Nor is it conceived as a unitary organic object – another conventional notion present in humanistic approaches. Least of all it is seen as a tessera in the mosaic of Dasein. It is evaluated instead in connection with what it is capable of, what assemblages can create, what kind of changes it undergoes, the way it affects and is affected by other bodies. It is seen as a confluence of becomings or affects. This is an extraordinarily active, dynamic, and affirmative vision of the body. By recognizing how we are impacted by our interactions, we recognize our powers to act, our ability to transform affects from passive to active. The mind cannot know the body, Spinoza teaches us; it is not even aware of its existence, "except through ideas of affections by which the human body is affected".[9]

There is much to admire in body-oriented psychotherapies which in various ways attempt to address the Cartesian split and which refer to a body-mind unity, emphasizing embodiment and the close link between the body and affects. At the same time, what often happens with these approaches is a reification of the body and a near mystical belief in the unassailable truth of the felt sense. Whilst being sympathetic to the general ethos, it is important to remember that the body is not a *thing*, least of all a *res extensa*, the "extended thing" of Cartesian lore. It is important to remember that both mind and body are *becomings*, continually changed by novel encounters and continually creating new assemblages. The holistic unity of the body or the mind matters less than its ability to be affected by encounters with other bodies and minds and then to creatively activate them into new assemblages, deeds, connections. This is power in the true sense of the term: as *potentia*, as the ability to transmute what is received by the body and the mind into concerted creative action, rather than the moronic surrogate of power as domination over others. It is no surprise that this notion of power present in the counter-tradition has profound implications for the ethico-political domain too. It widens the scope of this domain beyond interhuman relations to encompass connections between humans and other sentient beings and becomings, between humans and organic and inorganic *bodies* in the widest sense of the term:

> Anything that exists or is capable of acting or being acted on is a body, whether this is a living body, a nonliving object, or psychological and moral characteristics like the soul, wisdom, virtue, and justice. These are not ideals that operate apart from objects but are the qualities and relations in and between bodies: they are what acts and is acted upon. Every reason, virtue, character, or psychology remains a body (or many), for each acts and can be acted upon.[10]

This vision of ethics and politics, inspired by Spinoza, places encounters with other bodies – human, nonhuman, living, nonliving, institutions, etc. – at the very centre. It emphasizes a porous notion of the world, moving beyond the notions of autonomy and self-boundedness dear to the tradition. It underscores the experimental nature of our actions, the way these may heighten or lessen our powers. In the process, our bodies and minds undergo a transformation.

*

It is difficult to study the self – avowedly one of the tasks of the psychotherapeutic endeavour – while conceiving it as an entirely self-existing, solid entity. This is why, in a sense, to study the self is to decentre the self. The self cannot be truly examined without taking in the phenomenal field of experience. To solely focus on the violin soloist or the singer during an orchestral performance is to miss the richness and intricate texture of the ensemble. The self-construct is that soloist or singer and the field of experience is the entire orchestra.

Throughout its history, psychotherapy (accidentally?) envisaged a *threshold*, a "site" out of which subjectivity arises and to which it relates dialectically. Descriptions of the threshold vary as do its names and attributes; they vary according to the theoretical lenses adopted. I will look at two of them. The first is found in the humanistic/existential tradition, the second in psychoanalysis. Neither of them succeeds in providing the necessary blueprint for a form of psychical investigation that is free of the current neoliberal diktat afflicting our profession. This is why I will then introduce a third notion, the brainchild of playwright and writer Antonin Artaud and one that was later articulated in the work of Deleuze and Guattari: the *body-without-organs* (BWO). This ambiguous and pregnant notion presents us with a fluid map that may be useful in digging a way out of our newly refurbished, evidence-based prison. Within the extensive corpus of the philosophical *counter*-tradition, the BWO represents an imaginative adjunct to the theory of the *affective body* instigated in the seventeenth century by Spinoza in his *Ethics*. Like Nietzsche and Bergson, Spinoza too gives Deleuze an intermittently steady, quivering rhythm to his imaginative thought, particularly in relation to his "treatment" of the body. No primacy of mind over body is found in Spinoza. He convincingly refutes the mind/body divide: for him, a passion in the body *is* passion in the mind, and an action in the mind *is* an action in the body.

In *Anti-Oedipus*, the BWO is mentioned within a discourse that critically expounds on Marx's formulation of capital and Freud's articulation of the unconscious. But it is in a later work, *A Thousand Plateaus*[11] that Deleuze and Guattari present us with examples on how to *make* a BWOs.

To give (psychical/political) transformation a chance, the actual (the "given", the reality we often supinely accepted, as in our obeisance to biology, instinct, and the presumed facticity of the existing order) is transcended: we ascend (and sometimes descend) to the virtual, the site of revolution, subversion, and innovation. A scandalous thought:

could that mean that even the terrain, the obligatory, sensible, and sensuous "field" can and must be evaded in order to create a new terrain? Could it be that terrains of conventional psychotherapy are not, properly speaking, thresholds? We will see. Let us first examine these two: the *organism* and the *unconscious*.

The Organism

With its expert melding of psychology and neurology, Kurt Goldstein's classic study *The Organism*[12] instigated a minor paradigm shift in phenomenology, establishing some of the tenets of what was to become Gestalt and humanistic psychology. That he happened to be a philosopher too, and one with an enthusiasm for Goethe, meant that his scientific rigour was less prone to the fallacies of scientism. His notion of the organism may be etched within a particularly stimulating trend within phenomenology: a keen interest in organic life, as found in the writings of Merleau-Ponty[13] and Canguilhem.[14] For those keen on keeping an arbitrarily clear-cut separation between disciplines, Goldstein's approach can be baffling. Is it science? Is it philosophy? But then the category of organism was itself ambivalent from the start,[15] as seen in the late seventeenth-, early eighteenth-century debate between Leibniz and the chemist and physician Georg-Ernest Stahl, where the term emerges as a winning secular replacement for "semantic equivalents" to the abiding notion of the soul. Implicit in the idea of the organism is the alluring promise of a "functional unity of a system of integrated parts".[16]

It is no surprise that the notion would exert considerable influence on Carl Rogers[17] who strived to harmonize spirituality and science. The clinical applications of "organism" in the work of psychotherapy are clear. When linked dialectically to the self-concept (self-construct, ego-self, etc.), it does the trick of keeping the self-construct from morphing into a walled, self-bound object whose actualization rests solely on vague prospects of cosmetic improvement and/or the repair of disturbances and obstructions. Thought in this way, it is useful in reminding us that there exists a wider domain of experiencing, a *threshold* from which transformation may occur. Cultural and political pressures to align psychotherapy with the prevailing neo-liberal ethos and the agenda of our societies of control sadly mean that the threshold becomes a terrain to be colonized instead of a source of learning and transformation. An example of this is the dubious notion of an "organismic self", a self that in *seizing* the complex and multiple life of the organism confidently proclaims full alignment (congruence) with it. This trajectory is probably delusional at best, but useful in exemplifying the positivist ethos at work. Rather than becoming slowly and patiently acquainted with the darkness and multiplicity of the organism, we go in, as it were, bringing a light. This mode of understanding is not particular to person-centred or humanistic psychology but constitutes a widespread cultural phenomenon: "the idea that '*to see is to know*'" so firmly grounds our current way of being in and understanding the world it is "hard to imagine otherwise".[18]

The Unconscious

The wish to colonize an unknown domain rather than learning from it happened in psychoanalysis too, this time in relation to another threshold, the unconscious. Here a positivist agenda crept in, arguably taking hold of a potentially transformative science. Already since Freud (approximately around the time of his abandonment of the generalized theory of seduction in 1897), a widespread tendency to give in to cultural pressure towards positivism meant that the unconscious was now understood as a terrain whose content, once deemed inaccessible via the conscious mind, is analogous to and retrievable by consciousness. "Making the unconscious conscious", became the popular motto of positivist psychodynamic practice, intent at tracking down, interpreting and denouncing any semblance of transferential phenomena, rewriting the unconscious in phylogenetic terms: as the "ground of being", with humanity enthroned at its evolutionary peak, a move strangely reminiscent of Teilhard de Chardin's metaphysics,[19] unwittingly making the case for psychoanalysis as ersatz religion. The result is baffling: it pathologizes the unconscious as something to be understood, translated, and properly cleansed from the conscious life of the subject, equipping the latter with the societal and relational skills which may enable it to live an incongruously good life in a bad world and, in the process, curtailing the opportunity for psychical transformation.

The Body-without-Organs

At this point of our investigation, one might suggest that the once transformative notions of organism and unconscious have been seized by what Deleuze calls *reactive forces*, i.e., "utilitarian forces of adaptation" that prevent the body "from what it can do".[20] We may recognize how these notions have been hijacked by an epistemology rooted in fear (of the unknown, of the dark/multiple body; of becoming; but isn't epistemology *as such* rooted in fear?). We may then ascertain how domesticated and tame they have become within a thoroughly domesticated psychotherapeutic discourse – how thoroughly co-opted by the neoliberal agenda psychotherapy, psychology, and psychoanalysis have become. It is at this point that another notion is called for.

Deleuze helps us understand that to speak of an organism is to speak of a body conceived holistically, as an organization of organs. The term "organism" (and, increasingly, "body" too) often refers to an integrated repository of knowledge and wisdom: the body is said to know and remember – it keeps the score, this body of ours, a bookkeeping machine riddled with nostalgia and resentment. All we need to do, we are told, is increase our awareness, access a felt sense, tuning in to innate and real organismic evaluation, access a virgin domain untainted by cultural conditioning and disentangled from the various ways in which mum and dad fucked us up as children. This holistic, integrated body becomes a worthy candidate, a substitute for the soul. What this romantic, Rousseauian trajectory bypasses is the high degree to which the body is constrained and disciplined by societal forces – with prisons, hospitals, schools, and various other institutions regimenting and constricting the subject.

The BWO presents us with an appealing and difficult way out of the prison. It is appealing because it describes corporeality in a way that is convincingly at variance with the traditional restrictive notions of body/mind polarities. It is appealing because it rewrites *desire* in dynamic and life-affirming ways, bravely refuting the versions advertised by the tradition which from Plato to Lacan to hypermodern spirituality regards desire as lack or cavernous repressed material. It presents instead *desire as generator of reality*, as dynamic and immanent, no longer allied with fantasy, let alone "phantasy", or longing. It is appealing because it presents desire as actualization, as a range of practices and creative deeds which shape rather than shun the Real. Traditionally, whether in relation to consciousness or the unconscious, Elizabeth Grosz explains,

> desire is a property of the subject; it is enacted through representation, and is thwarted or frustrated by the Real ... By contrast, for Deleuze and Guattari desire is primary ... it is not produced ... but productive of reality.[21]

Rather than being focused on lack, on an external other, as in most erotic vicissitudes of all persuasions, desire is aimless, its only scope being the joy of self-augmentation and proliferation, its modus operandi being experimentation rather than the fabrication of static constructs.

The notion of the BWO is appealing because it does not fall back on either the getaway offered by transcendence nor on the false immanence of reactive narcotic descent.

It is difficult because it is not wedded to hope, the greatest of evil if we are to believe Nietzsche's interpretation of Pandora's tale. It is born out of despair, a tunnel at the end of the light. At the psychiatric hospital in Rodez where Artaud was subjected to electroshock treatment and where the other inmates poured ink on his papers as he was trying to write, he nevertheless carried on writing.

The BWO is not a concept referring to a distinct object. It demarcates a threshold, and it does so more convincingly than the organism and the unconscious. The BWO is not necessarily an alternative to both the organism and the unconscious; it represents a line of flight which more accurately fulfils the failed promise implicit in the other two notions. It signals the *zone of intensity* emerging when the limits of what a body can do are extended. Even though it signifies a *transcendental* shift, it nevertheless occurs within the field of immanence. There is no capitulation to ready-to-wear transcendent narratives, be they coated in the literalist, bad poetry of institutionalized religion, the precious silence of mysticism or the objectifications of positivist science. Its expression escapes the strictures of language, its hierarchical display of order words to which the subject is subjected and by which it comes to be defined. It traces and encourages the fugue on a funny bone, the flow traversing warm flesh, pulsating organs, and the living breath. It sends oblique memos from the brink. It is a blueprint, animated by an aspiration to strip away those practices which constrain the subject. It is an ambitious project at variance from the set of current practices which nowadays constitute and define psychotherapy. The term "body-without-organs" was coined by Antonin Artaud in his never-to be aired 1947 radio play *To have done with the judgement of God*. The last passage of this short play reads:

> Man is sick because he is badly constructed. We must make up our minds to strip him bare in order to scrape off that animalcule that itches him mortally, god, and with god his organs. For you can tie me up if you wish, but there is nothing more useless than an organ. When you will have made him a body without organs, then you will have delivered him from all his automatic reactions and restored him to his true freedom. Then you will teach him again to dance wrong-side out as in the frenzy of dance halls and this wrong side out will be his real place.[22]

Certainly, anyone wishing to come anywhere near this sort of endeavour must proceed with caution. The BWO dismantles our conventional sense of what a body is and how it is used. It even encourages us towards a kind of escape, a line of flight that in finding new avenues creates reality anew. Mainstream culture and psychotherapy look down on escape; it is swiftly diagnosed as avoidance, denial, manic defence, not wanting to confront "reality". But there is great value in escape. Following a line of flight, Deleuze teaches us, *creates* reality.

Riffing on Artaud, Deleuze first used the term body-without-organs in *Logic of Sense*,[23] a book which Foucault greeted as the cheekiest and most impertinent of metaphysical treatises ever written.[24] Among other things, the book is preoccupied with the dynamic genesis of sense in primary language. The *infant* experiences a *weatherscape*, to use Daniel Stern's memorable image,[25] constituted of fluid successions of varying degrees of intensity: the shudder of a piercing noise and a dazzling light, the overpowering blast of hunger, the soothing tone of a voice. This pre-verbal life of intensities-in-motion evokes the atmosphere for approaching the BWO.

In Deleuze's vision the organism is the first of three crucial strata or layers through which the subject becomes ensnared. Below is a brief step-by-step user guide through the three layers. This process is one of dismantling – a delicate and risky process to be sure, one which does not imply that anything goes. Freedom requires discipline. We must work diligently towards our emancipation and engage the three domains "that most directly bind us: the *organism*, *signifiance*, and *subjectification*".[26] On every layer discipline (practice, dedication, *studium*) is needed:

> You will [discipline] your body – otherwise you're just depraved. You will be signifier and signified, interpreter and interpreted – otherwise you're just a deviant. You will be a subject, nailed down as one, a subject of the enunciation recoiled into a subject of the statement – otherwise you're just a tramp.[27]

The First Layer: The Organism

The notion of the organism is vital in decentring and "updating" the self-construct. Within the frame of organismic psychologies and experiential approaches such as person-centred therapy, Focusing, Gestalt and others, the notion provides the practitioner with the first necessary step in the nomadic crossing towards the BWO.

Even within the frame of the experiential psychotherapies mentioned here, misted over as they often are by naïve Rousseauian leanings, the organism ends up becoming little else than a secular surrogate for the *soul*. What was meant to be a name for a more expansive threshold – an uncertain terrain of education and transformation – morphs into a "thing" duly outfitted with purpose, unity, and being – all three typical attributes, for Nietzsche, of nihilism, a slant on life characterized by the infliction of strategies of control and consolation upon the ever-changing, multiple, and contingent world.

Giving pride of place to the organism or the body is evidently a necessary first step on the journey out of the venerable Cartesian mansion within whose redecorated walls psychotherapy still lives and breathes: think of the Kleinian seemingly autonomous psyche where others are mere introjects; or of Husserl's notion of the *habitus*,[28] and the chronic subjectivism currently impairing existential therapy.

All the same, the first step towards the organism is crucial. It helps reframe psychotherapy within a naturalistic appreciation of the body and of the complexity of its affects. The body is, after all, the *great reason*.

Using the terms "body" and "organism" interchangeably, as I do here, may well be an oversimplification. Certainly, unbounded appreciation (love, study) of the body/organism is an important step away from the Christian doctrine founded on hatred of the body, a stance echoed in the "objectivity" of medicine and science towards this unruly "object", specimen, or enfleshed robot. And yet, both terms are riddled with metaphysical assumptions. The body is itself an abstraction, a nominal simplification of multiple pre-individual assemblages and processes of subjectification. As for the organism, this notion too is driven by the positivist ambition to match the perceived certainties of theology to take into account the insubstantiality and sheer randomness of its coming-into-form.

The second important step implies a *dismantling* of the organism with the aim of restoring it to its ontology of becoming and unrest, of "chaos" understood as "creative self-genesis"[29] devoid of a creator. One way of understanding the process we are invited to undergo is by perceiving the organism as nothing more than a particularly robust form of sedimentation. The task is to work through the sedimentation and begin a delicate (and potentially dangerous) process of dismantling. In psychological terms, this is akin to the migration from individuation to *dividuation*– from *monad to nomad*, the journey from the necessary affirmation of one's subjectivity – a place of irreplaceability and ethico-political emergence – to the recognition of one's inherent multiplicity and subsequent refusal to chase a delusional, coercive "integration". This equals to the appreciation that the fundamentally fragmented nature of the self does not necessitate integration. Dismantling the organism means refusing, in Artaud's words, the judgement of God and of God's shadows – the hefty baggage of guilt and shame about bodily functions, the eternalist resentment towards this perishable and flawed existence, the tall shadow of sin cast on our modest joys during a hurried transit on the

Earth's crust. It means refusing to both suppress or crush the creative liberated body.

This may sound like the familiar mix of Freud and Marx in the service of the starry-eyed, supposedly emancipated libido of the 1960s, but here we face a different tune, a different kind of fusion. Narratives of freedom from the 1960s kept the two economies – libidinal (desire) and political (interest and capital) – distinctly separated. It worked like a charm, though not in the way we expected. *Desublimation* triumphed: as a result, our current sexual liberty is politically powerless. Soaking up a wide range of cyberporn products, freely acting out the fantasies emanating from them via dating apps *and* cheerfully allowing the latest reactionary blockhead to strut his stuff in government. No sir. They are not two. For Deleuze and Guattari, libidinal and political economy are one and the same; it is "an economy of flows".[30]

Within the domain of sexuality, the BWO invites us to extend and radicalize *drive* over *instinct*, culture (in the wider sense) over biology. What happens in Taoist sex when a man does not ejaculate and the energy between the lovers is allowed to circulate and expand? What happens if the supposed goal of sex is put aside? What if we no longer conceive of desire as lack but are open to see what a body can do and experience, transcending the limits of biology without resorting to transcendence? Procreation is one possible direction: the direction of biological organisms, of State and family; the perpetuation of the species. What happens if the direction changes, if drive takes over instinct, if we reach the limits of what a body can do? We come near an *ecstatic* experience (from the Greek *existanai*, "to put out of place"), a *threshold*. And that threshold, that unmapped country is the BWO.

Sexuality is culture, Merleau-Ponty reminded us; it pirouettes effortlessly on the necessity of biology. This is not to say that biology is devoid of its own unabashed poetry. Deleuze takes it one step further. In his critical study of Sacher-Masoch's classic novel *Venus in Furs,* he points out that explicit in the text is found a "transcendence of the imperative … toward a higher function"[31]; *sex as theatre*: one more step away from biology and one step closer to that threshold of intensity that is the BWO where this body gets a taste of what it can do. Kraft-Ebing, the Austrian psychiatrist responsible for coining the term "masochism", pathologized this form of sexual theatre and with it the sacredness of mutual contractual vows. And there is more: masochism, Deleuze tells us, does not rest on the alleged centrality of the father. Instead, it regales us with a cultured view of eroticism, and it is not surprising that this heightened form of sexual expression "should seek historical and cultural confirmation in mystical or idealistic initiation rites".[32]

The Second Layer: Signifiance (Not Significance)

Merleau-Ponty famously wrote of the distinction between "*le dit*, the common coin of social exchange, and *le dire*, the newly minted, emergent language of a specific encounter".[33] Plateau 5 of *A Thousand Plateaus* takes us one step further: conventional language (*le dit*, or "the spoken") is not quite a *neutral* entity but a form of comprehensive indoctrination. School teaches us *order words,* the social hierarchies implicit within them and how to "know our place"; this deep process of socialization grips our very soul. For that reason, *le dire*, a living speech, might take a little more than the good will of two individuals in the therapy room. It may require the dismantling of conventional language. The way out is experimentation, creating a world anew by fashioning a new language.

Art, poetry, literature, plus experimental forms of theatre and performance all provide us with tremendous inspiration so that (I am being optimistic) even the hackneyed world of research in psychotherapy may one day come alive. It may leave behind the jaded formulas of both quantitative and qualitative research methods. The permission to roam freely, starting from a deep questioning of the speaking subject/researcher may push research towards a threshold: a tentative name for this being none other than postqualitative inquiry.[34]

The Third Layer: Subjectification

We become a subject through a difficult process of individualization, by accessing an internal locus of evaluation, through a healthy connection with our own experience. We become a subject through acknowledgement/recognition in an encounter with the other, whether through conflict or kinship.[35] We become a subject against a backdrop that sees the "interpenetration of minds, conscious and unconscious".[36] All the above viewpoints are valid to a degree, but they bypass an essential factor, highlighted in *Anti-Oedipus*: we become subjects through acquiescence. To be a *subject* – even the more sagacious "body-subject" of phenomenology – is to be *subjected* to interpellation[37]: the policeman calling my name in the street, demanding to verify my identity; the doctor holding the files of my clinical history; the psychiatrist charting the graph of my societal adaptation; the professional body regaling me with a membership number for a sum of money and the implicit promise to comply with the status quo; the theoretical parish in whose bosom I am truly welcome *if* I don't abstain from faithfully chanting the names of the holy trinity – empathy, congruence, and unconditional positive regard – or the Capitalized Teutonic Abstracts – Being, Authenticity, Universal Relatedness – shadows of God all of them, homesickness for an Eden that never was, the holistic dream of harmony that twists and thwarts our sacrosanct struggle for liberation.

The way out, once again, is experimentation: nomadism of the subject, acknowledgement of the rhizomatic multiplicity which *constitutes* the self rather than going back to arboreal roots in the self. The latter view, found in several psychotherapeutic approaches, acknowledges multiplicity but solely as an attribute of a substantial entity called the self. They all concur – whether they speak of parts, personifications, objects, configurations, or subpersonalities – in their describing what are essentially vassal epigones to the alleged sovereign, and usurper, of the psychical domain: the subject. It may be worth mentioning here, albeit only in passing, recent studies linking Deleuzian thought to the work of Fernando Pessoa[38] and the latter's use, in his writings, of *heteronyms*. These are entirely autonomous, with different names, different personalities and genders, different styles and worldviews. Each one tracing a distinctive *line of flight*. Contemporary psychotherapy would no doubt want to integrate these allegedly fragmented parts, using its insights and expertise in the service of control and the constipated discontent of the civilization it believes it serves. But with Pessoa, as with Deleuze, the artist, philosopher, or analyst chooses a different role: not as the constabulary of psyche but as a fellow explorer.

Notes

1 Elizabeth Grosz, *On Ontogenesis and the Ethics of Becoming*. Interviewed by Kathryn Yusoff, Society and Space, 22 May 2014, https://www.societyandspace.org/articles/on-ontogenesis-and-the-ethics-of-becoming, retrieved 8 May 2022. See also: Elizabeth Grosz, *The Incorporeal: Ontology, Ethics, and the Limits of Materialism*. New York: Columbia University Press, 2018.
2 Gilles Deleuze and Félix Guattari, *A Thousand Plateaus: Capitalism and Schizophrenia*. London: Continuum. Translation and Foreword by Brian Massumi. London: Continuum, 2003.
3 Elizabeth Grosz, *On Ontogenesis and the Ethics of Becoming*, op. cit.
4 Gilles Deleuze and Claire Parnet, *Dialogues*. New York: University of Columbia Press, 1987, p. 74, emphasis added.
5 Elizabeth Grosz, 'A Thousand Tiny Sexes', Constantin V. Boundas and Dorothea Olkowski (Eds), *Gilles Deleuze and the Theatre of Philosophy*. New York and London: Routledge, 1994, pp. 187–212.
6 Gilles Deleuze, *Difference and Repetition*. London: Athlone Press, 1994, p. xii.
7 Ibid, pp. xii–xiii.
8 Gilles Deleuze and Felix Guattari, *A Thousand Plateaus*, translated by Brian Massumi. Minneapolis: University of Minnesota Press, 1987, p. 8.
9 Benedict Spinoza, *Ethics*, II, P19 https://www.gutenberg.org/files/3800/3800-h/3800-h.htm#chap02, retrieved 27 Jan. 22.
10 Elizabeth Grosz, *Incorporeal: Ontology, Ethics and the Limits of Materialism*. New York: Columbia University Press, 2017, p. 25.
11 *A Thousand Plateaus*, op. cit.
12 Kurt Goldstein, *The Organism*. New York: American Book Company, 1939.
13 Maurice Merleau-Ponty, *Phenomenology of Perception*. London: Routledge, 1989.
14 Georges Canguilhem, *Knowledge of Life*, trans. S. Geroulanos and D. Ginsburg, New York: Fordham University Press, 2008.
15 Charles T. Wolfe, *Do organisms have ontological status?* http://philsci-archive.pitt.edu/5410/1/CW-Organism_HPLS_2010.pdf, 2010, Retrieved 20 Dec. 2020.
16 Georges Canguilhem, "Vie", *Encyclopaedia Universalis*, 1989, 23: 546–553; p. 551.
17 Carl R. Rogers, 'The actualizing tendency in relation to "motives" and consciousness – Nebraska symposium'. In Brian E. Levitt (Ed.), *Reflections on Human Potential: Bridging the Person-Centered Approach and Positive Psychology*. Ross-on-Wye, UK: PCCS Books, 2008, pp. 17–32.
18 Rosemary Rizq, 'A plea for a measure of opacity: Psychoanalysis in an age of transparency', *Psychodynamic Practice*, 25 (2), 2019, p. 113.
19 Teilhard De Chardin, *Selected Writings*. London: Orbis Books, 1999.
20 Gilles Deleuze, *Nietzsche and Philosophy*. Trans. Hugh Tomlinson, London: Continuum, 2006, p. 57.
21 Elizabeth Grosz, 'A Thousand Tiny Sexes' op. cit., p. 198.
22 Antonin Artaud, *To have done with the judgment of god*, 1947. Retrieved 26 December 2020, from https://www.surrealism-plays.com/Artaud.html.11
A Thousand Plateaus, op. cit., p. 21.
23 Gilles Deleuze, *Logic of Sense*. New York: Columbia University Press, 1990.
24 Michel Foucault, 'Theatrum Philosophicum'. In J. D. Faubion (Ed.), *Michel Foucault: Aesthetics, Method, and Epistemology: The Essential Works*, 1998, Vol. 2, 343–368. Penguin.
25 Daniel Stern, *Diary of a Baby: What Your Child Sees, Feels, and Experiences*. New York: Basic Books, 1992.

Gilles Deleuze and Felix Guattari. *Anti-Oedipus: Capitalism and Schizophrenia.* Minneapolis: University of Minnesota Press, 2000.

26 *A Thousands Plateaus*, op. cit., pp. 176–177, emphasis added.

27 Ibid, p. 177.

28 Edmund Husserl, *Cartesian Meditations: An Introduction to Phenomenology.* Leiden, Belgium: Martinus Nijhoff, 2013 pp. 66–67.

29 Babette Babich, 'Nietzsche's Critique of Scientific Reason and Scientific Culture: On Science as a Problem and Nature as Chaos'. In Gregory Moore & Thomas H. Brobjer (Eds.), *Nietzsche and Science*, Farnham, Sy: Ashgate, 2004, pp. 133–153; p. 144.

30 Gilles Deleuze and Felix Guattari, *Anti-Oedipus*, op. cit., p. xviii. 13 Baruch Spinoza. *Ethics*, op. cit.

31 Gilles Deleuze, *Coldness and Cruelty.* New York: Zone Books, 1991, pp. 20.21.

32 Ibid, p. 22.

33 Jeff Harrison, 'Talking Cure and Curing Talk: Therapy, Theory and the Already Dead'. In Manu Bazzano (Ed.), *Re-visioning Existential Therapy: Counter-Traditional Perspectives.* Abingdon, OX: Routledge, 2020, pp. 204–215; p. 206.

34 Elizabeth Adams St Pierre, 'Why post qualitative inquiry?' *Qualitative Inquiry*, 27, 2, 2021. London: Sage, https://doi.org/10.1177/107780042093114226

35 W. F. Hegel, *Phenomenology of Spirit* (A.V. Miller, Trans.). Oxford University Press, 1977.

36 Jessica Benjamin, *Beyond Doing and Being Done to: Recognition Theory, Intersubjectivity, and the Third.* Abingdon, OX: Routledge, 2018. p. 1.

37 Louis Althusser, *On the Reproduction of Capitalism: Ideology and Ideological State Apparatuses.* Transl. G. M. Goshgarian. London: Verso, 2014.

38 Fernando Pessoa, *A Little Larger than the Entire Universe: Selected Poems.* London: Penguin, 2016; Fernando Pessoa, *The Complete Poems of Alberto Caeiro.* New York: New Directions, 2020. See also J. Gil, *O imperceptível devir da imanência – Sobre a Filosofia de Deleuze.* Lisbon: Relógio D'Água, 2008. Also: N. D. Kennedy, *The intercessor or heteronym in Gilles Deleuze and Fernando Pessoa*, 2019. Retrieved 28 December 2020, from https://orpheusinstituut.be/assets/files/news-events/DARE-2019-book-of-abstracts-FINAL.pdf

Chapter 6

Power, Psyche, and Poisoned Solidarities

Whenever I suppress my natural capacity for joy, I feel annoyed by those who take pleasure in life. I think of them as shallow and greedy – a happy-go-lucky bunch of suckers who pay no heed to the depth of suffering in the world. Once I get going, I turn into a fully functioning expert in the crooked craft of mowing down those who "specialize in having fun" – to quote the worst song lyric ever in the otherwise pristine poetry of Lizard King Jim Morrison. I suspect I am not alone in this; strange things happen to those who repress joy and desire. Soon enough, we find ourselves straddling the high horse of resentment. In my case, I may come alarmingly close to calling on Lacan's dubious notion of the *name-of-the-father*, pretending to subscribe to his essentialist praise of the Oedipal prohibition. I will waffle lyrical on its indisputable value as necessary obeisance of the law within the symbolic order; I'll fall in with the even sillier idea that without Mum & Dad's hetero double-act kids won't stand a chance in hell to grow up as reputable citizens and potential Tory voters. Some resenters will no doubt join the structuralist chorus that made some psychoanalysts in France argue against *homoparentalité*, or gay parenthood.

Thankfully, I don't resent happy people that often. Being resentful feels to me more like being briefly in the grip of a foul mood. In the end, joy (or *tragic* joy, to distinguish it from the moronic glee of plutocrats) always peers through those grey London clouds.

So far, so subjectivistic. But what happens if an entire society or culture is doggedly detained by a resentful mood? And what if this mood were the *foundation* of that society or culture? I confess that I see this not as mere speculation but as something which may

DOI: 10.4324/9781003280262-7

approximate a description (diagnosis?) of mainstream culture at this particular conjuncture. If so, then let me ask: What happens when the majority of people within society, stooped by guilt, hatred, and fear succeed in suppressing joy and desire in themselves? One possible answer is: the *spirit of revenge* takes over. Nietzsche, who loved French, called the spirit of revenge *ressentiment* (the two expressions are interchangeable). What is *ressentiment*? It is much more than mere "resentment": to be animated by *ressentiment* is to nurture a stance of venomous denigration of life – to despise existence because it is found wanting, not "moral" enough perhaps, not complying with one's narrow and all-too-human notions of unity, direction, and purpose.

Normally it's easy to discern the spirit of revenge at work. Take for instance hatred of difference. Racism, sexism, homophobia, transphobia, contempt for the poor, the homeless, the exiles; fear of foreigners, strangers, and those who are different from "us". Consider the case of envy towards those who give the impression to be flourishing or are fairly content with their lot or seem to embody attributes we feel we lack. In these cases, the spirit of revenge represents a mean-minded state of being that wants others *not* to have what they have. It displays a sanctimonious worldview from which some of us feel authorized to apportion blame and dish out sanctions.

In all of the above, the workings of *reactive* forces are self-evident, given that these examples are to various degrees forms of defensiveness, of re-action against something appearing to threaten our shaky notions of identity and its retinue of knick-knacks and discreet charms, of delusions and ruddy hallucinations: property, propriety, the laughable belief in self-possession and cognitive mastery. The popular, reactive version of identity now in vogue advertises a notion of an "autonomous" self whose survival depends on a narrow set of uniformly servile choices: (a) become a consumer; (b) become a producer; (c) become a consumer/producer. No matter what we do, it ends up strengthening capitalism. What happened to the lofty promises of liberalism promoted by mainstream therapy culture (authenticity, independence, and self-actualizing-in-a-safe-environment)? They crumble miserably (with special effects and a cheesy soundtrack) under the pressure of a social apparatus dominated by the twin devils of competition and acceleration.

Autonomy? Authenticity? In your dreams! This is growth totalitarianism, baby, the jovial diktat of acceleration.

The spirit of revenge is dominated by reactivity, and a genuinely critical theory and practice must be alert to whether active or reactive forces have taken hold of a particular entity – be it a person, an event, a political or cultural movement. An active force is affirming and liberating; it asserts and enjoys its difference. In contrast, a reactive force is merely utilitarian, adaptive; it rejects what the active force can do, turning it against itself. The consequences for us humans are disastrous: we become the laughingstock in the whole of creation, the only animals who turn against themselves in the name of handful of silly ideas.

Sometimes it's hard to spot the spirit of revenge at work. Rapid changes in cultural perceptions and values mean that it will take hold of a variety of political expressions, *including* those with ostensibly progressive agendas. Like everything else, language mutates and travels alongside societal and political shifts. Corporate institutions will adopt the lingo of anti-sexism, antiracism, and green-thinking while merrily perpetuating sexism, racism, and environmental pollution. Academic psychology may apply terms such as the *actualizing tendency* or *individuation* while curtailing the very space where these ideas can breathe.

Then there is the case of privately-run, self-governing organizations which may ostentatiously berate the patriarchy but end up supporting it in other ways. What these associations tend to ignore is how closely associated the patriarchy is with a generalized politics of *protection* and *regulation* and how ubiquitous these are in social policies.

A more controversial instance of the above is the *#MeToo* movement. It is vital and long overdue that misogyny dating back centuries is fiercely opposed and stamped out. Yet the poisonous solidarities[1] emerging over the last decade or so – between white mainstream feminism and the evangelical far-right, especially in the US, give pause for thought. In a recent book, Aya Gruber, professor of law at the University of Colorado, writes that when studying as a law student and looking at issues of sexual harassment and sexual crime she was caught in a dilemma: on the one hand, knowing that "gender crimes reflected and reinforced women's second-class status", she felt these had to be actively pursued and dealt with. On the other, she was "involved in public defence and anti-incarceration work and had come to regard the prison as a primary site of violence, racism, and degradation in society".[2] It was after becoming a public defender that she "witnessed first-hand the prosecutorial machine". She goes on to say:

> I felt a sense of disillusionment that the feminist movement I so admired played such a distinctive role in broadening and legitimizing the unconscionable penal state. As an academic, I was increasingly concerned that women's criminal law activism had not made prosecution and punishment more feminist. It had made feminism more prosecutorial and punishing.[3]

As other feminist writers who drew on the legacies of Angela Davis and Beth Richie have pointed out,[4] this prosecutorial streak did not *start* with #*MeToo* in 2017 but it did come to a crescendo around that time. Then as now, the assumption of what is often called "carceral feminism" (from the Latin *carcer* for jail) is that women's safety can be ensured via state oppression and violence. What animates this kind of poisoned solidarity is *sex panic*, a particular form of fear which is rife both on the Left and the Right of political discourse. A sex panic is a social outbreak fuelled by the media and typified by the fear of innocence being endangered, an innocence habitually attributed to white women and children. An outbreak of sex panic usually requires the presence of the bad man, the predator – a loitering, changeable, social presence, a threat against which the righteous citizens can mobilize. The genealogy of this phenomenon is disturbing. It harks back to *The Birth of a Nation,* a 1915 film which glorifies racism and the KKK and which invariably depicts the bad man as black. With every case of sex panic – including the priests scandal, the prurient interests in the alleged "free and wild sex" going on in religious cults and the like, the same set of predictable reactions emerges, namely, huge media coverage; a simplistic narrative of good against evil which cannot be discussed, let alone questioned; collective permission given to indulge in the dreadful happiness of allocating blame – in short the very essence of *ressentiment*.

In her persuasive, impassioned, and poetic book, investigative journalist JoAnn Wypijewski[5] questions the omission of a critique of capitalism in mainstream feminist argument; she points out that in the US one in two black women love someone who is in jail; she questions the swift verdict with which too many different behaviours are shepherded into the sexual abuse definition and interrogates the glee with which Harvey Weinstein was described in the media and in the popular imagination: deformed, abnormal, intersex, with no balls but a vagina, disgusting, scarred, grunting, with bumpy skin, lumpy semen, fat, hairy, stinking of shit, sorry poop, a beast, unmanned, subhuman, and so forth.

It would be wholly wrong to blame young activists and their sac-rosanct anger for this upsurge of terrible enthusiasm, but Wypijewski doubts that in the victims' rights movements, the sympathetic aspect of the victim may disguise the real purpose of the campaigns, namely, *to affirm retaliation as a social good* – a sure sign of the spirit of revenge at work.

An important historical distinction has to be made between *Me Too*, a phrase devised by Tarana Burke, an American activist from the Bronx, and the hashtag *#MeToo* initiated by the actor Alyssa Milano. Burke worked for the last three decades with Black women and girls, survivors of sexual abuse, "talking about sex and life and violence and the hope for a measure of safety, pleasure, and power"[6] in a climate of exploration, emotional support, and em-powerment.[7] The phrase was hijacked, according to Wypijewski, and turned into a meme in 2017 when many instances of sexual assault emerged in Hollywood. When Burke was invited by the great and the good to the Golden Globes, her first incredulous response, before eventually accepting to join Meryl Streep, Natalie Portman, Jessica Chastain, and others and being hailed as the founder of the #MeToo movement was: "Why? I'm trying very hard not to be the black woman who is trotted out when you all need to validate your work".[8] For Wypijewski, there is a difference between Burke's work, dealing with "the mess of life" and its ambiguities, helping young women to talk about things they found difficult to talk about, and the "hammer" of #MeToo "used ... to exile the accused but also, perversely, put the accuser in a box, denying their messy humanity as well".[9] While Burke's Me Too acknowledged interlinked harassments, including violence in the family, #MeToo created a series of Hollywood and courtroom performances driven by simplistic scripts and accusatory glee.

In a similar vein, deconstructing the sexual panic around paedo-
philia which threatened the life of an innocent gay male teacher and
colleague, Roger Lancaster pointed out:

> Less about the protection of children than about the preservation
> of adult fantasies of childhood as a time of sexual innocence, sex
> panics give rise to bloated imaginings of risk, inflated conceptions
> of harm, and loose definitions of sex.[10]

Sex panic is defined by Wypijewski as "a social eruption fanned by
the media and characterized by alarm over innocence imperilled".[11]
As with other moral battles, the routinely simplistic narratives position good against evil, and to those who are seen as evil anything can
be done.

It would not be controversial to update Nietzsche's notion of
ressentiment[12] as the negative transference of the suffering that comes
with a sense of one's own mediocrity on to an external object on
which to assign blame. The creation of an external enemy often
comes in handy for explaining away one's own sense of failure,
particularly when raised through systematic cultivation of hatred,
that most perverse form of intimacy. The irresistible delight experienced in allocating blame is at the very heart of *ressentiment*, a breath
away from the so-called victim mentality of our age, and from
identity politics – both expressions in need of clarification, least we
join the poisonous chorus ranging from essentialists to positive psychologists. To some degree, politicized identity is necessary as dissent
against banishment and prejudice, but its roots are firmly within the
liberal tradition that strengthens the wounds it claims to heal, as
Wendy Brown attests:

> In locating a site of blame for its powerlessness over its past – a
> past of injury, a past as a hurt will – and locating a 'reason' for
> the 'unendurable pain' of social powerlessness in the present
> [politicized identity] converts this reasoning into an ethicizing
> politics, a politics of recrimination.[13]

While to some degree inevitable and even necessary, the current
triumph of identity politics as the primary socio-politico-libidinal

discourse of our day is also an unsettling sign of losses – of social context, of history, of class, of larger solidarities, of the vision of an emancipatory future in which the pain is overcome. Is there a way out? A first, difficult avenue of exploration is Nietzsche's encouragement to *forget*. As antidote to an identity built on *ressentiment*, learning to forget makes a lot of sense. Wendy Brown briefly considers this possibility before dismissing it through a pragmatist Rortyan move: Nietzsche is a valuable diagnostician in individual matters but questionable when applied to a collective programme of liberation. Her conclusions are nevertheless startling. After accepting the need for grievances to be acknowledged beyond the solipsistic claim of "I am" in favour of "I want this for us", her inspiring conclusion is that we must "*rehabilitate the memory of desire ... prior to its wounding*".[14]

At first glance, blank acknowledgement of difference in several contemporary Western societies appears as something to be praised, particularly when compared to the institutionalized misogyny, homophobia, and racism still rife in many parts of the world. Unfortunately, this kind of acknowledgement often tends to depoliticize difference to the point that the latter looks trivial, ineffectual, and entertainingly deviant – a matter of "lifestyle". Under neoliberalism, difference becomes a matter of the personal choice of the so-called free individual rather than a historical and intricate process of subjectivation which destabilizes traditional notions of identity. Once properly sterilized in this manner, difference ends up confirming normative identity. William Connolly explains:

> An identity is established in relation to a series of differences that have become socially recognized. These differences are essential to its being. If they did not coexist as differences, [identity] would not exist in its distinctiveness and solidity ... Identity requires difference in order to be and it converts difference into otherness in order to secure its own self-certainty.[15]

Can identity ever be liberating? Can it ever be disentangled from the managerial social order? In neoliberal societies, therapy has eagerly contributed to the bolstering of that very same social order; can therapy ever become a subversive practice in the service of an emancipatory notion of identity? This task is more difficult than ever, given that all mainstream theoretical orientations praise a taken-for-granted notion of relatedness that for the most part depends on the universalist notion of "we" promoted by the liberal state. To this "we", the "I" either bows meekly, accepting its role as an extra in the grandiose movie of the state, or else takes an entertaining stand as a "character", exulting in versions of eccentricity which confirm the rule after the fifteen minutes of fame and amusing controversy have passed. There are too many examples of "flamboyant" and "unique" individuals who go on supporting conservative policies. A necessary antidote is a politicization of identity which takes on board and learns from the emergence of new forms of radicalism – however fragmented and often isolated – which retain some link to the class struggle and the civil right struggle from the past. Considering what brought it about, considering what forms it and permeates it, we need to ask: what does politicized identity want?[16]

The crucial shift between reactive and active subjectivation does not automatically imply a movement from oppression to liberation. There are always "possibilities of resistance, disobedience, and oppositional groupings", Foucault reminds us, within most authoritarian formations. Equally, nothing is "functionally … absolutely liberating".[17]

Freedom is a practice; it cannot be bestowed on me by an avowedly democratic system. The guarantee of freedom is the *practice* of freedom. Clamouring for the Powers to accept my difference means accepting, in reactive mode, the universality of a "we" that is the bedrock of the liberal state and bolstered today by therapy culture's homogenous insistence on universal relatedness. This is precisely what a politicized identity opposes. The universal "we" is a sedimented historical construct assembled by the victors, the hegemonic forces writing history, the forces of stupidity, for stupidity always takes the winner's side. And even this "I" – different, marginalized – is still being conceived as autonomous and cohesive – all the more autonomous and cohesive because excluded and wanting to be admitted to a universal/ liberal community spouting platitudes as the oppressors continue to carpet bomb civilians with impunity. I want to be *recognized* as a "person"; a "person-centred" society obliges, acknowledging my existence reduced to quantifiable social traits and forgetting that is partly constructed by institutional power. The quantifiable social traits then become law and my entire existence becomes regulated.

The very fabric of the liberal state is imbued with *ressentiment* and the construction of identities – including politicized identities – within which the liberal state cannot escape *ressentiment*. The latter is not confined, as critics of Nietzsche antisocialist sentiments would have it, to the oppressed and the excluded. Everyone within the liberal state is subjected to *ressentiment* given that just behind the liberal state's empty promises of success and happiness, loom the shadow of failure. Grievances in the therapy room and beyond are then efficiently directed: either at oneself or against others. *Ressentiment* is very good at apportioning blame, and as a way to focus the mind, it works wonders. It succeeds, through anger and righteousness, in forgetting and glossing over our inherent vulnerability. It finds a perpetrator, the culprit who is to blame for our equally inherent sense of failure. It constructs an entire site of revenge where hurt can be conveniently displaced and buried.

With the advent of neoliberalism, this entire process became turbocharged. Escalating economic and political uncertainty on a global level brings about greater powerlessness and dependency. With human experiences shrunk to the level of commodities, the mystery and joy of everyday life vanish. This is the death of God without the freedom of a godless horizon; it is disenchantment as the twilight of all evaluative perspectives, prone to bureaucratic fossilization and with very little hope for re-enchantment through the heterogeneity of opposing gods.[18] Neoliberalism is the true nihilistic project, obliterating the unexpected openings envisioned by Nietzsche and Weber. Livid with resentment, classifying everything, turning everything into an article of trade, disciplining and regulating everything except the unsavoury freedom to ride on the trail to unlimited success on the bleached horse of failure. What affirmation of identity and difference is ever possible in this landscape? Nietzsche was right after all: identities are themselves the product of *ressentiment*; they are a reaction against a world perceived as external and worthy of blame, of the apportioning of causality and origins. Identities come into being by manufacturing an imaginary enemy. The "will" animating identities and the will itself has been poisoned, animated by the spirit of revenge, as Nietzsche's *Zarathustra* proclaims in *On Redemption*:

Thus the will, the liberator, became a doer of harm; and on everything that is capable of suffering it avenges itself for not being able to go back. This, yes this alone is revenge itself: the will's unwillingness toward time and time's 'it was.' Indeed, a great folly lives in our will; and it became the curse of all humankind that this folly acquired spirit! The spirit of revenge: my friends, that so far has been what mankind contemplate best; and wherever there was suffering, punishment was always supposed to be there as well.[19]

What to do when there is no ability or possibility to act? We react; revenge is a reaction, and through revenge our identity is strengthened, or more precisely re-created at every step. It may be useful to note briefly that the deconstructive power of contemplative practices such as *zazen* goes in the opposite direction, in the sense that they refrain from the painstaking and laborious endeavour we all engage in, namely constructing a subject every step of the way. Identity is (paradoxically?) what prevents redemption. The past may be redeemed the moment identity becomes no longer invested in it. But how can identity no longer invest in the past unless it gives up on "its identity as such, thus giving up its economy of avenging and at the same time perpetuating its hurt"?[20]

Identity giving itself up is nothing short of a catastrophe from the point of view of identity, in the same way as turning into a butterfly is a disaster for the caterpillar. It may be that no redemption is possible without catastrophe. Walter Benjamin would agree, and so would his friend Gershom Scholem: the forces of redemption may emerge not solely from divine intervention but, phoenix-like, from the heart of the ruins. For Benjamin, the new angel, the angel of history "preferred to free men by taking from them, rather than make them happy by giving to them",[21] by parcelling out de(con)structive critique, a task nowadays either trivialized by mercenary tabloid controversialists or timidly shunned by goody-two-shoes philosophers and psychotherapists.

The word "difference" is now *de rigueur*, beautifying the mission statements of many corporate institutions. But it is an empty concept; by the beginning of the millennium, it had lost all political meaning and intellectual substance. As poststructuralism slowly gave way to biological essentialism and its parade of unassailable trends – "genetics, molecular biology, evolutionary theories and the despotic authority of DNA"[22] – "difference" has been both overblown and objectified. It may be a curious fact, but it is no laughing matter that the term "differentialism" has now come to signify aggressive defence of provincialism, nationalism and all things parochial and ethnically "pure" against the threat of cosmopolitanism. It is as if poststructuralism and the materialist/deconstructive European phil-osophical (counter)tradition never existed. Which is one more reason to retrieve, capitalize, and build on the teachings and insights of these intellectual and political assemblages and texts. They give difference a different spin; their materialism grounds difference on the flesh and the body, giving priority to sexuality, an area of experience which has been legislated upon, quantified, apprehended but rarely given the philosophical depth it deserves. This process of retrieval and re-evaluation is all the more urgent at a time when *sexophobia* has become dominant in contemporary culture, whether disguising as edifying discourse in anti-pornography campaigns or making its bigotry known in the pronouncements of the Moral Majority, for instance in its attempts to criminalize sex workers.

Sexophobia and somatophobia are intriguing manifestations of overt, unsophisticated expressions of a narcissistic understanding of what a human being is. Sex and the body dangerously bridge the imaginary and artificial gap between the human and the animal. This bias originates in traditional metaphysics but is equally present in secular perspectives. For Heidegger, humans alone are able to weave a net of purposeful activity, belonging, and interconnectedness. Humans alone have a "world", he writes in *The Origin of the Work of Art*, whereas "a stone is worldless". Neither animal nor plant has a world according to Heidegger; they belong instead to "the covert throng of a surrounding into which they are linked". Humans have a world, we are told, because they dwell "in the overtness of things".[23] Infused with mesmeric jargon (what on earth does "overtness" mean?), his essay reveals to a considerable degree Heidegger's humanism, a curious find when one thinks of the overarching attempt in his philosophy to bypass the supremacy of the human subject. His humanism, though funda-mentalist in asserting the uniqueness and centrality of humans, is in some way unusual: what distinguishes humans from animals is not their rationality nor the immortality of their soul, as the more popular arguments would have it; it is instead *Ek-sistenz*, i.e., human capacity for what he calls "representational positioning",[24] its ecstatic position within the structure of "Being" characterizing the abysmal distance with "the beast",[25] its allegedly special language being no less than the house of Being. But "language isn't the House of Being"; it is "a fairground filled with hucksters and con artists".[26] There is no real understanding in Heidegger's philosophy of the bodily nature of the human subject – or body-subject – nor any remote imagining of the possibility of some form of bio-centred equality.

Current discourse is still dominated by an emphasis on the alleged supremacy of the human and on the glamorization of (human) language. These traditional stances present the human subject as a static entity rather than an assemblage of radical becomings. We are still a very long way from Nietzsche's *overhuman* – not a "higher" or "super" being but a threshold of unending becoming, a groundless project into an ineffable future.[27] Traditional views forget the richness and complexity of other species, including insects:

> Insects are well ahead of humans in this regard. Radical becomings take place routinely in their own lives. This is especially so in groups that pass through pupal metamorphosis. Their bodies are broken down and completely rebuilt in the course of transmutation from the larval to the mature stage. Is the butterfly "at one" with the caterpillar? Is this housefly buzzing around my head "the same" as the maggot it used to be?[28]

Nonhuman organisms are understood crudely in the philosophical and psychological tradition as simple multiple uncoilings of biological processes, as the passive recipient of *zoe,* while the "self-reflexive control of life"[29] is allocated to humans alone. And yet, whether or not represented by Logos, by human discourse, *zoe* inextricably links humans and animals, surpassing and exceeding Logos, presenting us with the richness of a life that encompasses and moves beyond the dismal and the divine.

There are admittedly Romantic overtones in this view of the overflowing power of Life. However, this is a Romanticism without a subject, animated by a reverence for the neutral and boundless flow

of Lifedeath traversing every sentient form. It is also a Romanticism
devoid of Rousseauian nostalgia for the wild and the uncontaminated,
a wildness and non-contamination that never were, other than in the
myths of unfettered childhood and the apportioned Eden of city al-
lotments. Openness to a future of radical becomings must mean taking
pleasure in the confusion of boundaries – be they in the direction of
plant/animal life or in the direction of the machine, particularly at a
time when the machine is already embedded in your daily existence.
Embracing this next step is possible once incarnate experience has been
understood and absorbed. Enter the cyborg.

I recognize that within a humanistic philosophical/psycho-
therapeutic culture, to even entertain the idea of the cyborg as one
possible aspect of liberative discourse is scandalous. The beauty of the
cyborg is that it is situated beyond narratives of salvation, moralizing
struggles of gender, tiresome oedipal agendas, and nostalgic yearnings
to go back to the Edenic womb where the melodrama of the heterosexual male can be duly restored and replayed ad infinitum – where
glorifications of family, country, and community are sung in unison.
The beauty of the cyborg is that "it is not made of mud and cannot
dream of returning to dust".[30]

By the late twentieth century, Donna Haraway argues, there have
been three important frontier breaks. The *first* is characterized by the
rise of animal rights activism which forced the mainstream to rethink
the boundaries between the human and the animal and to question
more deeply the bigotry inherent to creationism. The *second* has to do
with the creation of a stronger link between the animal-human
organism and the machine. This is parallel to the slow realization of
machines' autonomy, liveliness, and self-designing capabilities. While
our machines can be "disturbingly lively", we can on the other hand
be "frighteningly inert".[31] The *third* frontier break derives from the
second, namely the blurring of what is considered physical and non-
physical. It is at this point that the use of Nietzsche's hammer – its
priceless methodology of evaluation or *axiology* – becomes important. What would it mean, in other words, to put machines at the
service of *active* rather than *reactive* forces? And if active forces are
life-affirming, the advent of the cyborg would invite us to a
redefinition of *physis* and *zoe*, of what we call "body" and "life". This
is certainly a delicate balance. While there is at present every

indication that the cyborg is fitted out to serve policing, reactive forces, a cyborg world may also involve lived situations of "joint kinship with animals and machines", without the traditional dread of inhabiting "permanently partial identities".[32] The higher the risk, the greater the liberative potential to transform the socio-political dead end that is neoliberalism into a strategy of resistance.

*

Those involved in lefty political activism and/or various forms of emancipatory social protest may sooner or later encounter two crucial questions which will either complicate or enrich their struggle and political commitment: (a) "How does power infiltrate the psyche?" (b) "What shape and form does power take in one's inner life?". Hegel answered both questions by formulating the notion of the unhappy consciousness, that "dual consciousness [that is both] ... self-liberating ... and self-perverting",[33] forever in contradiction with itself as soon as the "master" has been transferred to the slave's psyche as *conscience* – as self-reproach, and self-flagellation and, in our day, as self-improvement – already prefiguring Nietzsche's view of conscience as bad conscience.[34] Certainly Nietzsche complicated and enriched things further by memorably suggesting that this quasi-originary split introduced by Christian morality – the birth of conscience – also constitutes the birth of the (dividual) self: there is no self without bad conscience. By turning back on and against itself through the entangled workings of conscience, the subject ends up profitably consolidating and perpetuating itself, fending off apprehensions about its own flimsy existence. And it does so grandly, nobly, in the same way as when, through grieving, ends up strengthening itself.

Self-reproach (in contemporary parlance self-regulation as much as affect-regulation) is in this sense a tangible symptom of the workings of power in the psyche. With (bad) conscience comfortably enthroned at the centre of our inner life, we respond happily to Althusser's proverbial policeman hailing our name and bringing us to life as a subject. The two are entwined: the inner policeman/woman greets its external double and off they go on a blind date. Whether or not the date goes smoothly, one thing is certain: the "theory of interpellation" (the subject is engendered by the policeman hailing my name in the street) – meets a "theory of conscience"[35] (I endeavour to reform myself through serving some time in jail, practising McMindfulness or seeing a neoliberal shrink). Could this constitute a potential frame for initiating Althusserian/Nietzschean comparative studies?

Punitive authority may look impressive as it strides and struts through rigid routines and deadening speeches and rolling tanks through city streets. But its efficacy becomes truly manifest when the subject eagerly declares its voluntary servitude and confirms its primaeval attachment to a good measure of consolatory order. Losing my passport a few years ago in Berlin was so unsettling that I had to exercise great restraint in wanting to hug and kiss the policeman who handed it back to me when it was eventually found.

Psychical reverberation of power is its most subtle and devious aspect. Power shrinking in the psychic vaults is what gives birth to the subject. And it is through subordination to parents, necessary for survival, that children learn the ways of obedience which in time turns them into submissive and passive members of society: better to survive in chains than ceasing to exist. Loving your parents becomes a matter of survival for the child. "Love" – the love that "matters", the love that creates secure attachment: this very same love, "bound up with the requirement for life",[36] is an absolute must for survival. You *must* love if you want to survive. Is this the dark side of attachment theory?

"No subject can emerge without this attachment, formed in dependency – Judith Butler writes – but no subject, in the course of its formation, can ever afford fully to see it".[37] Dependency must be denied so that from this enmeshment the subject can emerge. The price we pay during this process has far-reaching political implications. I must actively wish for my own subordination in order to continue existing as a subject. I must bow to repression, control, and restriction – the very things that threaten my existence – so that I can continue to exist as a subject. Even *before* the required acknowledgement/recognition of the other through encounter – the Hegelian *Anerkennung* which will confirm my subjectivity and unshackle it from mere solipsism, I am being shaped through childhood dependency by the introjected presence of power within me. Then as an adult I will have to deny this essential dependency, and by denying it destabilize a vital layer of my own sedimentation as a subject.

"Subject" is not the same as "person" and "individual" – at least not in the line of thought pursued here. Both the "person" – an idol in humanistic psychology – and the (authentic)"individual" – the hero of traditional existential therapy, may come to inhabit the place of the subject but it is with the subject (through language) that the person and the individual "achieve and reproduce intelligibility",[38] a process intrinsically bound to subjugation.

Is it possible, given this development, that *reactive* power, which appears to be constitutive of the subject, will ever become *active*? Can it ever express *agency*, a creative force which the subject is able to exercise rather than merely suffer? Is there continuity between these two aspects of power – between reactive and active power? For one to turn into the other – for the power *acted upon* the subject to turn into a power *enacted by* the subject, a fundamental transformation is needed, a transformation that is *in excess* of the reaches and modes of constitutive power. That does not mean, as liberal-humanistic thought would have it, that agency ("personal power") is not in some way or other implicated in power. There is no agency un-coupled from power-as-subjugation. Agency is not teleological nor can it be pragmatically saddled with a "project".

The subject's agency or, better still, the subject itself is a form of *excrescence*. The subject is *"neither* fully determined by power *nor* fully determining of power".[39] It surpasses logic at the same time as it is bound by it. The subject's agency is power revisited and re-constituted, yielding both subjugation and liberation – an instance perhaps of failing again, and failing better, of forever having a crack at sublating cynicism and idealism by acknowledging the presence of oppression and creation. In this instance, the "taking away" of sublation removes teleology: there isn't always a goal or a purpose to the way power constitutes the subject. It is not a straight story. Judith Butler alerts us to the possibility that the way the subject reframes power may be one instance of that *chain of signs* Nietzsche writes about in his *Genealogy*. No matter how thoroughly we may have absorbed the nature, efficacy, or function of a particular entity – be it a bodily organ, an institution, a political and social practice or, as in the present discussion, power and agency – its uses and purposes are subjected to changes, sometimes radical changes:

... all purposes, all uses, are only signs that a will to power has become master over something with less power and has stamped on it its own meaning of some function, and the entire history of a 'thing' ... can by this process be seen as a continuing chain of signs of constantly new interpretations and adjustments, whose causes need not be connected to each other – they rather follow and take over from each other under merely contingent circumstances.[40]

The personal is political, so went the old refrain, and it is still valid today. Does that imply that there is a continuum between the "outside" – political, external power – and "an inside" of personal, agentic power? If so, where do we locate power, and more specifically normative power? Does it emerge in the *agora* first and then insinuate itself in the inner dominion, itself an ambivalent locus encompassing both contingent "internal" relations and constitutive "interiority"? Or does the assumption of the existence of an inner life invent the very demarcation between the personal and the political? And how does, finally, this merry and intricate dance involve desire (power) and its suppression (domination)?

One often ignored aspect of the patriarchy, despite many articulate critiques of its structure and harmful effects, is how closely associated it is with a generalized politics of *protection* and *regulation* and how ubiquitous the latter are in social policy. It does not matter whether we are contending with "the state, the Mafia, parents, pimps, police, or husbands", Wendy Brown says, "the heavy price of institutionalized protection is always a measure of dependence and agreement to abide by the protector's rule".[41] It is tempting to ask whether this feminist reading could also be extended to self-governed professional bodies – say, in the world of therapy – which, for all the obeisance they exhibit to considerate, even feminist ethics (albeit watered-down to appease the Powers), are also prone to the very same patriarchal rule of thumb, founded on Rousseau's notion of civil slavery masquerading as communal ethics. "I know that oppressed people do nothing but boast without pause about the peace and repose they enjoy in their chains – he wrote – and that they call the most miserable slavery peace".[42] This is all the more disturbing when the protection afforded to the individual practitioner is next to nothing, something which reveals the wholly fraudulent nature of the contract between the professional body and the practitioner.

Bureaucracy and managerialism reign supreme in the liberal, capitalist state justly critiqued by feminist theory. This may partly have to do with the fact that male dominance no longer needs to constantly flex its muscles in cartoonish, primitive fashion; it can now prolong its control via a soft lingo of acceptance, respect for diversity and the environment. Wendy Brown again:

> The elements of the state identifiable as masculinist correspond not to some property contained within men but to the conventions of power and privilege *constitutive* of gender within an order of male dominance ... [T]he masculinism of the state refers to those features of the state that signify, enact, sustain and represent masculine power as a form of dominance.[43]

Then there is that other notion, so closely linked to protection, a notion riotously popular in therapy culture and beyond, one that is even more damaging than protection because of its insidiousness and "soft power": I am referring to *regulation*. Weber, Marcuse, and more recently Foucault have painstakingly charted "the increasing organization of everything as the central issue of our time"[44] illustrating the emptying out of human connection carried out by this process alongside the sinister normalization it manages to produce. Compared for instance with the monstrous expansion of rationalization and the levelling out of human experience carried out by contemporary use of metrics, old-fashioned ways of domination look naïve at best. We no longer inhabit a Hobbesian "state of nature" where masculinist power exerts brute force and dishes out crude discrimination, cruelty, and exploitation. Subjection – the unfreedom of women, blacks, the poor, the disenfranchised, and the oppressed – is now fully rationalized by bureaucratic supervision and adorned with liberal, eco-friendly, diversity-loving lingo and the verbiage of "authenticity". Given the choice, most of us will go for the second option of a smoother servitude: better to be under the stultifying yoke of the state – a broad, disjointed assemblage of power dealings and a conduit of vast control over our existence – than be the bruised recipients of the thuggery of unmediated power. The crucial insight from critical feminist theory is that "all dimensions of state power, and not merely some overtly 'patriarchal' aspects, figure in the gendering of the state".[45] A masculinist state is not simply one that pursues the interests of men but one whose very structures are constituted by fossilized modes of power founded on constructed forms of masculinity. There are, according to Wendy Brown's incisive analysis, four dimensions of masculinist state power: *liberal, capitalist, prerogative*, and *bureaucratic*, an analysis that is worthwhile summarizing.

The *liberal dimension* (and its attendant ideology and legislation) sees the family as pre-political, a natural, or religiously decreed entity separated from the public sphere and where woman is the key worker. This paradigm is encouraged and perpetuated by the overwhelming majority of therapeutic orientations through their uncritical adherence to attachment theory. The liberal storyline tells us that people – men – left behind a hypothetical "state of nature" and secured their individual rights within society. They did so, however, without safeguarding or empowering individuals within the family. Men gained the right to move at liberty between the family and the public sphere, a scenario which is at the very heart of masculinism. The bad news for liberals (including feminist liberals who delight in visions of a free and just society devoid of the imprint of masculine domination) is that between masculinity and liberalism there is an "interconstitutive"[46] relationship.

The *capitalist dimension* is similar to the liberal dimension in that it presents a division between the private and the public sphere. The difference is that the capitalist dimension traditionally moves "along a different axis":[47] the men do paid work while the women do the unpaid work of producing new labourers for the capitalist machine.

The *prerogative dimension* echoes the ancient but still resilient notion expounded in Niccolò Machiavelli's *The Prince* in validating the indiscriminate power of the state as princely power. Liberal/capitalist narratives are routinely keen to emphasize that a political organization centred around the power of few privileged men is a thing of the past, that it has been superseded by liberal democracy where justification for policies is supposedly no longer grounded on subjugation but instead motivated towards welfare. This explanation, however, bypasses the great ability the liberal state has to camouflage its deep-seated prerogative: from war to budget, institutional aggression continues to be asserted, with the full support of the police and the armed forces. This explanation also conveniently forgets that like other political institutions the state, as charted by the great sociologist and political realist Max Weber, has its origins in gangs of prowling warriors who depend on, without contributing to, a regional population and who arbitrarily intimidate their own as well as next-door peoples. Unlike many of his contemporaries who attributed moral quality to the state, he defines it in no uncertain terms as "a human community that [effectively] claims the *monopoly of the legitimate use of violence* within a certain territory".[48] This view is amplified by Charles Tilly, who writes: "If protection rackets represent organized crime at its smoothest, then war making and state making – quintessential protection rackets with the advantage of legitimacy – qualify as our largest examples of organized crime".[49] Without quite labelling all heads of state and the military as an assorted bunch of crooks and killers, Tilly nevertheless makes a compelling case for the great resemblance that exists between war makers and state makers on one hand and "coercive and self-seeking entrepreneurs"[50] on the other. Within this frame, the very notion of authority is *patrimonial* (from patrimony = paternal estate), grounded in the ability to guard the family against plundering warrior leagues, much in "the same way of street gangs, rationalized and legitimized in most international state activity".[51]

If we are to follow Weber's authoritative account, the very foundation of the state, including the liberal state, is *violence*. Plundering gangs of warriors gathered at the periphery of local communities become part of those communities and their joining announces the beginning of political communities. While the nomadic aspect is dissolved, the violent characteristics remain and become the important future of the nascent state. It is at this juncture that the local community changes "from one of mother-children groups to father-headed households"[52]: And it is at this juncture that for Weber the authority of the male emerges proportional with his aptitude to rule over as well as protect his family. While the economic factor plays an important role in the structure of the patriarchal family, the latter is also built on the need to erect a fence between the violence of the external world and the existence of vulnerable people. Paradoxically, the authority of the male within the family is predicated on his ability to protect the proverbial castle, kids, and home against external, i.e., *institutional* male violence.

The picture Weber describes accords not only with Sophocles and Dostoevsky but also with Freud's depiction of the totem meal after patricide in the fourth chapter of *Totem and Taboo*. "One day – he famously writes – the brothers who had been driven out came together, killed and devoured their father and so made an end of the patriarchal horde. United, they had the courage to do and succeed in doing what would have been impossible for them individually".[53]

The brothers had been driven out and together plot the assassination of their father. In order to avoid the situation that occurred before the patricide – their being driven out – they establish the state, its rules, and regulations, including not having sex with each other's women so as to release "the tension that an absent father introduces into a brotherhood".[54]

That threshold, the dividing line between state and family, external political life and domestic interiority is the very same area where most battles are fought and talked about in the therapy room – domestic violence and rape, property and money, access to children and so forth. Prerogative power implies, in Weber's terms, that at heart the state's *raison* d'*être* is not the welfare of its people but what he calls "the prestige of domination".[55] Safeguarding human life is not high in the priorities of the state, despite the cherished illusions of liberalism. The very existence of the (masculinist) state is grounded on self-perpetuation and self-glorification, even when supreme human value is accorded, in de Beauvoir's account, not to "giving life but [to] risking life" and superiority given not to women but to men, "not to sex that brings forth but to that which kills".[56] The difficulty in challenging the coercive power of the prerogative state consists in the fact that the power to destroy is inextricably linked to the power to protect – even when the latter entirely coincides with policing.

As for the bureaucratic dimension, this may be of more immediate relevance to those involved in the "helping professions", an area where the damaging effects of managerialism have been acutely felt. These developments have proven Weber and Foucault right when they each asserted in their own way the pervasiveness of bureaucratism in the social order, its sinister blurring of state and civil society, its coercive, disciplining traits.[57] But not even Weber and

Foucault could have predicted the dizzy heights of absurdity of measuring authenticity on an authenticity scale,[58] nor could they have foreseen how the only hotbeds of resistance left to the encroaching of managerialism appear to be our own futile attempts at humanizing the bureaucratic beast. In her 1984 seminal study, Kathy Ferguson denounced how, long before digitalization and the advent of managerialism-on-steroids, bureaucracies created their own language in order to control information, defended their associates, side-stepped accountability, created smoke screens to make their activities inaccessible to outsiders, explained and disciplined our experiences, looked after themselves and preserved prejudices and inequalities.[59] I believe some of these characteristics may be reasonably applied to certain professional bodies regulating therapy today.

For Ferguson, there are two distinctive aspects of masculinism at work within bureaucratic power:

a   Bureaucracy bullies workforce and customers alike into neediness and docility. In a way, it "feminizes" them. It teaches tactics of "impression management" to its staff. The example Ferguson gives is that of flight attendants who are trained by their companies to accept inequitable power relations and to ascribe difficulties in their work to their own "unsuccessful management of feeling and personae rather than to the conditions of work and the expectations of customers". Faced with rude customers or patronizing training programmes, attendants have no right to be angry: "They are paid, in fact, to forfeit that right".[60] I wonder how much of "impression management" is integral to the ethos of counselling and psychotherapy trainings in our neoliberal world, despite profusive avowals of congruence and authenticity.

b   Bureaucratic power endorses rationalization – a far cry from the "clearing of clouds" brought by the liberating power of reason – as well as officious legalism and hierarchy. Control is the supreme value: domination through systems of regularity, measurability, and manipulation. Again, the inevitable question is: how useful has therapy culture been in aiding rather than obstructing this process? This question is all the more important when one considers the paradox of contemporary institutional power, in many ways reflecting the paradox of contemporary masculinity.

Power and privilege in both areas operate more and more through "disavowal of potency, repudiation of responsibility, and diffusion of sites and operations of control".[61] To this state of affairs, therapy culture has sadly provided a ready-made lingo of authenticity and an ethical varnish instrumental in perpetuating and upgrading the very same operations of control.

Notes

1 Roger Lancaster, *Sex Panic and the Punitive State*, Oakland: University of California Press, 2011.
2 Aya Gruber, *The Feminist War on Crime: The Unexpected Role of Women's Liberation in Mass Incarceration.* Oakland: University of California Press, 2020, p. 1.
3 Ibid.
4 Judith Levine and Erica R. Meiners, *The Feminist and the Sex Offender: Confronting Sexual Harm, Ending State Violence.* London and New York: Verso, 2020; Maia Hibbett, 'Who keeps us Safe?' *The Baffler,* New York, September 2020, N. 53.
5 JoAnn Wypijewski, *What We Don't Talk About: Sex and the Messiness of Life.* London: Verso, 2021.

 1 Wendy Brown, *States of Injury: Power and Freedom in Late Modernity.* Princeton, NJ: Princeton University Press, 1995, p. 169.
6 Emma Brockes, Interview with Tarana Burke, *The Guardian.* 15 January 2018 https://www.theguardian.com/world/2018/jan/15/me-too-founder-tarana-burke-women-sexual-assault retrieved 28 Nov. 21.
7 M. Buna, 'Life isn't a Narrative: a Conversation with JoAnn Wypijewski'. *Los Angeles Review of Books*, 26 November 2020, Life Isn't a Narrative: A Conversation with JoAnn Wypijewski (lareviewofbooks.org), retrieved 28 Nov. 2021.
8 Interview with Tarana Burke, op. cit.
9 'Life isn't a Narrative' op. cit.
10 Roger Lancaster, *Sex Panic and the Punitive State*, Oakland: University of California Press, 2011, p. 2.
11 *What We Don't Talk About*, op. cit.
12 Friedrich Nietzsche *On the Genealogy of Morals: A Polemic.* Trans. D. Smith. New York: Oxford University Press, 1996, 1st Treatise.
13 Wendy Brown, *States of Injury: Power and Freedom in Late Modernity.* Princeton, NJ: Princeton University Press, 1995, p. 74.
14 Ibid., p. 75, emphasis added.
15 William Connolly, *Identity/Difference: Negotiations of Political Paradox.* Ithaca: Cornell University Press, 1991, p. 64. Jean-Jacques Rousseau, *Discourse on the Origins and the Foundations of Inequality*, London: Create Space Publication, 2018, p. 56.
16 *States of Injury*, p. 66.
17 Michel Foucault, *The Foucault Reader*, edited by P. Rabinow, New York: Pantheon, 1984, p. 245.

 Ibid., p. 67.

18 See Max Weber, 'Objectivity in Social Science and Social Policy' in *The Methodology of the Social Sciences*, edited and translated by E. A. Shils & H. A. Finch, New York: Free Press, 1949.
19 Friedrich Nietzsche, *Thus Spoke Zarathustra*, edited by Adrian Del Caro and Robert P. Pippin, Cambridge University Press, 2006, p. 111.
20 *States of Injury*, op. cit, p. 73.
21 Walter Benjamin, *Reflections Essays, Aphorisms, and Autobiographical Writings* Edited by Peter Demetz. Translated by Edmund Jephcott. New York: Harcourt, Brace, Jovanovich, 1978, p. 273.
22 Rosi Braidotti, *Metamorphoses: Towards a Materialist Theory of Becoming.* Cambridge: Polity, 2002, p. 4.
23 Martin Heidegger, *Basic Writings*. San Francisco, CA: Harper Collins, p. 231.
24 Ibid., p. 231.
25 Ibid., p. 230.
26 Steven Shaviro, 'Two Lessons from William Burroughs', in Judith Halberstam & Ira Livingston (Eds) *Posthuman Bodies*. Bloomington and Indianapolis: Indiana University Press, 1995, pp. 38–56; p. 44.
27 This point is discussed at length in Manu Bazzano, 'Against Humanism', *Nietzsche and Psychotherapy*. Abingdon, OX: Routledge, 2019, pp. 75–99.
28 Steven Shaviro, 'Two Lessons' op. cit., p. 48.
29 Rosi Braidotti, *Metamorphoses*, op. cit., p. 132.
30 Donna Haraway, *Manifestly Haraway*. Minneapolis, MN: University of Minnesota Press, 2016, p. 9.
31 Ibid., p. 11.
32 Ibid., p. 15.
33 G. W. F. Hegel, *Phenomenology of Spirit*. Trans. A. V. Miller. Oxford: Oxford University Press, 1977, p. 126.
34 Friedrich Nietzsche, *On the Genealogy of Morals: A Polemic*. Trans. D. Smith Oxford and New York: Oxford University Press, 1996.
35 Judith Butler, *The Psychic Life of Power: Theories in Subjection*. Stanford, CA: Stanford University Press, pp. 3–4.
36 Ibid., p. 8.
37 Ibid., p. 8.
38 Ibid., p. 10.
39 Ibid., p. 18.
40 Friedrich Nietzsche, *On the Genealogy of Morals: A Polemic*, London, Penguin, p. 59.
41 Wendy Brown, *States of Injury: Power and Freedom in Late Modernity*. Princeton, NJ: Princeton University Press, 1995, p. 169.
42 Jean-Jacques Rousseau, *Discourse on the Origins and the Foundations of Inequality*, London: Create Space Publication, 2018, p. 56.
43 *States of Injury*, p. 167.
44 Hubert L. Dreyfus, Paul Rabinow, *Michel Foucault Beyond Structuralism and Hermeneutics*. Chicago, ILL: University of Chicago Press, 1982, p. xxii.
45 *States of Injury*, p. 177.
46 Ibid., p. 183.
47 Ibid., p. 184.
48 *Max Weber, Political Writings. Cambridge University Press,* 1994, p.310.
49 Charles Tilly, 'War Making and State Making as Organized Crime', pp. 169–191 in Peter B. Evans, Dietrich Ruschenmeyer, Theda Skocpol (eds), *Bringing the State back in*, Cambridge University Press, p. 169.
50 Ibid., p. 169.

51 *States of Injury*, op. cit., p. 187.
52 Ibid., p. 188.
53 Sigmund Freud, *Totem and Taboo*, London, Routledge, 1983, p. 141.
54 *States of Injury*, p. 189.
55 Max Weber, *Economy and Society*, edited by G. Roth and C. Wittich. Berkeley, University of California Press, p. 82.
56 Simone de Beauvoir, *The Second Sex*, translated by H. B. Parshley. New York, Random House, 1952, p. 72.
57 Max Weber, *The Vocation Lectures*, Indianapolis, IN: Hackett Publishing, 2004; Michel Foucault, *Discipline and Punish: The Birth of the Prison*. London, Penguin, 2020.
58 See for example Alex M. Wood, Alex Linley, John Maltby, Michael Baliousis, Stephen Joseph, 'The Authentic Personality: A Theoretical and Empirical Conceptualization and the Development of the Authenticity Scale' in *Journal of Counselling Psychology* July 2008 55(3), pp. 385–399.
59 Kathy E. Ferguson, *The Feminist Case Against Bureaucracy*, Philadelphia, Temple University Press, 1984.
60 Ibid., p. 105.
61 *States of Injury*, op. cit., p. 194.

Chapter 7

Transformer

There is a difference between transformation and change. Mainstream therapy tends to promote what it calls positive change. This is a patently desirable, realistic, if somewhat cosy-sounding goal, yielding in some cases a degree of social adaptation and a handful of feel-good outcomes. These often revolve around the client's own wishes and projects (even when they themselves may constitute a hindrance to wellbeing), all the while contending with the self's phobias and hindrances along the "journey". This type of investigation remains superficial. It is, strictly speaking, *ego-therapy* rather than *psyche-therapy*. It is driven by the conscious *ego-self*; it is managerial, dealing with adjustments in response to the injuries and aspirations of the ego-self while staying well clear of *psyche* – a lavish term whose meaning include *organism, soul* (Heraclitus' ψυχῇ), the *existential unknown*, the conscious as well as the *unconscious mind*. In discarding psyche, out of fear, laziness, compliance with cultural/political pressures, we also discard its close ally *eros*. We discount from the outset the possibility of transformation.

Oddly for a practice that at its origins did not shy away from the vagaries and complexity of human experience, contemporary therapy's promotion of positive change ends up shunning eros, the universal élan which drives transformation. Why? My educated guess is that exploration of eros is complex and risky but ultimately more rewarding.

Transformation is literally changing *form*, the equivalent of metamorphosis, even though the latter is usually associated with magic or divine intervention. Change is on the other hand related to *barter*, to

DOI: 10.4324/9781003280262-8

the trading of an old lifestyle for a new one in the arcade of discarded archetypes: usually from bad to good or from dodgy to goody-two-shoes. The media is awash with thoroughly dull and edifying tales of redemption scripted in the soporific lingo of pop psychology. Transformation is a different ballgame; it is almost never ascensional, its trajectory is often wayward and may not be accompanied by inspirational muzak. It may lead us to a different understanding of the body as *bodying*; it may focus on an ontology of becoming; it may implement and expand critical feminist and queer perspectives on sexual difference. It may formulate methods of political activism un-fettered by liberal and neoliberal notions of the subject.[1]

There is no transformation without incarnate experience. It is important to resist the implied *somatophobia* of contemporary culture with its varied and concerted attempts to bypass bodily experience. It is important to trust the senses – a simple but powerful blow to Platonisms old and new. Even so, one doesn't have to fall for the sentimental pre-technological fables of a past where the wisdom of the natural and unfettered body is said to reign supreme. The "body" is (a notion) riddled with problems. Too many psychotherapeutic narratives deviate towards idealizations of the body – a gnostic entity magically gifted with near-divinatory power, be they felt sense, organismic congruence, authenticity and truth.

Yet the very notion of the body, demarcated from the flesh of the world and understood within the religious/philosophical/psychological tradition as incasement of the soul, betrays an attitude of denigration of the flesh and a transcendentalist wish to bypass our inherent human mortality as well as censure the humble and wondrous joys of sex.

The other problem to contend with is that in mainstream discourse it is assumed that there cannot be agency without a positioned, *unitary* subject. There is however a compelling and exhilarating case running through Spinoza, Nietzsche, Deleuze, and post-structuralism which has shown that the *conatus vivendi*, the will to live and affirm life is manifested at best not via a unitary self but at the crossing points of a *multiplicity* of forces: far from being the "the death of agency" multiplicity is "its very condition".[2]

The unitary subject gets in the way of transformation. What produces transformation is "a play of forces … working through bodily means". The *new* emerges as "a result of an activity that precedes the knowing subject but is not ... fully external to the subject".[3] This sounds counterintuitive in an age like ours, dominated by the idolatry of consciousness and of the ego-self. What makes us who we are is something that *precedes* us. Who we are cannot be reduced to consciousness.

*

Refusing to ensconce the unitary conscious subject at the heart of experience has far-reaching implications for how one understands transformation: it cannot mean for instance transcending or merely accepting sexual difference from the vantage point of an allegedly autonomous male subject. It implies instead affirmation of the nomadism of the subject: a positive, life-enhancing vision of the subject as dynamic and traversed by the intensity of affect. The body-subject becomes vehicle and means of transformation without a centre or fix (at)ed identity – a stance reverberating in various forms throughout the silver stream of the counter-traditional mode of thought and praxis. Feminism and critical queer theory have greatly contributed to this stream, helping foster an understanding of the more repressive, mor-alizing, anti-sexual strands within the legalistic, punitive feminism initiated by Dworkin and McKinnon, the latter effectively constituting a threat against feminism itself by underplaying "the more structural elements of patriarchal power" and denigrating "women's capacity for sexual agency and self-determination".[4]

*

Desire and transformation are bedfellows, both essential and both equally perverted and bullied into submission by the tradition. Desire transcends the Hegelian understanding that sees it solely in terms of a longing for recognition/acknowledgement, where desire is merely an aperture for the subject to turn into a "self" in the permitted sense: becoming a social being. In this progression, desire itself, the neutral current traversing bodies and minds, is overlooked, made subservient to the demands of the social contract. The social contract cannot be brazenly ignored of course. Consider transformation. Transformation follows a similar route to desire. Gay and lesbian love arrangements, for instance, may be seen to bracingly undermine at a fundamental level the structure and values of the oedipal family. Confronted with homophobic opposition to gay and lesbian marriages, however, one is faced with the difficult question of how to oppose the homophobia without adopting the marriage norm as "the exclusive or most highly valued social arrangement for queer sexual lives".[5]

Must kinship necessarily follow the marriage norm and abide by set notions of identity? What would it mean to stay close to desire itself, to transformation itself? In the case of the transexual yearning to become a woman or a man, this yearning can be a yearning for transformation itself,[6] a transformative endeavour affirming "desire itself as a transformative activity".[7] This is easy to say, especially for a heterosexual man like myself and despite my own profound misgivings about heterosexual identity. In reality, all lives require a certain degree of solidity and of social/legal recognition without which they become exposed to the violence and prejudice of the institutionalized norm. What is crucial then is that we "cease legislating for all lives what is liveable only for some", as well as refraining from forbidding "for all lives what is unliveable for some".[8]

This whole area is, needless to say, fraught with difficulties, tempting many of us into wanting to reach for the hasty and facile set of compulsions of essentialism ("a human being is a human being"; "a man is a man"; "a woman is a woman") rather than engaging with the more strenuous task of taking seriously into consideration the sedimentations of *culture* interwoven with our allegedly primeval "nature". When dwelling within this particular terrain, we are back, in a way, to have to discuss and critique all over again the resistant assumptions of anthropocentrism presiding over the religious, philosophical and psychological tradition. It is near impossible for the anthropocentric view to accept human life as that of a being who is both human and living, to accept that the presence and variety of living beings far exceeds the human, and that the very notion of the human is dependent on the nonhuman, on what is "outside itself but continuous with itself".[9] A similar form of essentialism is at work in debates about gender. The contention raised by some feminists that the yearning "to become a man or transman or to live transgendered is motivated by a repudiation of femininity" assumes that anyone who was "born with female anatomy is ... in possession of a proper femininity". The criticism of male-to-female transsexuality has focused on the appropriation of femininity, "as if it belongs properly to a given sex, as if sex is discreetly given, as if gender identity could and should be desired unequivocally from presumed anatomy".[10] Understanding gender as a historical categorization implies recognizing that gender, understood as "one way of culturally configuring a body, is open to a continual remaking, and that 'anatomy' and 'sex' are not without cultural framing".[11]

The time has been forever ripe for "gender controversy" – since Nietzsche, for instance, and his disputation of human sexuality founded on a binary opposition between women and men which opened the door to this important discussion a century and a half ago. The door was then left ajar and is now flung open by the rough winds of a long-deferred need for transformation. Taking up the baton – Nietzsche's as much as critical theorists such as Judith Butler – implies going beyond an essentialist view of "man" and "woman", widening the horizon and thinking more thoroughly about sex and gender. While the word *sex* has been used "to signify biological differences between females and males", the term *gender* usually denotes "social and cultural constructions of these differences".[12] This separation obliges us to think of them as being in two distinctive camps, the first providing the biological raw material, (the *raw*) the second constituting the performative, "aesthetic" dissemination of the natural body among other bodies (the *cooked*). But it may well be that this distinction has dissolved. There may be nothing raw, natural, or primordial about human sexual behaviour and it may not be possible to go back to a pristine state of nature.

Essentialism on gender reflects a more generalized essentialism on the human, a category sculpted in time and, as with sculpture, emerging from what is discarded, the rest of the sentient world that shares the immanent plane of existence. The tradition – including the psychoanalytic/psychotherapeutic tradition – has for the most part been employed in service of the essentialist position. This is unfortunate, because the insights accrued in investigating the psyche may also be utilized effectively to help us understand in a new light human experience in its interdependence with the world. It can help us understand better human sexuality and how it relates to the social mores by which it is controlled. A critical form of psychotherapy (one that is able to take on board the insights of the counter-tradition) can work in favour of a notion of the human as occupying a place of greater humility towards others and themselves.[13] It can help us understand that we don't know who we are or what motivates us; that what motivates us is not completely rational nor driven by the demands of social custom. This is particularly clear in relation to sexuality, which remains "lawless" and unregulated despite our every effort to regulate it. Not so much because it is wild and untamed but insofar as it is not "fully determined" but typified by displacement: it can easily "exceed regulation, take on new forms in response to regulation, even turn around and make it sexy".[14] The wonder (and trouble) of sex is that it arises as "an improvisational possibility within a field of constraints", both eclipsed and roused by them. There is comprehension but not understanding in the conventional sense, as Merleau-Ponty explains:

> There is an erotic 'comprehension' not of the order of under-standing, since understanding subsumes an experience, once perceived, under some idea, while desire comprehends blindly by linking body to body. Even in the case of sexuality ... we are concerned, not with a peripheral involuntary action, but with an intentionality which follows the general flow of existence and yields to its movements.[15]

Psychoanalysis, he goes on to say, has helped us grasp human ex-perience not "in terms of ... sexual substructure", but to an insight that in sexuality itself may reside "relations and attitudes" previously understood to be present in consciousness.[16]

The above is a controversial statement for our times – character-ized by excessive importance given – even within psychotherapeutic approaches who labelled themselves "existential" – to consciousness at the expense of the unknown, the unspoken, and the enigmatic. A return to existence cannot be apprehended as a return to con-sciousness, least we ignore the important lessons of psychoanalysis. "Existence" is not detained by consciousness. Clearly, Merleau-Ponty's statement is not a passing observation but a crucial point, as he makes abundantly clear:

> The return to existence, as to the setting in which the communi-cation between body and mind can be understood, is not a return

to consciousness or Spirit, and existential psychoanalysis must not serve as a pretext for a revival of mentalistic philosophy.[17]

For Merleau-Ponty this is a question above all of modesty, of curbing the hubristic claims of consciousness. Desire, love, and sexuality may be rightly thought of as residing within the domain of transcendental experience – of immanently transcendent experience. At the same time, this is no facile misunderstanding of the unconscious as the "ground of being" or the repository of all mysteries. Two mistakes are to be avoided:

> one is to fail to recognize in existence any content other than its obvious one, which is arranged in the form of distinct representations, as do philosophies of consciousness; the other is to duplicate this obvious content with a latent content, also consisting of representations, as do psychologies of the unconscious.[18]

To resist taking up either of these equally tantalizing positions means accepting *ambiguity* and *indeterminacy* as fundamental to human experience: all we do and think has several meanings. This is particularly true of sexuality, as there is no clear-cut way to determine what action or motivation is sexual and what is not. If this sounds controversial in our obdurate times, so be it. Sexuality may be ambiguous and indeterminate, but it is not fortuitous, for "existence has no fortuitous attributes, no content which does not contribute towards giving it its form".[19]

Sexuality, in short, decentres the self and its inherent complacency. The same applies to mourning when uncoupled from the hyperconscious smugness which in current culture very nearly prescribes a "natural" and "successful" sequence for grief and bereavement, the aim of which may be, unwittingly, to *prevent* transformation. The sanitization of emotional sorrow is one with the sanitization of sexual desire. It is also one with the sanitization of sacrosanct political fury at the ruling class. While it is bankable to have all three dramatized for consumption and vicarious pleasure in the entertainment industry, they remain taboo to the dominant hyper-rationalist ethos, for they depict being-beside-oneself.

Grief is a complex issue, and it is heartbreakingly sad to recall of how many who lost their loved ones were unable during the Covid pandemic to mourn and formally honour their passing. Despite the plurality of views present in contemporary psychotherapy, all interventions appear to corroborate Freud's rather too neat differentiation between mourning and melancholia (the latter upgraded in today's parlance as "depression"). The majority of approaches also seem to accept the notion of "prolonged grief disorder", a newly manufactured condition relegated by both the DSM-5 and the ICD-11 to the domain of pathologies, with its neatly allocated length of time of one year after which grief becomes an illness and therapeutic intervention necessary. I am sceptical of this opposition between "successful" and "unsuccessful" mourning. Freud tells us that while in the first instance the lost love object becomes eventually incorporated within the mourner's psyche, in melancholy or unsuccessful mourning this incorporation fails to happen. I don't know how many practitioners share my scepticism. I know some do. As I see it, the incorporation of the lost love object is impossible, even undesirable; all mourning remains "unsuccessful" and to a degree melancholic. The loss of a friend or a loved one is the irredeemable loss of an entire world. Of course, common sense will tell us that however painful the loss, life goes on for us, the living. But mourning begins long *before* death. It is already there at the beginning. The deeper the friendship, the more vivid and poignant the sense that one of us will die at some point in the future. The notion that melancholy has to be cured so that we may occupy our reserved seat in the traffic jam is risible.

Grief, sexual passion, and furious rebellion free up the space commandeered by the self, this dead ringer who paints eyeballs on chaos. The freed-up space can then become inhabited by a more immediate experience of finitude, vulnerability, and agency, all three educating the (individualistic) subject to the wisdom of solidarity and *Gemeinschaftsgefühl*, the communal feeling championed by Adler and which constitutes an actual basis for libidinal/political emancipatory action outside the dull environs of self-boundedness and private logic.[20]

Grief carries within it the opportunity of learning that embodiment – a much-touted subject in psychotherapy – is a *social* phenomenon. A new immanent cosmology could be established on the insights of finitude and imperfection. A living democracy may be built which understands sentient beings as ends rather than means and perceives this embodied human existence as on the same plane of immanence with other beings. But this would mean disrupting established norms and unsettling traditional knowledge. Precious openings do appear in personal and collective history and this is when transformation becomes possible. They are often indecipherable or mistaken as calamities. They are indecipherable because articulated in a new language; they are calamities when seen from a defensive point that is only adept at guarding the status quo. All the same, transformation invariably happens and unassailable norms are rewritten. We must take heart in remembering that power is often camouflaged: it wears the garments of being. "This is how things truly are" it proclaims. "This is the truth". We must remember Foucault's admonition and understand the connection "between the mechanism of coercion and elements of knowledge".[21] Traditional knowledge and coercion go hand in hand, and rebelling against coercion rewrites the rules. Rebellion in this sense implies articulation of embodied counter-fantasies, a way of "taking the body as a point of departure" without being "constrained by the body as it is".[22]

Transformation begins with the body – this sexual, ecstatic, vulnerable and mortal body. From the body, it then takes flights of fantasy (rather than flights of fancy), discovering the vital missing link dodged by prosaic realism; not illusion but the ability to reconsider ourselves and others beyond our prevailing philistine pragmatism: making the room ready for the guest. Becoming otherwise. Inhabiting the elsewhere that we already are, this body of difference that outstrips the abstract code dictated by the norm and by regulation. The norm operates within everyday social goings-on, by implicitly imposing social standards. This aging body, whether or not subjected to medical alterations, continues to contradict the norm by not being a *fait accompli*, the static reliable token of facile appraisal of the human. It also contradicts *regulation*, i.e., "the institutionalization of the process by which persons are made regular".[23] Norm and regulation are blissfully ignorant of difference. And if the body is not solely masculine nor solely feminine, norm and regulation contrapuntally command that it ought to be defined.

> Gender is not exactly what one 'is' nor is it precisely what one 'has'. Gender is the apparatus by which the production and normalization of masculine and feminine take place.[24]

The emphasis is on the valence of disorientation, of being exposed to what I do not know rather than on manufacturing a new "differential" normative that pretends to understand the field of our experience of gender merely by prescribing the usage of correct pronouns.

Regulation won't simply go away by us remonstrating against it; this is because it is enmeshed with the symbolic domain. But a shrewd critique of the symbolic (particularly as depicted in Lacan) might help disentangle ourselves from regulatory restrictions and our connivance with the norm. For Lacan, the symbolic is the province of the Law, and its aim is to "regulate desire in the Oedipus complex",[25] a regulation based on symbolic injunction against incest, a stance at the very centre of the *structuralist* influence still overriding psychoanalysis and most humanistic/existential/transpersonal approaches. While mummy-daddy oedipal scenarios dominate the former, the latter largely comply (each in their own not-so-unique way) with the norm of relatedness as a given, which is but an appendix of mummy-daddy scenarios.

Structuralism still rules the roost in most therapeutic orientations – despite jostling claims of innovation. Nothing new; no horizon hence no future; only upgrades of structuralist leitmotifs. Levi-Strauss made it clear: the incest may not be biological but it is cultural, hence universal and final.[26] There is much to be admired in Levi-Strauss's work. The eccentric ingenuity and sheer inventiveness of this proverbial bricoleur is all the more tantalizing for being disdained by hard science. Even more encouraging is the notion of anthropology's task as "reintegrating culture into nature, and finally life into the set of its physico-chemical conditions",[27] a notion not wholly at variance with the tenets of surrealism and teasingly close to Alfred Jarry's pataphysics, if one is willing to entertain the idea that the study of *physis* requires imaginary leaps.

The move from biology to culture was the first slip, as it were, and 1970s mainstream feminism followed suit, affirming a "universal and primordial law".[28] The second slip was from culture to language, a move we owe to Lacan for whom the symbolic is characterized by linguistic structures that cannot be framed within the social forms of language.[29] This is no mere semantic, for it entails a restless aspiration to fully obey the law – the law of the Father. In the psychical as in the political domain, there is a payoff for such ecstasy of obedience: appeasement of the existential anxiety of finding oneself in an open playing field of multiple gendered potentialities. To erase the norm, it will be predictably objected, would mean a return to the deluded liberalism and even libertarianism of the ego-self. To displace the God archetype, Jungians may add, could well mean doing away with integrating psychical parts and aspects. But the point is not removing the norm but superseding it, seeing it, if not as a movable feast, then as the ever-changing entity that it appears to be. The open, unresolved question is where to place the human subject, and whether it is to be incorporated within the pre-determined design of the symbolic. Levi-Strauss sees every culture as a collection of symbolic systems regulating language, marriage rules, economic relations, religion, science, and art. But is it a given that the social sphere specified by the symbolic must be dominated by the name of the father, and that losing a psychical space dominated by the name of the father necessarily implies insanity?

Norm, etymology suggests, describes mathematical and architectural patterns (*norma* = the carpenter's square) imagined by the first century BC Roman architect Vitruvius and by Cicero alike as an imitation of nature. Naturalization and universalization often go hand in hand with normalization and legitimation of coercion – of imperial power in the case of the Romans; of disciplinary powers in today's bureaucratization and policing of the psychical and political spheres.[30] All of this in the name of the edifying purpose of producing a common standard, the flipside of which is to be subjected to a vague ideological notion as the length of a body is shortened or stretched to fit Procrustes' bed. By the end of the 18th century, a significant section of the UK's population was duly demarcated and effectively marshalled through comparisons and quantitative measurements into constituting a social sphere. Comparisons and quantitative measurements result in the fabrication of what is average, normal, and ideal and literally make a social body,[31] which in turn becomes a defensive tribal body inaugurated by self-referential or even endogamous criteria according to which the abnormal is any "external" individual or body worshipping the wrong god or loving the wrong person. Norm-manufacturing operates through exclusion and, cunningly, through inclusion – a cosy, liberal term for which a more accurate name is *engulfment*. The norm "integrates anything which might attempt to go beyond it", François Ewald writes. Nothing, nobody, no matter how different they may be, can ever assert "to be exterior, or claim to possess an otherness".[32] This is the very same insidious inclusiveness present in the ubiquitous and unbending notion of "relatedness" in contemporary psychotherapy discourse which only understands difference in *relation to* the same and tends to engulf opposition to the norm within the norm's terrain and mode of functioning. This position leads to an impasse. It precludes the possibility of any alternative to the norm, unless one is willing to conceive the norm as immanent and subjected to change rather than an objective entity against which one rebels or to which one obeys, both instances reifying and reinforcing the norm.

In terms of relatedness, a normative ideal in contemporary therapy[33] (especially conventional existential therapy) which relies unsteadily on vague versions of Heidegger's notion of *Dasein*, the problem is that recognition is *presumed*; it is understood as a given, instead of a precarious attainment. In more sophisticated forms of this stance such as intersubjectivity in relational psychoanalysis, the dialectical genealogy of recognition is acknowledged. In Jessica Benjamin and others, the reference to Hegel's *Anerkennung* (recognition/acknowledgement) is explicit. Even when recognition is presented as an aspiration, reference to Hegel implies by default the agonic element present in any en*counter*. Similarly, the other is acknowledged as external to the subject rather than the projection of an internal object.

Yet this approach relies too heavily on the subject's conscious effort of communication, encouraged by a Habermasian assumption of the ever-present possibility of a symmetrical encounter. The other is not me, relational psychoanalysis asserts. So far so good. But there is more to it: the other is capable of negating the self, and it is in the very potentiality of negation that the possibility of a transformative encounter lies:

> Recognition is at once the norm towards which we invariably strive, the norm that ought to govern therapeutic practice, and

the ideal form that communication takes when it becomes a transformative process. Recognition is, however, also the name given to the process that constantly risks destruction and which ... could not be recognition without a defining or constitutive risk of destruction.[34]

The assumption (in both intersubjective psychoanalysis and humanistic/ existential approaches relying on notion of relatedness) is *complementarity*, sometimes clutched as an aspiration, other times regarded as an object of faith, keeping at bay with militant gusto any threat to the heteronormativity implicit in the very notion of complementarity. Unsurprisingly, the latter carries (half-buried within an often-forgotten theological underpinning) *complementarianism*, the notion that men and women were assigned by God different roles in the family and in public roles, including religious leadership. One of the problems with the supremacy of complementarity in psychotherapeutic discourse is that the psychical landscape shrinks to a claustrophobic parlour game ping-ponging between the phallus and the maternal, and even when the bias falls on the latter (be they via Winnicottian, Kleinian, or Jungian leanings) we still haven't left the oedipal room. Even when the bias falls on "inclusiveness", with professional bodies spelling out the new rules about the usage of correct pronouns, we still haven't left the oedipal room. Inclusiveness is in turn a faint echo of overinclusiveness, the wish that the preoedipal state may be restored, a psychical place where one identification with one gender need not imply rejection of the other. But is it really true that there are no other ways to conceptualize kinship, gender, and desire?

The aforementioned question assumes particular significance in relation to transgender persons. It is difficult to say with any degree of certainty "whether the sexuality of the transgender person is homosexual or heterosexual". There are "moments of undecidability" which the world of conventional psychotherapy has not even begun to conceive, let alone wrestle with. Undecidability is key, not only in the case of transsexuals who are in transition (when the new identity is not yet emerged), but all the more stronger for those transsexuals who see transition as "a permanent process".[35] Allowing for undecidability in psychotherapeutic work would necessarily imply leaving behind complementarity as well as the presumption of complementarity. It would imply abandoning the consolations of intersubjectivity and relatedness that have become the foundation of conventional psychotherapy theory and practice across most orientations. A truly important question was asked twenty years ago by Judith Butler and it has still remained unanswered, namely:

> [Is] intersubjective space ever free of destruction? And if it is free of destruction, is it also beyond the psyche in a way that is no longer of use for [psychotherapy and] psychoanalysis?[36]

There are good reasons for the wide popularity enjoyed by the notions of intersubjectivity, relatedness, and mutual recognition in psychotherapy. The idea that congruent dialogue gives rise to the harmonious music of the *third*, an echo of the early nonverbal experience of earliest exchanges between mother and child, is enticing, but many other "thirds" are overlooked, including "the past that cannot be reversed, the future that cannot be contained, the unconscious itself".[37] There is much that cannot be processed, resolved, or, to use Hegel's original term, *sublated*, i.e., both preserved and changed through dialectical agon and assimilation. Dialectics was never meant to be smooth, nor dialectical synthesis straightforward. The music of the third forgets the beauty of dissonance and the fact that relationship cannot be merely derivative of complementarity, and that emergent phenomena can ever be reduced to the abstract unity of "Being". Unless, that is, one is only able to conceive relatedness in terms of the self, in terms of incorporating the other or projecting onto the other. Hegel's *Anerkennung* can never be, in other words, a variation on yet another narcissistic motif, and in the way it plays out, the self always risks dislodgement. The realization that the other is *other* – that the self is not the centre – is nothing less than a traumatic revelation to an overwhelmingly narcissistic perspective prevalent in psychotherapy and in the wider culture, despite their relational lingo. Encounter with the other implies loss of self and a reformulation of self in terms of the reflection seen in the other. There is no return to the Ithaca of the self-that-was. Encounter with otherness necessarily implies separation as well as *negation*, a negation that can never be entirely outlived other than in the pleasant fantasies of bourgeois psychotherapy and liberal political thought. This does not mean that aggression and destruction are the basis of human reality or the foundation of who we are. But it is vital that we entertain the thought that violence is an ever-present risk. Aspiring to constructive dialogue is a worthy aspiration, but is not the same as believing in dialogue as a given, as an entity pre-dating the encounter. Self-loss is essential to self-knowledge; without it, there cannot be either a future nor "experience", unless we think of the future as upgrade and of experience as repetition. Self-loss means vulnerability. It means relinquishment. No recognition is possible without it. Recognition, understood with Hegel as the self undergoing transformation through encounter hence beyond the solipsism of the inner life of the beautiful soul (or tormented, accursed, self-bound soul), means being recognized by the other and recognizing the other in turn. But this cannot be either mutuality or inclusion because, far from being a unity and a container, the self is other to itself and ever-changing.

Appreciation of otherness is ecstatic: it implies being moved outside of oneself. This form of displacement is what a self is. The tradition will be at pains to distance itself from this view no doubt deemed "aberrant". It will call it "splitting". It will mount an assault against postmodern deviant views. It will summon the holy trinity of unity, integrity, and holism, which is the foundation of nihilism, the understanding that human experience is nothing – nihil – without the application of these lofty principles. The naïve Cartesianism of the tradition is as endearing as it is witless: it presupposes the existence of a self who then "splits". It believes that the self is self-existing and autonomous, that its ontological status is rightfully granted from the start. The tradition then extends this solipsistic view into the relational domain, understood within the narcissistic frame, ignoring in the process the internal duality and originally divided nature of the self but more importantly forgetting how the self comes to be properly constituted through encounter with otherness. Another way of considering relatedness is as the relativization of the self or subject. As with the Buddha's notion of paticca samutpada or dependent co-arising, this view of relatedness emphasises the unsubstantial nature of the self.[38] What's more, it is fairly easy to think of relatedness in abstract dyadic terms without taking on board the intricate legacy of history and the unpredictability of the future, i.e., without considering: (a) that the dyad is a provisional form in a "temporal chain of desire"[39] which escapes the binary model of relatedness, and (b) that the notion of an equal, horizontal encounter between two people is at best wishful thinking and at worst collusion with the Powers.

It is not easy for the stance advocated here to gain traction when the dominant "invisible" ideologies are liberalism in politics and structuralism in psychology, both views lending each other a hand in legitimizing the status quo. That liberalism might be complicit in maintaining the status quo shouldn't surprise anyone but structuralism? The claim may sound excessive; but it is structuralism in its many guises and across psychotherapeutic and philosophical orientations which supports the symbolic position of Mum and Dad. It elevates them to the role of defenders of the prohibition, sanctifying the male and female positions within an aura of unassailability and quasi-eternality. The setting is endogamic, for even though the prohibition forbids us to sleep with mum or dad, it incites us to marry their surrogate. Ideological endogamy is pervasive. A similar endogamic perspective prevails in the western ideological foundations set in the Bible, where a dialectics between the disparate narratives of nomadism and idolatry of the soil found its violent conclusion, still alive and thriving today, in consecrating suspicion of (outer and inner) otherness, hatred of strangers and their foreign gods, and agitated incitement to intermarriage within the hallowed tribe of the faithful. "Rootedness [often] puffs itself up".[40] Can it be said without fear of reprisals in our current puritanical and treacherously inclusive cultural climate that a similar logic is at work in the popular notion that kinship is instituted via "neutral" language and other "objective" or "archetypal" symbolic processes, forgetting that these coming-into-beings are both social and contingent? Can it be said without being excommunicated by the society of the righteous that this notion of kinship blatantly ignores that any symbolic or archetypal positions (male and female included) are glorifications and fossilizations of socially contingent norms? Have psychology, psychotherapy, and psychoanalysis become entirely *idiotic*, by relying on an insular *idiom* divorced from society and the world as well as from sociology and history?

*

Risk plays a significant role not only within the ethico-political realm explored above but in biology too. While a normative view of health presupposes homeostasis (an ideal state of continuous optimal functioning in the living organism), non-normative views (such as the one expounded by Canguilhem) tend to determine health by a "margin of tolerance in relation to the unreliabilities of the milieu".[41] One vital implication of this stance would go towards constituting the foundations for a humanist medical discipline as active defence against iatrocracy, with the verdict of what constitutes health residing with the patient rather than the doctor. Far from being negligible, this non-normative perspective belongs to that *ethics of risk* found within a formidable lineage that runs from Kurt Goldstein to Georges Canguilhem to Michel Foucault. In complete disagreement with the morality of equilibrium and conservation touted by the tradition, this perspective draws on the "great health" expounded by Nietzsche in section 382 of Joyful Science, a health that is

> stronger, more seasoned, tougher, more audacious, and gayer than any previous health ... [a health that] one does not merely have but also acquires continually, and must acquire because one gives it up again and again, and must give it up.[42]

*

While the championing of transformation over cosmetic change and social adjustment may imply a critique of technology and its dehumanizing aspects, this does not mean that the task should be informed by a romanticization of our pre-technological past. The question is first of all axiological, calling for an evaluation of the forces that take hold of technology. These are reactive, dominated by a desire to increase capital for the few rather than expanding the actualizing potential of living organisms. Secondly, some limits must be in place to an ever-expanding technology which seeks to recoup the old Platonist hope of bypassing bodily reality and bodily difference altogether. A transformative technology that were to sidestep sexual difference would reinforce both phallocentrism and somatophobia. It would reinstate the illusion of a neutral nongendered domain behind which unreconstructed notions of masculine autonomy would once again prevail. It would reinforce a flight from the incarnate body. It would do away with any possibility of transformation, for there is no transformation that is not rooted in the living body. However, the living body must be understood as the locus traversed by and constituted by multiple forces, a locus without a unitary subject at its centre. To the predictable objection that a lack of a unitary subject means no possibility of agency and affirmation, the answer is simple: no transformative affirmation can emerge without the existence of multiple forces at play. A powerful yes to life emerges only through the fray and frisson of multiplicity. Transformation implies dynamism; it cannot stem from the project of a unitary subject that would lose its privileged seat in the psychical domain were it to allow the playful confluence of multiple forces. Which is why incidentally what goes under the name of psychotherapy has almost ceased to be a force for transformation and has become instead entrenched in its ancillary role as agent of the norm and the status quo. True agency comes from the agonistic involvement of multiple forces, many of them unconscious and pre-conscious, which are not fully graspable by the subject but from whose reservoir a finely attuned and non-defensive subject can intuit the new. It is baffling that the transformative stance explored here – arguably "poststructuralist" – has very rarely been part of the conversation within contemporary psychotherapy. The understandable fear around de-centring the self and giving prominence to the play of multiplicity is a fear of fragmentation and the anguish this can bring. At the same time, it is from an acceptance of the intrinsic multiple nature of psychical life that transformation can take place. It is also one of the more effective ways in which oedipalization can be disrupted, something to be welcomed and celebrated if one is serious about difference. Some will object to this and assert that the notion of a unitary subject is necessary in terms of accountability. Accepting the existence of a self-bound "I" at the centre of psyche and experience means that someone will be answerable; it allows the sanctification of norms and regulations without which there can be no *order*. And without order, so the argument goes, no human community can exist, let alone thrive. What this "liberal" argument overlooks is that the inherently conservative drive to establish and preserve order is dominated by reactive forces, that is, by forces which mistrust the dynamic unfolding of life. It also overlooks the fact that the establishment and preservation of order is by definition violent and exclusionary.

Notes

1 This catalogue of what transformation might do takes its cue from Judith Butler's discussion of Rosi Braidotti's book *Metamorphosis: Towards a Materialist Theory of Becoming*, in *Undoing Gender*, Abingdon, OX: Routledge, 2004, pp. 174–203.
2 Judith Butler, *Undoing Gender*. Abingdon, OX: Routledge, 2004, p. 194.
3 Ibid, p. 194.
4 Rosi Braidotti, *Metamorphosis: Towards a Materialist Theory of Becoming*. Cambridge: Polity, 2002, p. 30.
5 Judith Butler, *Undoing Gender*, op. cit., p. 5.
6 Kate Bornstein, *Gender Outlaw*. New York, Routledge, 1994.
7 *Undoing Gender*, op. cit., 8.
8 Ibid, p. 8.
9 Ibid, p. 12.
10 Ibid, pp. 9–10.
11 Ibid, p. 10.
12 Francis Nesbitt Oppel, *Nietzsche on Gender: Beyond Man and Woman*. Charlottesville and London: University of Virginia Press, 2005, p. 2.
13 *Undoing Gender*, op. cit., p. 15.
14 Ibid, p. 15.
15 Maurice Merleau-Ponty, *Phenomenology of Perception*. Abingdon, OX: Routledge, 2010, p. 181.
16 Ibid, p. 182.
17 Ibid, p. 185.
18 Ibid, p. 195.
19 Ibid, pp. 196–197.
20 Despite the fact that my root training was in person-centred therapy, I remain grateful to Alfred Adler for this and many more insights. An indispensable reading on Adlerian psychology is H.L. Ansbacher & R.R Ansbacher. *The Individual Psychology of Alfred Adler: A Systematic Presentation in Selection from His Writings*. New York: Harper & Row, 1964.
21 Michel Foucault, *The Politics of Truth*. New York: Semiotext(e), 1997, p. 50.
22 Judith Butler, *Undoing Gender*, op. cit., p. 28.
23 Ibid, p. 40.
24 Ibid, p. 42.
25 Dylan Evans, *An Introductory Dictionary of Lacanian Psychoanalysis*. London: Routledge, 1996, p. 202.
26 Claude Levi-Strauss, *Elementary Structures of Kinship*. Beacon Press, 1971.
27 Claude Levi-Strauss, *Wild Thought: A New Translation of 'La Pensée Sauvage'*. Chicago, Ill: Chicago University Press, 2021, p. 281.
28 Juliet Mitchell, *Psychoanalysis and Feminism: a Radical Reassessment of Freudian Psychoanalysis*. New York: Vintage, 1975, p. 370.
29 Jacques Lacan (1966), 'Of Structure as the Inmixing of an Otherness Prerequisite to Any Subject Whatever', in Richard Macksey and Eugenio Donato (Eds), *The Structuralist Controversy*. Baltimore: John Hopkins, 1970.

30 On the norm, see Georges Canguilhem, *The Normal and the Pathological,* introduction by Michel Foucault. Princeton, NJ: Zone Books, 1991. On normalization, see François Ewald, 'Norms, Discipline, and the Law', in Robert Post (Ed.), *Law and the Order of Culture*. Berkeley, CA: University of California Press, 1991, pp. 138–161.

31 Mary Poovey, *Making a Social Body: British Cultural Formation 1830–1994.* University of Chicago Press, 1995.

32 François Ewald, 'Norms, Discipline, and the Law', op. cit., p. 173.

33 John Mackessy & Manu Bazzano, 'Is Relatedness a Normative Ideal?' in Manu Bazzano (Ed.), *Re-visioning Existential Therapy: Counter-traditional Perspective.* Abingdon, OX: Routledge, 2020, pp. 11–23.

34 Judith Butler, *Undoing Gender*, op. cit., p. 133.

35 Ibid, p. 140.

36 Ibid, p. 145.

37 Ibid, pp. 145–146.

38 Manu Bazzano, *Zen and Therapy: Heretical Perspectives.* Abingdon, OX: Routledge, 2017, p. 111.

39 Undoing Gender, op. cit., p. 151.

40 Theodor W. Adorno, *The Jargon of Authenticity*, translated by Knut Tarnowski and Frederic Will. Evanston, ILL: Northwestern University Press, 1973, p. 54.

41 Georges Canguilhem, *The Normal and the Pathological*, op. cit., p. 170.

42 Friedrich Nietzsche, *The Gay Science. With a Prelude in Rhymes and an Appendix of Songs.* New York: Vintage, 1974, p. 346.

Chapter 8

Of the Devil's Party

In *The Marriage of Heaven and Hell*, William Blake famously wrote:

> The reason Milton wrote in fetters when he wrote of Angels & Gods, and at liberty when he wrote of Devils & Hell, is because he was a true Poet and of the Devil's party without knowing it.[1]

To encounter Milton's Satan, as portrayed in the first two books of *Paradise Lost*, is exhilarating. Milton takes great delight in introducing this fallen angel, brave combatant, and leader of a valiant brigade of demons. William Blake's own admiration contributed to the building of one of two main interpretive strands. The other, championed by C. S. Lewis and others, is more overtly "Christian", pointing at Satan's pride and his being a master of delusion for daring to challenge the unchallengeable. Blake places the mythical devil-in-chief firmly in the Romantic tradition and in doing so influenced other writers, including, most significantly, William Empson.

Empson does not deny that envy and pride play a role in Satan's rebellious stance but he also emphasizes that "as Satan believes God to be a usurper, he genuinely does believe him to be envious". The moment "we waive our metaphysical presumptions, we easily recognize that the motivation will be complex as in human affairs".[2] What's more, there is "in [Satan's] address to his troops an impressive degree of sincerity [not found] in a politician".[3] Empson sums up his defence of Satan and his rebellious troops by saying:

DOI: 10.4324/9781003280262-9

Whether the rebels deserve blame for their initial doubt of God's credentials, before God had supplied false evidence to encourage the doubt, is hard for us to tell; but once they have arrived at a conviction, they are not to be blamed for having the courage to act upon it.[4]

Within this interpretive line, Milton's Satan is a trespasser endowed with tremendous eloquence, a Byronic hero to whom the very notion of submission is thoroughly alien.[5] "Better to reign in Hell than serve in Heaven", he proudly declares,[6] and in his speech to the Sun he similarly proclaims that any form of acquiescence on his part would only be insincere. He personifies all the mighty passions, those upheavals of thought and magnificent monsters[7] forever chastised by religion, morality, and psychology. Strangely for an art and a science which professes the understanding of emotions and encourages their healthy expression, psychology has sustained of late a tendency to confine powerful emotions – often alongside what used to be called the unconscious (its repressed as much as its creative part) – to the secular purgatory of diagnostics and arbitrarily assorted pathologies.

The irrationally rational hope is that inner upheavals can be behaviourally modified and sensibly mitigated by the power of reason, all the while forgetting that reason is but one more affect among many: useful when skilfully employed, but tricky when enthroned at the centre of the psyche. Milton's Satan is fierce in battle yet stirred with intricate feelings when eavesdropping on the innocent love-making of Adam and Eve, and in his tragic plight he bravely dismisses hope: "So farewell hope, and with hope farewell fear".[8] These are the words of a tragic hero, troubled by inner discord. Yet without inner discord, without *agon*, what chance does one have of giving birth to oneself, of giving birth to a creative inner life, and/or contribute something to the world? "So farewell hope, and with hope farewell fear": these are not the words of a compliant bourgeois but of a true poet and artist, a poet in William Blake's sense: of the devil's party, a tragic anti-hero, ill-equipped to accept the empty promises of integration, homeostasis, and "wellbeing".

*

Devilish energies have been allowed to tiptoe around the edges of the tradition. In psychotherapy, via the notion of the daimonic. What is the daimonic? The etymology of *daimon* points towards the meanings "divider" and "allotter", and its use in ancient Greek literature suggests the irruption of a force that is perceived as external to humans – unpredictable, impersonal, often disruptive. From daimon comes the adjective *daimonios* – meaning odd, unfathomable, and *uncanny*, the last one being a key term (*Unheimlich* in Freud) now expediently, catastrophically consigned to oblivion. A connection between the daimon and the dead, which I will discuss later, also appears in ancient Greek texts. Hesiod suggested a new meaning of daimones as protective spirits bringing either blessings or damage, a good daimon (*eudaimon*) and a bad daimon (*kakodaimon*). This dualistic and moralizing view found its zenith a few centuries later with Christian theologians rounding up and exiling all pagan gods as evil. This had repercussions in the psychical landscape; it meant a pathologizing of multiplicity within psyche itself in favour of a "unitary" view linked to the "one and only God" – the very birth of what today most approaches refer to as "integration".

We pay a high price when we keep daimonic intensity at bay, however: jouissance disappears from one's existence and life becomes just doing one damn thing after another.

Naturally, being open to daimonic intensity does not mean giving it free rein. There is a big difference between being "possessed" and being "in possession" or between being a plaything and being a player. While the first option is problematic (the irruption of uncanny energies often leading to psychosis – what Sperber calls the *dysdaimonic*[9]), the second option is desirable, not in the sense of gaining egoic control over the richness of affects, but in the sense of being able to accept and humbly learn from daimonic experience. Sadly, within contemporary culture the approved state, endorsed by various forms of psycho-technology – whether pharmacological, behavioural, or mainstream psychotherapeutic – is that of the *antidaimonic,* i.e., the a-pathy (no pathos) of an everyday normotic (normally neurotic) existence which is the result of the suppression of the daimonic and which makes all of us cogs in the capitalist wheel. The normotic/antidaimonic model – the *homo neo-liberalis* ideal – is fast becoming the grail of shiny homeostatic daydreams. If only we could attain a viable degree of control over our emotions; if only we could bridle the unruliness of affects and temper their intensity; if only we could focus on our "goals", aided by pluralistic therapists who allow us to pick and choose from the wide range of methods available on the shelves of the psych supermarket! Instead, time and again life shows up in all its messiness and splendour, refusing to adhere to our sensible plans or obey to our premature interpretive ejaculations.

Each in their own way psychoanalytic/psychodynamic, Jungian, and humanistic/existential approaches tend to emphasize the importance of "integrating" the daimonic and aspire to *eudaimonia*, the human flourishing celebrated by the philosophical tradition since Plato and Aristotle. But for too long eudaimonia has been adulterated by the notion of happiness, a superficial notion dished out with the daily bread by ideological apparatuses the world over. Long before the advent of Hollywood, it had been pointed out that humankind does not really strive for happiness; that only a certain type of (utilitarian) human does.[10] That particular type has now been elevated to a universal, and officially endorsed by (evolutionary, positive, positivist) psychology. The jury has been out for centuries as to the true meaning of eudaimonia, given that none of the three terms usually ascribed to it – happiness, well-being, flourishing – adequately describes it. Happiness and well-being are too subjective and can imply self-deception or a narrow-minded, avaricious view of existence, whereas flourishing can also refer to animals and plants and is reminiscent of that lame notion, "growth" more fitting for broccoli or cancer cells than humans, but wildly popular all the same (psychological growth, spiritual growth, and now post-traumatic growth).

The notion of eudaimonia is fastened to virtue ethics and to the philosophical tradition and for that reason encrusted with philosophical biases allied to value-laden, moralizing worldviews. Like most avowedly secularist and empirical approaches to ethics, even psychology, the alleged queen of the sciences,[11] became entangled with religious and moralizing ideas, relying on things outside nature and forgetting the importance of applying (as Spinoza reminds us) nature's common laws when studying human experience.[12] Disappointingly, all boils down to arguments about "character", to projecting our beliefs onto experience, rather than suspending those beliefs in the attempt to study experience.

There are of course very good reasons to separate virtue ethics from scientism[13] and for paying close attention to philosophy, art, and literature. But we should be suspicious of practices which tend to neglect vital links to the organismic and naturalistic foundations of experience and opt instead for some form of moral, "ontological", or spiritual bypass. What is at stake here is the need to create a strong reformulation of psychology's link to naturalism and the biological sciences. Historically, this link meant that psychology gave in to scientism – excessive belief in positivist, quantitative, "evidence-based" procedures and in the power of scientific knowledge and alleged objectivity. Opposition has often come from vaguely "spiritual" stances and "human-centred" generalities. While scientism reifies nature, spirituality ignores it. Caught in the middle, psychology takes on an ancillary role, serving alternate masters, losing sight of the ambitious tasks which is rightfully hers as the queen of the sciences: (a) attempting a naturalistic re-evaluation of values themselves; (b) recognizing with Nietzsche the presence of cowardice under the layer of humility, of lust for power under the layer of uprightness; (c) paying heed to his exhortation to put powerful emotions to good creative use (towards self-creation as much as artistic creation).

This predicament deepens when faced with the cluster of experiences defined as daimonic, for within this sphere nature and spirit are entwined in the form of natural archetypes. I am referring for the time being to the modern, existential description the daimonic as "any *natural* function which has the power to take over the whole person [as well as] an *archetypal* function of human experience".[14] This assertion, contradictory for some, with its clustering together of nature and archetype, of materiality and Platonic Idea, will seem correct to those who pay heed to Spinoza's reminder, *Deus sive Natura*, that Nature is God and God is Nature – a brilliantly ambivalent and exacting assertion which cuts through the superficial divisions between religion and secularism, one which earned Spinoza banishment from both camps.

Speaking of the daimonic through an existential lexicon is a way of tipping my hat to an approach that has acknowledged this domain, even though it did so vaguely and without recognizing its link to the autonomous dimension of affect. While it is true that Heidegger (a mystifying influence in existential therapy) does focus on the affective register of experience, that focus is confined to anxiety (*Angst*) and worry (*Sorge*, often translated as "care") and is oblivious of desire.

Come to think of it, the very demarcation of a "daimonic" locus, though potentially useful for an initial investigation, becomes problematic in the end. There are two frequent misreadings: the daimonic is either perceived as *peripheral* in relation to subjectivity (usually as a threat) or as *foundational*, i.e., as stemming from an alleged "ground of being" out of which subjectivity is then supposedly carved. These misreadings are useful, provided we can develop their implications. The first mode may help us think of the daimonic as otherness, on an intrapsychic as well as interpsychic level. Convention, morality, and our own learned good manners all emphasize the welcoming of foreigners. Yet something about the way we enforce, regulate, systematize our welcome of difference and regard for others is problematic because "we end up ignoring their foreignness" as Jean-Luc Nancy pithily says in a short film by Claire Denis.[15] The otherness of the foreigner is overlooked. Perceived as an intruder, the foreigner is routinely told to assimilate and integrate. Nancy is right: there is no difference between assimilation and integration. Our common-sense acceptance of differences ends up *erasing* differences; they become undetectable. The stronger the identity, the more solid its historical layers, or one's identification with clan, state, and dwindled empire, the stronger the need to assimilate and integrate what is seen as foreign, and as such intrusive.

I believe something similar happens in relation to the daimonic. Otherness in ourselves, that otherness which partly constitutes us, is ignored and pathologized. When well-intentioned therapists declare that the task is to make the unconscious conscious, or to bring to the light and integrate the shadow elements in the psyche, or to accept and integrate the powerful energies at work within the daimonic, the very same conventional moral imperative operates of keeping the intruder(s) away from the self's tip-of-the-iceberg consciousness and trajectory, projects, and plans. The second useful mistake (i.e., of the daimonic as stemming from an imagined "ground of being") forgets that on one important level the daimonic represents the vivid if mysterious presence of the other within the self. As with the pathologizing of the unconscious, pathologizing the daimonic is the act of forceful rejection of an intrusive presence within the confines of an atomistic self. Laplanche has a lot to teach us on this subject, including the fact that the unconscious is effectively *implanted* in the infant's psyche in the shape of the parents/caregivers' enigmatic messages. The "task" in this case is not to make the unconscious conscious, to sanitize it, least of all to relegate it to the limbo of pathology, but to transmute it instead into our own message to the world through love, work, and self-creation. Clearly, carefully chosen segments of psychoanalysis are useful to this investigation. Not only Laplanche, deemed by some to be rather unorthodox, but Freud himself.

*

Curiously considered by Ernest Jones to be an example of "non-medical applications of psychoanalysis",[16] and by Freud himself as the best book he had written, *Totem and Taboo*, published in 1913, is rarely quoted nowadays.[17] Yet it constitutes, alongside the more popular *Mourning and Melancholia* and *On Transience,* an important text on mourning, one where Freud weaves interesting connections to the *daimonic* – in early psychoanalysis and psychology termed *demonic*. Usually mentioned in relation to the great drama of the horde, the problem of the totem and the murder of the father, in *Totem and Taboo* Freud also writes of the great enigma of the taboo, in particular the taboo of the dead, from which, according to his analysis, other taboos derive. The closeness between the "demonic" and the dead appeared to be self-evident in this text. Freud writes of the notion of *réserve,* a French term he uses to describe temporal, spatial, and linguistic spaces freed from everyday transactions and useful in facilitating the work of mourning. While temporal *réserve* is the time allocated to mourning, spatial *réserve* is constituted by areas within the clan's territory where one is not allowed to enter and by objects one is not allowed to touch. As for linguistic *réserve*, this is characterized by the taboo of the name: the dead person is referred to by another name in order to deliberately confuse matters, cover the tracks, and "prevent the creation of an archive". Freud refers to the custom, among the Guaycuru people of Paraguay: "when a death has taken place – he writes – the chief used to change the names of every member of the tribe",[18] and from that moment on all remembered their new name as if they borne it for all their lives. There is, Freud comments, a perpetual change of vocabulary, which in turns raises profound questions about the proper name and its interpretability. "The proper name, like the dead person, is untranslatable – Laplanche comments – it could only be exchanged, in a rigorous sense, for the person himself".[19] The name of the dead person is also changed, and this allows for a space to exist, a space of non-mourning where mourning can begin to take place. Not everything can be metabolized, or, in the current lingo, "processed". Giving the dead a new name asserts the fact that the dead person is unassimilable. The new name houses their original name in a sacred space, that is, a non-serviceable, non-translatable space. The new name permits a constant mention of the dead person and with it a going-through; it permits the unfolding of the subtle work of mourning. There is a wide gulf between this type of understanding and that of conventional psychotherapy. While the former acknowledges the sheer impossibility of apprehending death and the dead person, the entire psychotherapeutic world in our neopositivist, neoliberal age seriously believes that just about everything can be duly processed, understood, and brought to the surgical light of a hypertrophied consciousness.

Freud's surprise in contemplating the mysterious process of mourning in his 1916 text *On Transience* consists in discovering that "libido clings to the object and will not renounce those that are lost when a substitute lies ready to hand",[20] an outrageous thought for the positivist, for whom the dead are really and truly dead. However, Freud's momentary wavering, which might have borne fascinating insights, does not last long and is soon placated. Mourning itself gets buried in the common grave where all pathologies are interred. This may have been the moment in the history of psychoanalysis when mourning started to be seen as pathological – a development which later intensified and expanded to include anything from stages of grief to "change management".

In a similar vein perhaps, the pathology (from *pathos* = passion) inherent within the daimonic is "apprehended" in existential/

humanistic/Jungian therapies through the compulsion to integrate it and make it work in the service of the self and its many projects. Both moves are standard conduct within the tradition. But any creed, it seems, harbours its double, i.e., a counter-traditional undercurrent which tells a different story. Eager to have psychoanalysis accepted as a science, Freud deserted the daimonic; Wilhelm Wundt (1832–1920), founder of experimental psychology, did not, and what he had to say still reverberates among those who have not swallowed whole the positivist/neo-positivist package. Unlike Freud, for whom the two aspects within this elusive domain are opposite and irreconcilable – love and hate, adoration and disgust – Wundt maintained that at the beginning there is a primary, indistinct domain. He also maintained that the cultural split occurred later on. He did so a hundred years before affect theory's suggestion that there exists a unity of affect *prior* to its translation into a socio-linguistic, adaptive set of individualized and often opposing emotions. Wundt arrived at his conclusion decades before the ethics of alterity developed by Levinas, Derrida, Jankélévitch, and others. Jean Laplanche pointedly remarks:

> Could it not be thought that what is prefigured in Wundt, what Freud could not have read there under the term 'demonic' was the original ambivalence – or rather 'pre-ambivalence' – of the message of the other? That which Freud rejects, in his disagreement with Wundt, under the pretext of obscurity and irrationality, is *a conception in which the dead become demons, reveal themselves in their enigmatic aspect, and being henceforth absent give way entirely to their enigmatic message.*[21]

The other re-emerges, this time in the form of alien enigmatic messages implanted in the virgin psyche by the long dead – be they Mom and Dad, significant others, lovers long vanished from sight, or benevolent/malevolent oneiric visitations. For the person in mourning, the enigmatic message from the deceased remains suspended, even though it still has the power to be strangely fertile. What would she have said? What did the dead person want of me? What were they trying to convey to me?

Laplanche makes an important distinction between *enigma*, *riddle*, and *mystery*. Much like a riddle, an enigma is offered by one person to another. The difference is that the person posing the riddle knows the answer, whereas the enigma is posed by someone who does not and cannot know its full meaning because the enigmatic message they are transmitting is a compound of both conscious and unconscious contents. As for mystery, that is a matter for theologians, mystics, and metaphysicians.

In this sense, we cannot say, for instance, that a natural event, however puzzling and unusual, is an enigma, or that an infant is able to pose an enigma. Neither the natural event nor the baby are endowed with an a priori unconscious, unless one believes with Melanie Klein that the infant comes into this world with a fully fledged psychical apparatus. Placing projections at the origin inflates interiority to gargantuan proportions: everything springs up from the magic box of inner life. In their instructive 1956 paper, Francis Pasche and Michel Renard remind us that it is the job of the therapist to pay attention to all aspects of psychic life, and that to reduce everything to the subject "without any reference to the real external object is to distort reality", which is what happens when the object is presented "as an emanation, a secretion or 'projection' of the subject".[22] This solipsistic notion is not limited to Kleinian analysis but seems to pervade the culture at large. For instance, invariably when working on dreams, a client will say matter of fact, "Anyway all these characters, places, and events, they are all *me*, are they not?".

True, instincts are hereditary, but so are the impressions – the imprint, the seal – from a concrete external world. To neglect this simple fact, "we lock the subject up within [their] own narcissistic world ... [condemning them] to create nothing other than object-phantoms".[23] Thus conceived, subjectivity becomes a watertight cast, inside which several things can take place, but none of it from the outside. One of the many problems with the Kleinian model is that in an insulated system such as this, the level of energy does not fundamentally change. This is closely related to this model's deeply *asexual* nature. Pasche and Renard explain:

> There is never anything other than the wish to destroy, the fear of being destroyed, the need to repair what has been destroyed, and the need to seek and be assured of protection against destruction. The fact that the breast and the penis are, anatomically, sex

organs appears to confer upon them nothing of an erotic nature. They are organs to bite, crush, lacerate, and expel.[24]

The above, overtly biological turn which understands the unconscious as endogenous is, however, in a more muted form, already present in Freud and is equal to modes of disavowal and foreclosing typical of a subject seeing itself as indestructible. Laplanche clarifies this point:

> To protect, to introject, to identify, to disavow, to foreclose ... all the verbs used by analytic theory to describe psychical processes share the feature of having as subject the individual in question: *I* project, *I* disavow, etc.[25]

Needless to say, what gets forgotten is where the process originates: the *other*.

*

Unlike the riddle and the mystery, the enigma takes us back to the otherness of the other, to their unconscious, to the otherness of themselves. The other-centred view presented here implies, quite simply, that the unconscious is not the core of our being. The unconscious is "the other implanted in me, the metabolized product of the other in me: forever an internal foreign body".[26] This is the most direct, uncompromising way to truly acknowledge otherness. Without this fundamental understanding, i.e., that *the other has a primary role in the making of subjectivity*, we remain shackled within our culture's liberal narcissism and its hollow appraisals of diversity, its championing of so-called mutuality and intersubjectivity and its treacherous political denial of the fundamental asymmetry of just about every human encounter. Some will no doubt object that by giving such unfettered primacy to the other, we end up forgetting the crucial questions of introjection and projection. But what is proposed here is a vital subversion: the subject's originary processes are external, steeped in the otherness of the other. There is no original root to be found after diligent and painstaking excavation of "my" unconscious. If there is a going back to the past in therapy (and how can there not be?), this does not mean a journey to an original source. Even if all our clinical resources and expertise are implemented in the resolution of a trauma through hermeneutic re-interpretation of a crucial past event, the investigation would be all the poorer if the enigmatic message from the other were absent. This is where the other-centred, counter-traditional approach championed here differs from hermeneutics. It is not possible to untangle the past unless we also attempt to decode the enigmatic message from the other. This is arguably more attuned to the origins of hermeneutics as "a hermeneutic of the message", i.e., the "religious interpretation of sacred texts".[27]

The dead may be truly dead, and to argue otherwise would mean pandering to irrationality. But the presence of the other in the psyche, whether alive or dead, persists throughout the wayward history of psychology, even though relegated to an undercurrent of thought. The orthodox view gives far greater attention to *projection*, often going all the way in accepting Melanie Klein's philosophical idealism of turning concrete others into external manifestations of a seemingly all-encompassing "inner" psyche. But in Freud himself we find some instances – Laplanche found two – where there is a break with the mainstream view. Firstly, the resemblance he detected in *Totem and Taboo* between the taboo and the Kantian categorical imperative (and the entire bourgeois moral edifice built on it) meant an "opening towards the other and towards the message of the other". Secondly, in his 1918 text *The Taboo of Virginity,* he interestingly links the fear of deflowering the woman with fear of castration. He wrote:

> Perhaps this dread is based on the fact that woman is different from man, for ever incomprehensible and mysterious, strange and therefore apparently hostile.[28]

Why is this important? Because (admittedly in the language and cultural biases of his time) Freud recognizes one concrete aspect of otherness, in this context, woman is other to man. For Laplanche, this is a "rare, in every sense *extra*-ordinary" occurrence. Projection is superseded by "a centripetal movement [from the other to the subject], by an originary injection of fear". Plus, hostility is not the final explanation. Otherness is. Otherness is perceived as hostile because it is other. Another name for this is the *demonic*, in Freud's and Wundt's language, and the *daimonic* in our current discussion.

This leads towards a movable hypothesis: the daimonic is the *otherwise*: in its hidden, uncanny manifestations, it is the impingement of otherness upon the self; "it is only secondarily that it is split into good and bad".[29] It is also constitutive of the self, which means as Clarice Lispector reminds us, that "I am ... taboo for myself, untouchable because forbidden".[30]

What Freud could do in relation to man/woman, Laplanche insists, he could not do in relation to the living and the dead. The positivist in Freud sees the woman as real and concrete but the dead person as truly gone, presenting no danger, no otherness, no impingement. As if the psyche makes a distinction between the living other and the dead other. As if the living is different from the dead in dreams. "A signifier – Laplanche concludes – remains a signifier, even if set down thousands of years ago, and found in the desert or in a pyramid. It could even be said to gain in otherness".[31]

*

The daimonic, i.e., a natural rather than Platonic archetype, is permeated by sex and death. More sex than death in fact, if we dare, as we must, interpret Freud's "oceanic feeling" as the ocean of the sexual, as the centripetal movement activating the psyche and giving impetus to its centrifugal motions – if we dare, as we must, contradict Freud and say that at its origins sexuality is *not* auto-erotic but arises from the encounter with the other's other, that is, the mother's unconscious.

In that sense then we could say, paraphrasing Sartre in a way that Richard Pearce would have liked, that *the daimonic is other people*. Whether we like it or not, others – with their infringements, their loves, and hatreds implanted on us – have primacy in the constitution of our psychical reality. Before it became thoroughly sanitized (whether by denying its emergence or by submerging it under simplistic reification), there used to be an apt word for this: *transference*, i.e., the carrying of the same thing elsewhere. Its discovery was something special, akin to a celestial or devilish event which, just like sexuality seen in its numinous guise, seriously threatens the subject's self-preservation. It threatens the reassuring notion of psychical unity psychology has been peddling for some time. It makes the familiar unfamiliar, the ordinary extraordinary. To go down this path, we need to accept with Laplanche that the "fundamental dimension of transference is the relation to the enigma of the other"[32] and consequently that the enigmatic message implanted by the other may be turned into one's own cultural message. This is when the daimonic can become a tremendous source of creative energy which may be put at the service of one's fellow travellers. Art, in the wide sense of the term, is a good example, and so are practices of engaged, emancipatory politics and liberative psychical work. By engaging in these practices, we go beyond ourselves and move ecstatically towards others. These others may not be *particular* others. The recipients are unknown. We do not know who is going be inspired (or disturbed) by that piece of music we composed, by that painting we painted, by a particular action we performed. *Recipient* is the right word, Laplanche suggests, a valid alternative to the prosaic term *consumer* and the more particularized term *addressee*. Recipients need no pedigree and will receive the enigmatic message in their own way, perceiving a content and an affect that was not consciously expressed by the messenger. The cultural dimension inundates our lives with its daily seductions, inductions, and inherently invasive, arousing and sexualized contents. A thorough understanding of the enigmatic message implanted from parent/caregiver to child would give psychology greater capability in navigating the cultural (and political) domain and offer new critical insights instead of being a simple transmission belt for dominant neoliberal values.

*

Despite the overwhelming centripetal pull towards the subject, the opposite movement of a centrifugal decentering away from the subject continues to emerge from time to time. An interesting example of this is what Freud calls *Nachträglichkeit*, rendered by James Strachey as "deferred action" and by Laplanche, more accurately, as *après-coup*, sometime rendered in English as "afterwardness". This is traditionally understood as an earlier event in one's life which can later on take on a new meaning, clarifying through present day awareness what was yet unknown at the time. Intriguingly, the etymology of the term shares a close link with physical dislocation, with *nach* indicating "after" and *träglich* "carrying", i.e., motion to and from a stable point.[33] Temporal dislocation becomes necessary in the act of naming, coming alive at times in poetry.

Walking after a lapse of time by a street once familiar, the heart is tangled up with past memories and renewed feelings in the present. It is a double time in action, a time in which a particular representation gains greater density and intensity. It is felt on the skin and from there expands and ripens. Emerging in Freud's writings two months after the relinquishment of the general theory of seduction, après-coup is an instance of a "powerful return of the organic"[34] – of a significant, if only temporary, centripetal move. It is temporary because, as it often happens with innovative and potentially subversive notions in the history of psychoanalysis and psychotherapy, interpretations soon emerge which succeed in diminishing and de-sexualizing the transformative valence of the insight, pushing psychical investigation safely back onto a traditionalist path. Laplanche notices two major ways in which this interpretive process takes place.

The first is the *retrogressive* path, "that of the so-called hermeneutical interpretation [which] completely dispenses with any postulation of infantile sexuality. Aspects of it have come to the fore more recently in the light of '#*MeToo* memories', a phenomenon tersely described by psychoanalyst Agvi Saketopoulou".[35] She begins by explaining après-coup with an example which I will briefly paraphrase. It's Christmas, and you are five years old. You call for your Mommy, but there is no response. Walking into the bathroom, you see her kissing Santa Claus. It doesn't bother you in the least; you too would kiss him; he brings such lovely gifts. All the same, you feel confused by Mommy's strange, embarrassed response and get the impression that something is not quite right even though you can't put your finger on it. This sensation lingers somewhere in the recesses of your memory as a trifling image. Then, sometime in your mid or late teens, as you begin to know more about sex, that trivial crumb of memory reappears, this time taking on a whole new meaning. The experience itself changes as a new interpretation emerges which could be called 'traumatic' because the realization dawning on you is overwhelming and brings up in its wake mixed feelings of embarrassment at having been so naïve and perhaps anger at having been deceived.

If one were to transpose *après-coup* to a cultural, collective dimension, the unwanted attentions of a male boss towards his female secretary would not be perceived in the same way in the 1970s, 1980s, or 1990s than they would in 2006 after the advent of #MeToo. The profound cultural shift #MeToo spearheaded means that they would be seen and felt as harassment. With the après-coup, the powerful return of the organic brings about new responses as well as new sexual ideas. A close link with the organic and the sexual, however, brings ambivalence into the picture and problematizes the often-black-and-white claims of the atomistic, self-preserving subject. In the context of the present discussion, it remains to be seen whether these bring in their wake a (centripetal, Ptolemaic) rejection of the organic and its intrinsic ambivalence – a good example, in my understanding, of the retrogressive path Laplanche describes. If so, it would end up directing the inviolable wish to right wrongs towards a conservative agenda. It would end up policing sexuality in the name of opposing sexism.

The second is the *progressive* path, the envisioning of a "succession of stages [which also] runs a risk of desexualisation". This path is evident in object relations theory, which sees the various infantile stages "even when they are termed 'sexual' … only so metaphorically". We are no more, Laplanche concludes, "in the presence of metamorphoses of sexuality, but of those of love and hate, rendering … obsolete all reference to an object, to pleasure, to the zones of sexual excitation".[36] In object relations theory, words such as "sexuality" and "erogeneity" are severed from their original meaning and no longer linked to actual erogenous zones and if there is for instance mention of the breast, it is never regarded as a source of sexual pleasure but mentioned at a merely "symbolic" and even allegorical level. It could be said that object relations provided the initial impetus to desexualization of the psychotherapeutic endeavour before the coup de grâce delivered by attachment theory.

We have come a long way down, from considering the disappearance of sexual desire more or less apar with the loss of vitality and of our intrinsic conatus vivendi, to the pathologizing of desire. *Aphanasis*, a term originally developed by Ernest Jones, has been unceremoniously relegated to the museum of psychoanalytic curiosities. The etymology of the term refers to the fading of brilliance and eventual disappearance of a star.

Après-coup is a temporal concept and as such invites a wider reflection on time itself. First of all, *we are time*. Secondly, time itself is *other*. Examining the link between historical, sexual time, and the time internal to sexuality in the light of the philosophical tradition, Laplanche poses *four levels* (interestingly named "fields" by his colleague Didier Anzieu) of development in the way time may be conceived. The *first* level is cosmological time, or world time. The *second* is perceptual time or the time of the living being's immediate consciousness. The *third* is the time of memory, the temporalization constructed by a person's projects and trajectory. The *fourth* is the time of history, of human collectivities, including that of humanity as a species. Usually, a thinker begins her inquiry from one of this vantage points and then the investigation begins to touch the other levels. Freud's "natural" level is the second, the realm of perceptual time, but he also ventures into the fourth level. This may be the reason why psychoanalysis has incisive and original things to say about culture and history. This is also why it maintains to this day (French psychoanalysis in particular) a vigorous dialogue with philosophy, to the point where it can occasionally wear the mantle of an antiphilosophy, when it succeeds, that is, as Justin Clemens writes, in "tear[ing] the mask from logos and testify[ing] to the deranging suffering of the animal subjected to language".[37] The third level, linked to the human being's temporalization, is only touched upon implicitly by Freud. It becomes central in existential therapy but, to my knowledge, not in relation to the *après-coup*.

Après-coup reinstates the other – and otherness – at the centre of psyche, in such a forceful, "traumatic" fashion that it provokes, again and again in the history of psychoanalysis and psychotherapy – an equally forceful relapse to a centripetal movement. The most persistent and insidious of these is seeing the unconscious as the primal, instinctual kernel of the person, as a proxy for the "ground of being" beloved of the tradition, secreting as it were outgrowths, or pseudopodia. No longer an alien – a daimon, an irreducible presence implanted in me, the unconscious now becomes my very foundation. Other theoretical approaches may be shy of using the term "unconscious", yet parallel foundational notions of "ground" are found alongside a craving for metaphysical validation, be they felt sense, organismic self, authentic self, being, ground of relatedness, the gnostic truth of the body and so forth. In all cases, otherness is routinely forgotten and the enigma and the perennial *awe* (as in awesome *and* awful) of existence is temporarily appeased. It is disheartening to see psychology trying to justify its existence by entreating metaphysics – any metaphysics, no matter whether second-hand or downright worthless. As a result, one can now say dismissively that a particular investigation into a cultural or psychical phenomenon is mere psychology or, worse, psychologism. We have come a long way – a long way *down* – from the second half of the nineteenth century when the hope of this novel science was to help humans see through the constructs of secular and religious systems.

Notes

1 William Blake, *The Marriage of Heaven and Hell.* London: CreateSpace, 2014, p. 9.
2 William Empson, *Milton's God.* London: Chatto & Windus, 1965, p. 40.
3 Ibid, p. 44.
4 Ibid, pp. 44–45.
5 Peter Mayo, 'Of the Devil's Party?' *Hyphen,* Vol. 4, No. 3, 1984.
6 John Milton, *Paradise Lost, I, 2. 262.* Oxford University Press.
7 The term "upheavals of thought" belongs to Proust and its implications are developed in Martha Nussbaum great study of the same title: *Upheavals of Thought: The Intelligence of Emotions,* Cambridge, MA: Cambridge University Press, 2003. The term "magnificent monsters" is used by Nietzsche to describe strong emotions and feelings. See Manu Bazzano, *Nietzsche and Psychotherapy.* Abingdon, OX: Routledge, 2019, pp. 48–49.
8 *Paradise Lost,* op.cit., IV 1, 108.
9 M. Sperber, 'The Daimonic: Freudian, Jungian, and Existential Perspectives'. *Analytical Psychology* 20, No. 1, January 1975, pp. 41–49.
10 "Humankind does not strive for happiness; only the Englishman does". Friedrich Nietzsche, *Twilight of the Idols or How to Philosophize with a Hammer,* translated by R. Polt, introduction by Tracy Strong. Indianapolis: Hackett, 1998, p. 3.
11 Friedrich Nietzsche, *Beyond Good and Evil: Prelude to a Philosophy of the Future,* translated by R. J. Hollingdale. London: Penguin, 1978, p. 36.
12 Benedict Spinoza, *Ethics.* London: Penguin, 1996.
13 Richard Hamilton, 'Naturalistic Virtue Ethics and the New Biology'. In Stan Van Hooft (Ed.), *The Handbook of Virtue Ethics,* Acumen Publishing, 2013, pp. 42–52.
14 Rollo May, *Love and Will.* New York: Norton, 1969, p. 6.
15 Claire Denis, *Vers Nancy* ('Towards Nancy'), Vers Nancy (Towards Nancy) - YouTube, 2008, retrieved 4 Jan. 2022.
16 Ernest Jones, *The Life and Work of Sigmund Freud,* Vol. 2. London: Hogarth Press.
17 Sigmund Freud, *Totem and Taboo.* London: Routledge, 1983, p. 64.
18 Jean Laplanche, *Essays on Otherness,* edited by John Fletcher. London and New York: Routledge, 1999, p. 244.

19 Sigmund Freud, *Totem and Taboo*, op.cit., p. 70.
20 *Essays on Otherness*, op.cit., p. 248.
21 Ibid, p. 246, emphasis in the original.
22 Ibid, p. 243.
23 Ibid, p. 256.
24 Francis Pasche and Michel Renard, 'The Reality of the Object and Economic Point of View. Translated by Joyce McDougall'. *International Journal of Psycho-Analysis*, 37, 1956, pp. 282–285, p. 282.
25 *Essays on Otherness,* op.cit., p. 135.
26 Ibid, p. 265.
27 Ibid, p. 265.
28 Ibid, p. 247.
29 Ibid, p. 248.
30 Clarice Lispector, *Água Viva*, translated by Stefan Tobler, edited by Benjamin Moser. London: Penguin, 2012.
31 *Essays on Otherness*, op.cit., p. 248.
32 Ibid, p. 222.
33 Judy Kendall, *Edward Thomas: The Origins of His Poetry*. Cardiff, GLA: University of Wales Press, 2012.
34 E*ssays on Otherness*, p. 236.
35 Agvi Saketopoulou, 'Using Psychoanalysis to Understand #MeToo Memories'. *New York Review of Books*, 11 Oct. 2018.
36 *Essays on Otherness*, op.cit., p. 237.
37 Justin Clemens, *Psychoanalysis Is an Antiphilosophy*. Edinburgh: Edinburgh University Press, 2013, p. 13 (man/animal quote). Wilhelm Wundt, *Elements of Folk Psychology: Outlines of a Psychological History of the Development of Mankind* (trans. E. L. Schaub). New York: The Macmillan Co., 1916, p. 8.

Chapter 9

A Conspiracy of Orphans

For Riva

The manuscript of the first draft of *Le Premier Homme*, 150 semi-autobiographical pages, was found in a bag in Albert Camus' car after the road accident that killed him, aged 46, in January 1960. It was to be a historical novel about Algeria, from the arrival of French settlers in the 1840s to the Second World War and beyond, woven with memories where his alter ego Jacques Cormery searches for the seeds of his life as a writer. We read of his birth in 1913 during a rainstorm on the kitchen floor of a derelict farm, of his visit many years later to his father's grave (who died when Camus was only one) in the cemetery of St Brieuc, and of his fear of the dark and of death. As he tracks his younger self, he finds himself marvelling at the boy's ingenuity and unruliness when roaming the streets or playing football with a ball made of tatters. There was no secure attachment between the young boy and his mother. The boy loved his mother with despair. She never hug him because she did not know how; they would be physically close to one another only when he slept the sleep of the poor, in the same room with her and his brother. In the evening, his grandmother would tell him it was time to go to bed; he kissed her first, then his uncle, and last his mother. She kissed him absent-mindedly, then went back to stare at the street below;

> her son, endlessly, watched her in the shadows with a lump in his throat, staring at her thin bent back, filled with an obscure anxiety in the presence of adversity he could not understand.[1]

DOI: 10.4324/9781003280262-10

In many ways, the young boy lived like an orphan, negotiating alone his relationship with history and the world. When Camus returned to visit many years later, his mother showed the same ethereal affection and elusiveness.

*

Some will be familiar with Mary Ainsworth's *strange situation procedure*, the experimental set-up used to appraise differences in children's attachment. Ainsworth was keen to understand the child's anxiety potential in relation to the caregiver and utilized signals of separation and novelty, activating the child's intuitive expectations. This experiment highlighted the ever-present likelihood of the child accessing a state of abandonment. What went unnoticed is that this state of abandonment – factual, symbolic, or psychological – can have a positive side. If we can entertain for a moment the notion that the traditional nuclear family thwarts our creative desires and tries to make young people submissive and ready to merge with the capitalist machine, then the condition of "becoming-orphan" – factually or symbolically – may yield a positive, emancipatory potential. Being faced with the fear of separation and abandonment in the "strange situation" also opens the possibility for deterritorialization: of happy, expansive, and combinatory play – a dimension strangely neglected in a psychology culture bent on preserving the status quo and reiterating the alleged relevance of the Oedipal nuclear family.

*

The family has been back in fashion for some time, to the point where one may wonder whether its natural, cultural, and political legitimacy was ever questioned. But questioned it was, fiercely and fluently over 150 years of influential socialist and feminist writings which cast rightful suspicion on this hierarchical bastion of patriarchal power and enforcer of capitalist ideology. From Fourier to Engels to the great Clara Zetkin, the family has been thoroughly deconstructed, all the way to the Combahee River Collective's compelling argument in the late 1970s that the liberation of all oppressed peoples requires the demolition of the political-economic systems of capitalism, imperialism, and the patriarchy. Most women's liberationists would agree,

I think, with this last statement. So why does it now sound quaint, even archaic? Could it be that a different approach has prevailed, namely the liberal, well-mannered "anti-discrimination" view which no longer calls for the disbanding of hierarchical structures but is content with genteel reassessment plus a handful of discreet entreaties (if ... ahem ... at all possible) to be "included", to be allowed to push an Oedipal pram in the suburbs, to renew our subscription to a secularist resurrection and our overrated species' joyride to nowhere, and above all to "join the conversation", as the hollow mantra *du jour* has it.

Psychology rushed in to lend scientific legitimacy not only to the family but to the corrosive takeover of humans and humanities which crept up since the zombification of the world put in place by Reagan and Thatcher. How did psychology come to legitimize global neo-liberal vampirism? It did so in countless ways, and one example among many is having bought wholesale and then broadcasted to the colonies the Anglophone Gospel of Attachment Theory. In so doing, it reintroduced biologism, essentialism, and the century-old tradition of keeping women down and thwarting any shred of liberation for all humans for decades to come. The overwhelming presence of the warm duvet of consensus – cosy, comforting, and cuddly – is sure indication of ideology at work just under it – bourgeois, liberal, neoliberal, positivist, conservative, reductionist, essentialist, founda-tionalist, ethnocentric ideology, that is.

*

What Camus learned in the Algerian streets of his youth is the precious freedom which emerges at times through the physical or emotional absence of parents. It was the seed of his unique voice as a writer. This condition of "becoming-orphan" (an expression I borrow from Deleuze and Guattari) represents the creation of a fresh territory out of a loss of territory. By finding oneself in con-crete or symbolic exile, becoming a freelancer, and learning self-sufficiency, a person recreates a new terrain. "Individuation" (a notion bullied to the margins by the false need for social, political, and intrapsychic "integration") may be linked to this. To become oneself, one mustn't have the faintest idea of what one is. To become oneself, one must wave goodbye to the dubious haven of

identity and find a joyous and risky dimension of play and experimentation. Here is John Berger:

> I propose a conspiracy of orphans. We exchange winks. We reject
> hierarchies. All hierarchies. We take the shit of the world for
> granted and we exchange stories about how we nevertheless get
> by. We are impertinent. More than half the stars in the universe
> are orphan stars belonging to no constellation. And they give off
> more light than all the constellation stars.[2]

To be "the first man" – or woman or person – in Camus' sense is to
bring oneself up outside the parental sphere; to transubstantiate
the parents' ambivalent message by turning social conditioning into a
line of flight towards emancipation. Today, it means to stand up to the
banality, compliance, and conservatism of contemporary culture –
including psychotherapy culture, that new fortress of surveillance of
the populace set up in the name of protecting "the public". For all the
talk of measuring authenticity on authenticity scales, an authentic
person is hard to find. If found, she'll be told to seek counselling for
chances are she won't fit the peer-reviewed requirements. For all the
scientific appropriateness of peer-reviewed articles in academic journals, an original article is hard to find. If found, it will probably be
considered "unscientific".

*

Earlier on I dredged up the mighty word *individuation* as a cursor to
what I am trying to describe. A more exact term would be *existential
individuation*, closer to Kierkegaard's testing theology than to Jung's
pious socio-religious adaptation. Try it sometime: stick your neck
outside the precincts of your tribe, snub the dusty hymn sheet others
are half-heartedly crooning from. Now tell me, how does it feel, to get
on your face the icy blast of abuse, scorn, and defamation? How does
it feel "to be on your own, with no direction home"?

At this point, you join the conspiracy of orphans. Like the
Kierkegaard of *Fear and Trembling*, accused of madness by sanctimonious psychotherapists. Like Riva Joffe, tireless campaigner
against apartheid and racism and committed activist in Jeremy
Corbyn's Labour party, a Jewish woman – wait for this – investigated

for antisemitism by Keir Starmer's faction for criticizing Israel's brutal treatment of Palestinians and for rightly denouncing Zionism as an "inherently racist ideology".[3] Riva was in her eighties when she passed away in September 2021. If for instance you are getting on and nevertheless refusing to go meekly into that good night, you are an orphan too, an exile from the confederacy of docile dunces who supinely accept whatever a thoroughly inept government tells you – or for that matter the BACP (does the acronym stand for Banal Assemblages of Constipated Platitudes?).

Life might be a lot less cosy then, but you'd be in good company. Think of Beethoven. Sure, very few can "self-actualize" into a genius, least of all an overrated psychologist like Maslow who coined that dodgy term. All the same, Beethoven's example may be an inspiration. Contrary to the expectation that in old age you should recline in religiose reconciliation or "acceptance" of the ridiculous "power of now", in his late years Beethoven produced delightfully gnarled and unconventional pieces which transgress conventions, express defiance, and set the ball rolling for the avant-garde. In his unfinished book on the composer, Adorno marvels at the fact that it is not disquiet for his impending death that drives these late works, but the desire to create a new aesthetic that values fragmentation and challenges the norms of his era. Without daring visions of the new, what chances are there for genuinely progressive politics and truly transformative psychology?

Notes

1 Albert Camus, *The First Man*. London, Penguin, 2001, p. 178.
2 John Berger, *Confabulations*. London, Penguin, 2016, pp. 29–30.
3 Jewish Voice for Labour, *Riva Joffe – in memoriam*. https://www.jewishvoice forlabour.org.uk/article/riva-joffe-in-memoriam/

Chapter 10

Men Going Down

*

Personal experience of men's work, first as a participant in the early 1990s and later as a facilitator, alerted me to a rather disturbing trajectory. At the origins of men's work, the influential mythopoetic work of Bly, Hillman, and Meade[1] had at its core *katabasis*, from the Greek *Katá* (down) and *Báino* (go), representing the necessary process of a man's *descent*: a "going under", a journey to the land of mourning (the mourning of absent fathers the world over, the mourning of one's own sense of direction and purpose as a man) which alone could prevent and/or cure the onset of unremitting melancholia. In its original acceptation, katabasis is not allied with any of the notions prevalent today in a culture permeated by neopositivism. It is not resilience, that equivocal term popularized by Positive Psychology and eagerly embraced by neoliberal culture at large. It has little to do with the trauma industry and its reductive understanding of attachment theory and addiction. Finally, katabasis is not allied to a *politics of injury* which classifies individuals and entire communities on their trauma alone rather than their ambitions and their humanity.[2]

Katabasis is a term rich in meaning: Socrates used it when referring to his journey away from Athens to the port city of Piraeus. He might have used it when going down on the young men infected by his dangerously virulent love of wisdom, or *philo-sophia*. Every man who falls in love falls down, slips up, goes under, and undergoes the affirmative masochism of a being-in-love divorced from the ubiquitous grip of narcissism. He becomes "feminized" not "because he is

DOI: 10.4324/9781003280262-11

inverted but because he is in love".[3] He is no shrewd speculator, man-about-town, reactionary hipster hungry for green credentials, toying with veganism and diversity while remaining a corporate swindler through and through, mistaking larceny for daring, rape for passion, a manicured beard for manliness, eventually designing a paranoid spaceship to the indifferent stars.

The man in love is the one who no longer hunts and journeys but waits. He waits for the beloved. In any man, Roland Barthes tells us "who utters the other's absence, *something feminine* is declared". The man who waits and hurts because of waiting is "miraculously feminized".[4] Waiting for the beloved while feeling their absence is akin to the practice of meditation. There is no guarantee in either case that the longing will be allayed. *A letter in your writing does not mean you are not dead.*[5] For the child, there is only a small gap between the realization that the mother is absent and the belief that she is dead.

The man in love is ashamed when he is lucky at cards, for he then wonders if he is a cheat.[6] A man in love invites a magnificent *catastrophe* – a word of Greek origins whose etymology (overturn) suggests close affinity with subversion (overthrow) – which may shield him from the exhausting superficiality of "coteries, ambitions, advancements, interferences, alliances, secessions, roles, and powers".[7]

This stance, ethico-political as much as a matter of aesthetics, is at variance with the wide resurgence, after 9/11, of cartoonish manhood models à la Indiana Jones and *Die Hard*'s John McClane as it is with the upgraded softer version of the very same unreconstructed masculinity displayed by the postmodern mawkishness of Thor, "hammer-wielding Asgardian with the disconcertingly Oxbridge accent".[8]

It also differs from the scientism now prevalent in the humanities which, not unlike gossip or Ovidian *Fama*, coldly claims objectivity and knowledge, belittling "what I love [and speaking] of love according to truth",[9] that "evidence-based" truth so dear to dominant discourse in psychology. With its crude appeal to measurements, biologism, and idolatrous belief in "facts", scientism is, like gossip, utterly unsuitable when dealing with the subtleties of gender and the irreducibility of human experience:

> Gossip reduces the other to he/she and this reduction is intolerable ... [T]he other is neither he nor she ... The third

person pronoun is a wicked pronoun: it is the pronoun of the non-person ... When I realize that common discourse takes possession of my other and restores that other to me in the bloodless form of a universal substitute, applied to all the things which are not here, it is as if I saw my other dead, reduced, shelved in an urn upon the wall of the great mausoleum of language.[10]

Katabasis also denotes, among other things: a sobering of tone from the shady peaks of cunning rhetoric, the sinking of the sun or the wind, a military retreat, and, crucially, a journey to the underworld. In the men's work of the 1990s, it often meant a journey to the land of sorrow, of eating ashes, of suffering on one's own skin the irremediable limitations of being a mortal body laden with the pressure of having to perform as a "real" man. It retranslated and condensed several ancient mythologies – Egyptian, Mesopotamian, Greek, Roman, and Japanese – and fused them with contemporary anxieties. It felt crucial at the time that this delicate and often painful process be experienced first-hand, with the help of a mentor or a group of men engaged in creative ritual space, in storytelling, in the communal expression of poetry and of personal struggle, rather than vicariously, through dependence on someone else's wisdom, including the tender and fierce wisdom of women. Descent, going down, going under: the notion of katabasis implies that there may be considerable value in *failure* – a counterintuitive, even countercultural position, particularly at a time when the archetype of the "loser" is more reviled than ever in a culture hooked on ascensional success. There may be considerable value in the experience of defeat, as many writers have testified, from Christopher Hill's seminal study of Milton[11] to T.J. Clark's reflections on the contemporary Left,[12] to Aeschylus[13] who invites compassion for the Persians defeated by the Athenians.

Unlike positivist and neopositivist narratives, katabasis implies at best an embracing of the tragic dimension of existence, with the tragic understood as the profoundly enigmatic rather than mere horrific nature of existence. It potentially implies appreciation of the wayward ways in which individual and collective destiny moves. Crucially, it is removed from the present infantilization of human needs in the language of politics and in the language of psychotherapy alike. Taking on board the lessons of katabasis might mean constructing a *psychotherapy in a tragic key* rather than in obeisance to the dictates of "mental health".

*

The trajectory of men's work over the last three decades uncannily reflects the trajectory of psychotherapy as a practice and a culture. There is a world of difference between journeying to the underworld in the attempt to sanitize it and descending to that realm in order to learn. The initial stirrings of men's work were all about receptivity and humility or the depth of learning present in sadness, mourning, and in the eventual loss of a naïve ideal of manhood. The general feel of the work also implied a naïve desire to dismantle the patriarchy – naïve because unaware of the wider implications of the necessarily *homosocial* nature of the work. Patriarchy is "the structured system of gender inequality that privileges males over women and others".[14] It is constituted by relations between men with a material base which, even though hierarchical, determine solidarity among men that allow them to dominate women.[15] Traditionally, the tacit intent of male bonding in a patriarchal society is to bolster heterosexism by repressing potential homoerotic desire and by interrupting the link between the homosocial and homosexual domains. While the men's work of the early 1990s at least allowed these insights to peak through, more recent manifestations for the most part trampled them defensively. It became all about controlling and managing those very same deep feelings.

A parallel process has taken place in mainstream psychotherapy: the unconscious has been variously ignored, reified, and pathologized. What was glimpsed for a brief moment in early men's work was that darkness could be a place of enlightenment rather than an experience to be mastered: facing one's demons, rather than facing them down. Even the bravest of men shudder, as the stoics are fond of reminding us.[16] The "best" men are then those who can openly shudder. And there is more: from Emily Dickinson's letters, we learn that shuddering is a sure premonition of poetry as much as of pain, a deep act of imagination and an emotional affair as much as a muscular reaction to a pain that is yet to happen:

If I read a book and it makes my whole body so cold no fire can warm me, I know that is poetry ... if I feel physically as if the top of my head were taken off, I know that is poetry.[17]

I would go one step further: Katabasis is in fact a necessary form of *self-destitution*, a finely honed technique of the self, a practice that, in a Foucauldian sense, *constitutes* the self.[18]

*

For a while at least, texts like *Iron John*[19] and *The Rag and Bone Shop of the Heart*[20] captured the zeitgeist. They answered the tangible need (especially for men weakened by obsequiousness to the female archetype and disoriented by indulging for too long with Jungianism) to "man up" in more intelligent ways than a dumb collective imaginary could ever provide.

It is easy to assert now with hindsight that these texts (and the men's work loosely inspired by them) overlooked the symbolic nature of the homosocial bond and its implicit homoerotic component. It may be downright pedantic to refer to Levi-Strauss's theory of the exchange of women by which male clan members establish a symbolic relation between each other by desiring the same woman.[21] Nevertheless, the near total absence of acknowledgement of homoeroticism in these expressions of men's work turned out to be a weakness, in my view, for which men's group paid a high price.

The other factor closely linked to the above and which those of us involved in men's work in the 1990s overlooked is *triangulation*. Absent women in men's homosocial meetings propel an implicit rivalry in relation to them which in turn cements a stronger bond between men whose hidden music is homoeroticism, a phenomenon which I believe was implied by Freud for whom "libidinal impulses can take both [heterosexual and homosexual] directions without producing a clash",[22] and perhaps by René Girard, who understood the triangle as a "systematic metaphor, systematically pursued",[23] becoming alive in rivalry:

In the quarrel that puts him in opposition to his rival, the subject reverses the logical and chronological order of desires in order to hide his imitation. He asserts that his own desire is prior to that of

> his rival; according to him it is the mediator who is responsible for the rivalry. Everything that originates with this mediator is systematically belittled although still secretly desired. Now the mediator is a shrewd and diabolical enemy; he tries to rob the adverse object of his most prized possessions; he obstinately thwarts his most legitimate ambitions.[24]

In the animosity towards an erotic rival, the subject construes an intimacy of sorts whose undertone and intensity are symmetrical to the intensity of the erotic experience.

Neoliberalism later appropriated the soft power of mythopoetic work and sold it back to us through the faux naiveté and the malignant obliviousness of *Facebook* culture. There are antecedents dating back a long time, for it could be argued that one of the key mythical figures who announces civilization is an insecure and "soft" young man named Jason, the hero who acquired the Golden Fleece through scheming, cool rationality, and treachery towards Medea. His great achievement is that his cruelty is cloaked in sensitive language. Similarly, the touchy-feely interface of Facebook hides what is really running the show: algorithms and the greedy dictates of the market. It is often difficult to see ideology at work while it is in full swing and even more difficult when dealing with an ideology which speaks of the end of ideology if not the end of history. By the time its deleterious effects become clear, it is almost too late. As Marx and Engels indicated, the function of ideology is to obscure inconsistencies in the status quo by reorganizing them into a pseudo-historical narrative of origins.[25] A similar warning is found in Marx's *Grundrisse* where he discusses historically decontextualized abstractions:

> Since bourgeois society is itself only a contradictory form of development, relations derived from earlier forms will often be found within it only in an entirely stunted form, or even travestied. For example, communal property. Although it is true, therefore, that the categories of bourgeois economics possess a truth for all other forms of society, this is to be taken only with a grain of salt. They can contain them in a developed, or stunted, or caricatured form etc., but always with an essential difference.[26]

The presumption of historical truth is contentious and one-sided:

> The so-called historical presentation of development is founded,
> as a rule, on the fact that the latest form regards the previous ones
> as steps leading up to itself, and, since it is only rarely and only
> under quite specific conditions able to criticize itself ... it always
> conceives them one-sidedly.[27]

An important aspect of these modes of mystification is the glorification of outmoded ideals of a bygone era in defence of a contemporary system of inequality with the scope of occluding the material
basis of these values. Gender essentialism, the ever-present pitfall of
men's work, may be understood within the above parameters. A lack
of historicizing analysis is often paired to a tendency to take gender
alone to be the most defining feature of human experience. In this
sense, contemporary men's work could still learn much from *reading
history* alongside *reading sex*. It could learn from the ethos of socialist
feminism (now nearly obliterated by red-carpet feminism) and in the
process come to realize perhaps the liberative potential of studying
masculinity experientially rather than ending up reinforcing patriarchal stereotypes. Liberation starts at home, with the dismantling of
the family, or rather the *ideology* of the family. When capitalism
replaced feudalism, Juliet Mitchell writes, "the family changed from
being the economic basis of individual private property ... to being
the focal point of the *idea* of individual private property under a
system that banished such an economic form from its central mode of
production".[28] Or: *a man's home is his castle*, a cunning instance of
ideological construction, disentombing a simulacrum of power for
the powerless so as to flatter and encourage the befuddled male wage
worker into more barren fields of alienation, from labour to the
battlefield to the vast array of bullshit jobs. The reward? Becoming a
king in one's home. But the labourer is not a lord: the forms of
property are very different (rented or mortgaged home versus
inherited castle) as well as contradictory. The contradiction is mol-
lified by an ideological formulation which transfers the "political and
economic control [of the lord] over the environs of his castle to an

image of the father's personal control over the inmates of his home".[29] As if by magic, ideology traverses agency, time, and space.

Like ideology, sexuality too is contingent on the alteration of historical and contemporary formulations (in Sedgwick's language, diachronic and synchronic): it operates in retrospect with regards to most feelings and emotions that comprise it. One immediate consequence of the imbrication of ideology and sexuality is that sexuality is not as fixed as the tradition would like us to think. It is an uncertain space, a space that keeps shifting over time. This makes it playable to ideological formations but also to emancipatory transformation.

*

Was the mythopoetic project doomed from the start? It would be ungenerous to say so, especially considering how useful and inspiring it has been for many. To this day, I do find myself working with young male clients who have benefited from those insights and understood the confusion and sadness of their experience as a necessary step towards greater psychological maturity.

Perhaps mythopoetic men's work relied too heavily on the notion of the absent father, whose factual and/or symbolic re-enactment and restorative presence through mentorship and psychical/communal work could repair what did not need repairing in the first place. Perhaps excessive reliance on familialism as well as on Jungianism meant that the project remained moored within traditionalist rather than transformative narratives. Yet the spark and inspiration experienced by those of us involved in men's work are undeniable. The rare, precious mixture of vulnerability and strength remains valuable. And it is miles away from what is taking place now in current manifestations of masculinity. The fact that a psychologist such as Jordan Peterson should nowadays be an inspiration for several young men, some of them involved in men's work, should give pause for thought. There are differences as well as similarities between the men's groups of the 1990s and current incarnations. Let's have a look at differences first.

Early on in his first book, *Hölderlin and the Question of the Father*, Laplanche traces the poet's depression in Jena, during a crucial phase of his life, stating that while Hölderlin rightly perceived the difficulties he experienced "in terms of maturation, of passage ... [his reflections are] completely permeated with Kantian philosophy",[30] tarnished with a moralism and sternness that is evident in his letter to his brother of 21 August 1794 where he writes:

> It is through incessant activity that one matures into a man, through striving to act out of duty, even if it brings little joy with it and appears a petty duty, one matures into a man; by denying one's desires, renouncing, and overcoming the selfish part of our nature.[31]

While Hölderlin's stance is reasonable (a degree of austerity certainly assists the passage to adulthood), his "Kantian legalism is a totally inadequate mode of expression for his thinking": it is at variance with his own organismic proclivity "towards a much more holistic and naturalistic idea of individual fulfilment". Kantian moralism, let alone "a too-narrowly conceived Kantian moralism",[32] is inadequate in helping a man develop and realize what Hölderlin in his letters repeatedly refers to as *Bildung*, the drive to give shape to oneself. Setting "naturalism" against "morality" in this rather generalized way does not imply that the former is devoid of duty, but that it entails a different responsibility directed at "knowing one's own nature and needs, the necessity of 'nourishing [one's] heart and mind'",[33] rather than obeying to the voice of an interiorized sergeant-major spouting categorical imperatives. These two wholly different forms of answering the inner necessity of becoming a man neatly represent in my view the difference between the early men's work in the 1990s and contemporary men's work. The mythopoetic work of Bly and others emphasized working with soul, organism, and naturalness. It echoed somewhat the ethos of a humanistic, archetypal psychology open to experimentation, exploration, and prone to its inevitable pitfalls. Contemporary men's work, on the other hand, appears to regress towards a self-punitive, moralistic call to duty, steeped in that very same patriarchal worldview which decades of psychotherapy worked hard at deconstructing.

*

There is a wider, multifaceted cultural and political context within which the shift outlined above may be understood. Here is an example:

Google engineer James Damore was fired in August 2017 for writing a memo which stated that women are by nature less capable to sustain high-powered, high-stress jobs in technical employment. He gained instant status as hero of the alt-right and the manosphere (i.e., online forums, blogs, and websites promoting misogyny in the name of noxious and regressive notions of masculinity). He was feted by the likes of Jordan Peterson, Milo Yiannopoulos, and others and compared to the fifteenth-century theology professor Martin Luther for standing up against Google's "Vatican".[34] In addition, he was also flattered by the liberal press who predictably pop-psychologized and explained away his views in terms of his autism.[35]

Posted in a webpage studded with endorsements to books written by his heroes Steven Pinker and Jonathan Haidt, Damore's memo makes for a fascinating read. It eulogizes evolutionary psychology, a discipline critiqued by many feminist writers for defending and bio-logizing patriarchy.[36] It draws on sources such as the so-called new atheism movement, "an online subculture that moves between isla-mophobia and hyper-rationality"[37] inspired by authors such as Richard Dawkins, Sam Harris, and others. Damore berates a generic "dominant ideology" and its biases for "preventing honest discussion". The core of the argument is that "men and women biologically differ in many ways [and these] differences explain why we don't see equal representation of women in tech and leadership". Biological differences between men and women are "universal across human cultures". He goes on to say:

> [Biological differences] have clear biological causes and links to prenatal testosterone. Biological males that were castrated at birth and raised as females often still identify and act like males. The underlying traits are highly heritable. They're exactly what we would predict from an evolutionary psychology perspective.[38]

A study by Ben Little and Alison Winch[39] painstakingly traces a coherent linear continuum and the similarities not only between Damore and Google, but also between views uttered in the mano-sphere and within Google ideological echo chamber. The name of the ideology is *dataism,* the belief that the world and human experience within it can be reduced to quantifiable data and decontextualized information. Like all corporations, Google champions diversity,[40] while some of its employees invariably tell a different story, speaking of Silicon Valley as segregated valley.[41] Google's feat arguably consists in taking to another level the dot.com neoliberalism denounced years ago by Barbrook & Cameron in their seminal study of the Californian Ideology, in their view a successful example of "Jeffersonian democracy [morphing into] a hi-tech version of the plantation economy of the Old South".[42] The seeming neutrality of data betrays at close scrutiny a whole set of biases propagating misogyny, racism, and a lopsided view of masculinity.

> Data is not neutral – it is always an applied form of knowledge gathered (i.e., removed from context) and organised in specific ways. So not only is data radically decontextualized knowledge, but it is also constantly being recontextualized in the service of finding solutions to problems.[43]

While data may be useful in other contexts, it is inadequate and misleading when describing human experience, including the under-standing of complex notions such as gender. The decontextualization and recontextualization constantly at work in the way a corporation such as Google-Alphabet operates favours and augments existing racialized patriarchal constructs. It also provides, at this historical conjuncture, consistent support for the alt-right online network. There appears to be a continuum between the two: while the tech industry is set apart and ranked along the lines of race and gender by "formal and informal work practices", in online (sub)cultures "these exclusionary practices are exaggerated and amplified, harnessing ... hyperbolic language".[44] The problem is wider and it involves the increased use of Artificial Intelligence (AI). An added aggravation is that the use of algorithms, data, and cloud designs depends entirely on the use of minerals and other resources necessary for building computer components.[45] While it is useful to advocate the value of human compassion, intelligence, and creativity alongside a healthy revulsion of a technological take-over, it is important to remember that biases, including gender biases, are *introduced* into AI systems, as recent studies have shown.[46] Facial recognition systems, for instance, were found to fail to "identify gender just 1% of the time when the subject was a white male". However, "when the subject was a darker-skinned female ... the error rate was nearly 35% for the third".[47] For these reasons, it is not unreasonable to conceive of tech culture as providing a fertile ground for the manosphere and or to see a continuum between the two.

*

This continuum echoes to some extent the one between two "entities" which are often examined separately: the domain of *money* – the economy as it is conventionally understood – and the domain of *desire* – the libidinal economy. A set of theories and practices attempted in the 1930s and the 1960s to bridge two influential discourses which had offered a sophisticated critique of each: Marxism in relation to capital and psychoanalysis in relation to libido. One of the merits of writers such as Guattari – especially his seminal essay *Everybody wants to be a fascist*,[48] and of Deleuze & Guattari[49] is to have explained these two seemingly separate domains as one and the same, reconceptualized as the assembling of a necessary micropolitics of desire (detached from fashionable discourses on "pleasure" and its attendant associations with subjectivity), closely linked to an analysis of microfascism as an expedient way to police/control desire in political/private domains, including a domain that is currently idealized by most therapeutic orientations thanks to the acceptance of the alleged universality of Attachment Theory: the *family*. For Guattari, the tyranny present within family relationships emerges "from the same kind of libidinal dispositions that exists in the broadest social field". Similar authoritarian attitudes and dynamics are at work in the family as in public institutions, and "a struggle against the modern forms of totalitarianism can be organized only if we are prepared to recognize the continuity of this machine".[50] Men's work can potentially subvert the dominant role assigned to men by a patriarchal social milieu and in this way contribute to emancipation rather than perpetuation of stale narratives. What is a "patriarchal social milieu"? In the words of Kate Manne, author of *Down Girl:*

> A social milieu counts as patriarchal insofar as certain kinds of institutions or social structure both proliferate and enjoy widespread support within it ... These patriarchal institutions will

vary widely ... But they will be such that all or most women are positioned as subordinate in relation to some man or men therein.[51]

Despite its tremendous potential, the ways in which men's work has evolved in recent years give reason to believe that it is an expedient conduit for culturally and politically regressive positions. Can this doomed trajectory be averted? In order to do so, men's work would need to be coupled with an understanding (and a concomitant practice) of *emancipation*. To be effective, the latter must be apprehended as a political act. Politics is not the ratification of the principle, the law, or the identity of a community. It is intrinsically anarchic, i.e., devoid of an *arché*. Democracy itself has no arché or organizing principle. This notion comes not from the radical fringes but from the tradition's chief instigator himself, Plato. Jacques Ranciere writes:

> As Plato noted, democracy has no arché, no measure. The singularity of the act of the demos – a *cratein* [an act of ruling] instead of an *archein* – is dependent on an originary disorder or miscount: the *demos*, or people, is at the same time the name for a community and the name for its division, for the handling of a wrong.[52]

The handling of a wrong in a community of men must begin with an acknowledgement of the iniquities done by the patriarchy and with a genuine dismantling of the essentialist notion of "man" which has ideologically and materially bolstered centuries of oppression against women and anyone who is different. Only then, a door may open to an exploration which may be emancipatory for men rather than reinforcing the same tired and defensive narratives. There cannot be emancipation without a thoroughgoing questioning of identity – of an individual self as well as of a community – if one is to understand emancipation outside the jaded variations on the canon. These mostly rely either on congratulating oneself for being the rightful resident of abstract universality (the domain of the law and of liberal democracy) or to see oneself as part of a minority hungry for admission within the precincts of the ruling culture (the flip side of the same coin). Some of the narratives within contemporary men's work capitalized on the latter, presenting privileged, heterosexual white men as the oppressed minority – a feat of populist distortion with disastrous consequences in politics. The alternative to the ideological impasse is to conceive political emancipation of a group outside the confines of the self. It could be said that "self" and "emancipation" go together. "But the first motto of any self-emancipation movement is always the struggle against selfishness"[53] – a statement that is both logical and ethical. "The politics of emancipation is the politics of the self as another, or, in Greek terms, a *heteron*. The logic of emancipation is a *heterology*".[54] This is true of men's work as of any community or cultural/political movement whose guiding principles are emancipation (rather than defensiveness) and transformation (rather than superficial change).

Where are the most profound lessons learned from in the wider political sphere? From being able to listen to those who have undergone the injuries of history – "subjugation, domination, diaspora, displacement"[55] – and by listening to the experience of the marginalized and the oppressed, learning to problematize any cosy allegiance to universalism. What is wrong with universalism? It is, paradoxically, *tribal* – the provincialism of the human overblown to cosmic proportions. Where are the most profound lessons learned from in the "personal" experience of men? From being able to listen to the woes and struggles of women, trans, gay, and non-binary people and in the process slacken the tight hold the yoke of male identity has on men. Where are lessons learned historically from within the psychotherapeutic tradition? From those who have edged towards the threshold of psychical turmoil and anguish. In all cases, lessons are learned from outcasts. We should remember with Ranciere that "an outcast is not a poor wretch of humanity; outcast is the name of those who are denied an identity in a given order of policy".[56] Another word for outcast is the one used by the philosopher and revolutionary August Blanqui in response to the prosecution. When asked "What is your profession"? Blanqui replied "I am a proletarian". How could an educated bourgeois like him, a student of law and medicine, the son of a local government official, claim to belong to the poorest of the poor? Because he became an outcast through being a writer, an activist, and a prisoner of the state.

Because his lifelong commitment was the subversion of an unjust social order. Becoming an outcast through political subjectivation is precisely what becoming a subject means, escaping subjection through creative emancipatory participation to a collective project of subversion. Becoming a subject is to become attentive to the logic of otherness – to external others and to others within. It is a *heterology*. Subjectivization is not what liberalism and neoliberalism say it is: it is no mere declaration of identity. It implies refusal of the appellation given by the ruling order. It does not seek consensus because it does not presuppose relatedness nor mutuality. That does not mean there is no shared space, but this shared space is polemical, a place of necessary struggle and conflict in order to address a wrong. To forget this is to be either complacently naïve or complicit to injustice. It is to assert stupidly "all lives matter" in response to "black lives matter". It is to assert stupidly "men suffer too" in response to the centuries-old suffering of women. The stupidity in question is structural, the result of the crisis of emancipatory politics. One way forward is to assert heterology:

> [In May '68] we were 'all German Jews' ... we were in the heterological logic of 'wrong' names, in the political culture of conflict. Now we have only 'right' names. We are European and xenophobes.[57]

*

Guattari questioned the established notion, still rife today, that psychotherapy deals solely with so-called private matters (the realm of family and the person), whereas politics addresses the larger social domain. As he saw it, "there is a politics which addresses itself to the individual's desire, as well as to the desire which manifests itself in the broadest social field".[58] The formulation of a micropolitics of desire, paired with an analysis of how "private" and "public" institutions variously curb, corrupt, and co-opt the emancipatory force of desire, led him to a detailed analysis of microfascism. The latter was studied alongside what he called *bureaucratism*, another effective way in which desire is suppressed and, as present psychological language has it, "regulated". We would be wrong, he warned us nearly four decades ago, in believing that fascism has been defeated. Fascism is alive and well through new variants. One of these variants is provided by closely related forms of suppression, be they managerialism, dataism, and excessive reliance on decontextualized and biased knowledge and reading of experience. The overriding illusion in psychotherapy practice as in men's work is that if the mess of life could somehow be managed – if everybody could become a successful manager of their lived experience, things would be better. What is forgotten is that in doing so, we would turn psychotherapeutic exploration into another form of policing. Can psychotherapy theory and practice help construct new representations of masculinity as performative, fluid, and as turning point to a deeper form of inquiry? This is undoubtedly a difficult task, rendered almost impossible by the pervasiveness of neoliberal ideology. My attempt here has been to outline a series of questions that may help deconstruct long-held accepted theories about masculinity. This is the first necessary step. The second is to widen the conversation. Is there an appetite in contemporary culture for a reframing of masculinity? It is hoped that despite its limitations, the psychotherapy space, both individually and in groups, may still allow the emergence of the new and the unexpected. This may be possible if the psychotherapeutic field opens the door to the investigations present in other domains such as biology, spirituality, as well as psycho-social, political, and technological domains. If that happens, psychotherapy may play a role in helping clarify and foster emergent practices of difference and oppositionality, divorcing them from metaphysical and subjectivists stances. Truly differential and oppositional practices are as a rule ignored or fiercely rejected by the existing order because they cannot be easily turned into profit and/or co-opted into the dominant ideology.

Notes

1 Robert Bly, James Hillman, and Michael Meade (Eds.), *The Rag and Bone Shop of the Heart*. New York: Harper Perennial, 1993.
2 Nick Estes, *Our History Is the Future: Standing Rock Versus the Dakota Access Pipeline, and the Long Tradition of Indigenous Resistance*. London & New York: Verso, 2019.
3 Roland Barthes, *A Lover's Discourse*. Trans. R. Howard, London: Cape, 1979, p. 14.
4 Ibid, p. 14.
5 Black Francis, 'Cactus', *Surfer Rosa*, The Pixies, music album, Boston, MA: 1988.

6 "I love him who is ashamed when the dice fall in his favour and then asks: 'Am I a gambler who cheats?' For he wants to perish" Friedrich Nietzsche, *Thus Spoke Zarathustra*. Trans. A. Del Caro. Cambridge University Press, 2006, p. 15.

7 Roland Barthes, *A Lover's Discourse*, op. cit., p. 17.

8 Wendy Ide, 'Thor: Love and thunder review – sentimental multimillion-dollar romp', *The Guardian*, 9 July 2022 https://www.theguardian.com/film/2022/jul/09/thor-love-and-thunder-review-taika-waititi-chris-hemsworth-natalie-portman-sentimental-multimillion-dollar-romp.

9 *A Lover's Discourse*, op. cit., p. 184.

10 Ibid, p. 185.

11 Christopher Hill, *The Experience of Defeat: Milton and Some Contemporaries*. London & New York: Verso, 2017.

12 T.J. Clark, 'For a left with no future', *New Left Review* 72, March/April 2012, https://newleftreview.org/issues/ii74/articles/t-j-clark-for-a-left-with-no-future retrieved 22 Oct. 21.

13 Aeschylus, *Persians and Other Plays*. Oxford University Press, 2009.

14 Heidi Hartmann, 'The Unhappy marriage of Marxism and Feminism: Toward a more progressive union' In Lydia Sargent (Ed.) *Women and Revolution*. Boston, MA: South End Press, pp. 1–41; p. 14.

15 I am indebted to Eve Kosofsky Sedgwick for this insight, in particular *Between Men: English Literature and Male Homosocial Desire*. New York: Columbia University Press, 1895.

16 Seneca, *Dialogues and Essays*. Oxford, OX: Oxford University Press, 2008.

17 Joanne O'Leary, 'Bitchy little spinster'. *London Review of Books*. Vol. 43, no. 11, 2021. https://www.lrb.co.uk/the-paper/v43/n11/joanne-o-leary/bitchy-little-spinster retrieved 23 Oct. 21.

18 Michel Foucault, 'The care of the self'. Vol. 3, *The History of Sexuality*. London: Penguin, 1986.

19 Robert Bly, *Iron John: A Book About Men*. Boston, MA: Addison-Wesley, 1990.

20 Bly, Hillman, and Meade, op. cit.

21 This point is discussed in depth by E.K. Sedgwick in *Between Men: English Literature and Male Homosocial Desire*, op. cit.

22 Sigmund Freud, 'Analysis terminable and interminable' *International Journal of Psycho-Analysis*, 1937, 18, pp. 373–405, p. 349, https://icpla.edu/wp-content/uploads/2012/10/Freud-S.-Analysis-Terminable-and-Interminable.pdf, retrieved 01 Aug. 22.11.

23 René Girard, *Deceit, Desire, and the Novel: Self and Other in Literary Structure*. Baltimore, MD: John Hopkins University Press, 1972, p. 2.

24 Ibid, op. cit., p. 11.

25 Karl Marx and Friedrich Engels, *The German Ideology*. Santa Fe, CA: Martino Fine Books, 2011.

26 Karl Marx, *Grundrisse: Foundations of the Critique of Political Economy*. Tr. M. Nicolaus. London: Penguin, 1973, pp. 38–39.

27 Ibid, p. 39.

28 Juliet Mitchell, *Woman's Estate*. New York: Random House, 1973, p. 154.

29 Eve Kosofsky Sedgwick, *Between Men*, op. cit., p. 14.

30 Jean Laplanche, *Hölderlin and the Question of the Father*. Victoria, BC: ELS, 2007, p. 19.

31 ibid, p. 20.

32 Ibid, p. 20.

33 Ibid, p. 20.

34 Ben Little and Alison Winch, 'Patriarchy in the digital conjuncture: An analysis of Google's James Damore'. Lawrence & Wishart, London: *New Formations*, no. 102, 2020, pp. 44–63.

35 P. Lewis, 'I see things differently: James Damore on his autism and the Google memo'. *The Guardian,* 17 November 2017, https://www.theguardian.com/technology/2017/nov/16/james-damore-google-memo-interview-autism-regrets retrieved 17 Oct. 2.

Roland Barthes, *A Lover's Discourse*, op. cit., p. 185.

36 https://firedfortruth.com/ retrieved 20 Oct. 21.

37 'Patriarchy in the digital conjuncture', op. cit., p. 54.

38 https://firedfortruth.com, op. cit.

39 'Patriarchy in the digital conjuncture', op. cit.

40 https://diversity.google/annual-report/.

41 J. C. Wong, 'Segregated valley: The ugly truth about Google and diversity in tech', The Guardian, 7 August 2017, https://www.theguardian.com/technology/2017/aug/07/silicon-valley-google-diversity-black-women-workers retrieved 17 Aug. 21.

42 Richard Barbrook and Andy Cameron, 'The Californian ideology' *Science as Culture* 6.1, 1996, pp. 44–72.

43 'Patriarchy in the digital conjuncture' op. cit., p. 56.

44 Ibid, p. 58.

45 Kate Crawford, *Atlas of AI: Power, Politics, and the Planetary Costs of Artificial Intelligence*. New Have, CT: Yale University Press, 2021.

46 Simon Chesterman, *We, the Robots? Regulating Artificial Intelligence and the Limits of the Law*. Cambridge, MA: Cambridge University Press, 2021.

47 Sue Halpern, 'The human cost of AI', *New York Review of Books*, Vol. LXVIII, 2021, no. 16, pp. 29–30.

48 Felix Guattari, 'Everybody wants to be a fascist' in *Chaosophy: Texts and Interviews 1972–1977*. Los Angeles, CA: Semiotext(e), 2009, pp. 154–175.

49 Gilles Deleuze and Felix Guattari. *Anti-Oedipus: Capitalism and Schizophrenia*. Minneapolis: University of Minnesota Press, 2000. Also: Deleuze and Guattari, *A Thousand Plateaus: Capitalism and Schizophrenia*. London: University of Minnesota Press, 2005.

50 Felix Guattari, 'Everybody wants to be a fascist', op. cit., p. 162.

51 Kate Manne, *Down Girl: The Logic of Misogyny*. Oxford, OX: Oxford University Press, 2017, p. 88.

52 Jacques Ranciere, 'Politics, identification, and subjectivization' in John Rajchman (Ed.), *The Identity in Question*. New York: Routledge, 1995, pp. 63–70; p. 64.

53 Ibid, p. 65.

54 Ibid, p. 65.

55 Ibid, p. 48.

56 Ibid, p. 66.

57 Ibid, p. 69.

58 'Everybody wants to be a fascist' op. cit., p. 156.

Chapter 11

The Trauma Club

Leaflets on trauma, grief, and loss tumble out each time I open the envelope containing one of the many psychology magazines I subscribe to. Ads of summits and seminars on trauma, grief, and loss clog up most pages of these mags and journals, leaving some space for articles on trauma, grief, and loss, plus the regular interview with the newest expert on trauma, grief, and loss. Time and again, trainees and colleagues alike tell me about the last trauma, grief, and loss workshop they attended, of the trailblazing findings revealed from the screen of zesty zoom webinars. They tell me of the latest thrilling trends – from polyvagal theory to neurobiology to post-traumatic "growth". They graciously ignore my sceptical rejoinder, my pointing out that growth is for carrots rather than humans; that neuroscience is still in its cradle and that its claims feel a little too feverish. They won't have it; they are adamant that these smart new integrated schemes will tackle trauma, grief, and loss in unprecedented ways.

It's been hard in the past to work with trauma, the brightly coloured leaflets concede, but thankfully a winning permutation has just been devised that brings together and "integrates" (a key word in these narratives) the very best modalities. Prospective punters are told that this or that legendary clinician, whose fully integrated visage beams from the edges of these ornate ads, will confidently "curate" this freshly minted model for healing trauma. The word *curate* is apt, evoking both the stuffy ways of old ("more tea, vicar?") and the "curating" that goes on in art galleries, routinely pushing trauma-free and duly narcotized products. The terminally vapid iPad art by national treasure David Hockney comes to mind, his depiction of a beautified and orderly

DOI: 10.4324/9781003280262-12

"nature" perfectly matching the equally green and pleasant regulated affect so beloved of contemporary neuropsychology. Hockney's retro-melange of old and new in primary colours offers a gentrified vessel for the dull dream of aristocracy of the contemporary English middle class. His pretty pictures provide a fitting paradigm for keeping culture vultures and cultured philistines alike immunized from the trauma-ridden yet magnificent fury of far more significant artists like Francis Bacon.

*

Trauma is unquestionably, painfully real in the lives of individuals and entire communities. It is endemic in our ostensibly free world where the breezy illusion of free markets, individual liberties, and "healthy" competition makes all of us prone to an awful lot more than the injuries of fate and the existential grievances of anguish and uncertainty. What's more, trauma is often the upshot of wounds hatched and compounded within the family, that bedrock of bour-geois ideology so idealized by Attachment Theory and its current avatars across theoretical orientations, all of them applauding es-sentialism and biologism, (unwittingly?) endorsing the slow burning microfascism that goes down quietly and not-so quietly in every kitchen. Every therapy training that I know of is besieged by *dataism*, the PowerPoint-driven belief that the world can be shrunk to decontextualized data and measurable rationalization. This is not only ludicrous (as in the notion of measuring empathy on an empathy scale). It is also creepily attuned to the kind of defrosted Blairite baloney – the insipid, pseudo-progressive devotion in the almighty power of technology to save us all by replacing politics on the syn-thetic wings of a silicon chip.

In short, did reactive forces *usurp* the psych world? Now that I think of it, that question is naïve. It assumes that there once was a virgin terrain of transformative psychical enquiry before Corporate Mindfulness, Burning Man, Existential Therapy Inc., and Cyborg-centred Therapy took over. Could it be that despite its subversive and exploratory potential, the psych world was reactive from the start? A cursory glimpse at the trajectory of men's groups from the late 1980s to the present makes for an instructive read. We have travelled from the richly ambivalent mythopoetic work of Bly, Hillman, and Meade –

through *katabasis* (descent, going under), its questioning of stereo-types, a reclaiming of a masculinity of the heart – to the current narrow-minded essentialist defence of archaic and reactionary ideas about gender championed by Jordan Peterson. In both cases (it makes me wince to realize this), the key inspiration is Jung. Aspects may be found at the heart of the renowned Swiss doctor's work which are now advertised in the banal self-help lingo of Peterson, Jung's most sub-standard disciple: glorification of the Self with a capital "s", dependence on Platonism, fear of the Dionysian, flirtation with and eventual rejection of multiplicity, and to top it all, reactionary politics.

Like the followers of Ken Wilber before them, Petersonians, most of them fed on a diet of *YouTube* videos, loudly object to the dangers of "Marxist postmodernism" in the name of the blessed standards of identity, home ownership, and an officious defence of "Truth". What often drives them is fear of the foreign, of the non-binary, of the sexually and relationally ambivalent. No wonder a large section of men's groups has now tragically become undistinguishable from the alt-right and the noxious manosphere.

*

Meanwhile, in the commuter jungle, in the liquid world, in the rat-race fields of late-capitalist society, and among the work-from-home, Netflix-and-porn-addicted precariat, false hopes for thoroughly false needs are tendered in many forms, the last of which is the vastly touted, highly lucrative, and multitentacled *trauma industry* with its luxuriant roster of mini-gurus, its range of techniques, its ready-to-wear, monochrome worldview for befuddled counsellors the world over. Therapists are gradually morphing, in a grotesque reversal of Lenin's vision, into reactive *transmission belts* entrusted with the dreary task of instilling in society this pathetic illusion, this fatigued, third rate but well-varnished neoliberal hogwash: the pledge of becoming "fully-functioning" in a thoroughly dysfunctional world. Give me your tired, your poor, your huddled masses yearning to breathe free. I will send them to online trauma courses. That's what the Statue of Therapy says. There they'll learn that the body keeps the score, like some bounty killer in a spaghetti western. They'll learn that the body is emitting gnostic truths and an Ultimately True Felt Sense. Send the tempest-tossed to me, the Statue of Therapy says, I will teach them all about the autonomic nervous system. They will learn how to become a regulated presence. They will learn how to smile and dutifully adjust to an unjust world. They'll happily go back to that cherished seat in the traffic jam. They'll go back to the fast motorway to nowhere with a congruent smile on their face.

It is not the fault of trauma therapists if the psych world is deeply asleep in a comatose and compliant state. But the question remains as to what forces psychology and psychotherapy are serving. My guess is they are serving *reactive* rather than active forces. It could be argued that the whole psychotherapeutic enterprise, with the unconscious duly pathologized and relegated to the museum, now rests on a bed of reactive forces.

The problem is political, but what characterizes progressive politics in a "traumatic" climate governed by dangerous buffoons and racist tyrants is an overtly defensive position, with no vision other than a *politics of injury* which categorizes entire communities on their trauma alone rather than their desires, ambitions, and humanity. Joe Biden is the most noticeable representative of the politics of injury, a man who is genuinely empathic because he experienced tragedy: first the death of his first wife, Neilia, and their daughter, Naomi, in a car crash, and later the death of his son Beau. A man who strongly identified with the dead Kennedys who like him were of Irish descent. A man who, some hoped, would steer American foreign policy towards a more humane course and heal a nation under the yoke of bigotry, racism, and a cluster of evils sanctified by the Republican party. Fat chance. Biden has maintained the discriminatory policies against migrants set up by Trump and which outsourced US immigration control to Mexican and Central American security forces. He has not followed on his pre-election statement to tackle the Saudi authoritarian regime; he has bolstered the laughable claim of the United States as leaders of the so-called free world. He has done nothing to revive the Iran nuclear deal. The list could go on.

*

We live in wary times, both in politics and in the allegedly private realm of psyche. While past insurgencies aimed at *all power to the imagination* and the overthrow of capitalism, all we ask for nowadays is little else than the chance to survive on an overheated planet and to quietly enjoy a solipsistic and innocuous notion of "liberty". Similarly, in the psychotherapy world, the aspiration towards transformation, liberation, and living more fully in solidarity with others is waning fast. All we ask for is specialist knowledge for licking our wounds. The politics of injury are replicated in the psychotherapies of injury. And if Biden is the chief representative of the former, Gabor Maté is the guru-in-chief for the latter. His neuro-reductionism is currently all the rage, supplying a set of explanations that are like mellifluous music to the ears of therapists struggling with the heavy load of vicarious trauma. To be sure, Maté is an articulate, humane, hands-on practitioner in the field of addiction who worked with inner-city addicts in Vancouver. I don't know if it's the same now, but I vividly remember when I was there some fifteen years ago how (literally, physically) segregated drug users and homeless people were from the rest of the town. To a visitor stepping by mistake into this ghettoized area, it felt like entering a circle of Dante's hell. The Insite Injection Centre and the Portland Hotel, where Maté worked, provided invaluable help in the form of housing and psychological support.

"I feel your pain", a phrase made famous by Bill Clinton, might summarize Maté's approach. It certainly humanizes the other. It also glosses over an asymmetry of gargantuan proportion by assuming, as most of the therapy world does, that there exists somewhere a place of equality between two people or that this place can be created through our faith in relatedness à la Spinelli and in civic dialogue à la Habermas. You and I are not different, Maté is effectively saying, even though you may be penniless, homeless, and strung up on heroin while I am a well-off therapist "afflicted" by ADHD and shopping addiction like he was. You and I are the same also because all addictions are the same, are they not? They are effectively forms of brain dysfunction, the root of which is to be found in abuse suffered in early years, in unsatisfactory forms of attachment resulting in the insufficient processing of dopamine and endorphins. And so on and so forth. According to this model, drugs or other forms of addiction replace the missing stimuli. Why is this approach *reductive*? Because the problem, whatever that may be, is *reduced* to early abuse and conjectural biochemical alterations. These become the main reason and culprit. Never before the biomedical model had a more convincing advocate. Never before societal, political, and environmental contexts were so alluringly and convincingly bypassed. One way or another, the implication appears to be, we are all addicts. All we can hope for is the good fortune to alight on a safe hamlet where, guided by compassionate experts like Maté, we'll be directed to search for (and inevitably find) the traumatic root cause of our woes. Then we shall be healed. We shall be saved. We will become "integrated" and, regaining our precious seat in the traffic jam, we'll forget all about our desire for revolution.

Chapter 12

Therapy as Art and Praxis

Psychotherapy is an art: for many practitioners – I count myself among them – this claim has considerable appeal. This may be true even when, in deference to the scientism currently in vogue, some of us select a rather contrite version of the above statement, describing therapy as a "science of the art".[1] My intention here is not to merely defend the claim, but to see how far it can go. To vaguely endorse it feels apologetic; it also implies a facile polarization between art and science – between a (preferred) subjective, qualitative dimension and a seemingly objective and quantitative domain.

Besides, it would be wrong to bring art into the equation without some appreciation of the aesthetic experience. In relation to therapy, this requires developing a better grasp of the *craft* of therapy – of its imaginative response to the sheer elusiveness of mental distress. Appreciating our practice as a craft already frustrates to some degree the neoliberal robotic takeover to which most therapeutic orientations comply. But something more is needed: a pervasive *re-envisioning* of how we understand the craft of therapy and how it may relate to art and aesthetics. A good place to start when aligning therapy within the domain of art is the notion of *world feeling* articulated by Adorno.[2]

*

The prompt for choosing Adorno emerged partly from the sporadic but meaningful conversations I had with existential therapist Richard Pearce. Richard was keen to explore parallels and discrepancies between Adorno and Sartre, and we both found in the writings of the

DOI: 10.4324/9781003280262-13

Frankfurt School useful pointers for a salutary critique of existential therapy. This is admittedly an ambitious task, even more so if considering that England, where I live and work, "had no Frankfurt School, no Sartre, no Lefebvre, nor any Gramsci or Della Volpe",[3] and here I am merely drafting a handful of salient points, encouraged by Adorno's lectures and writings on aesthetics. I will be working on the assumption that much can be gained from parallels between the *aesthetic* response to the work of art and the *therapeutic* response in the clinic. Admittedly, the focus here shifts somewhat: therapy as art comes to mean an imaginative "aesthetic" rejoinder to the emergent phenomenon, to the matter at hand – including (and perhaps especially) when the latter is understood as a breakaway, a drift that challenges the subject's pretension to mastery. Therapy then becomes a *subversive* art insofar as it *interprets* the emergent phenomenon as an important moment of departure and deterritorialization. This is not as clear-cut as it sounds but it does entail "turning [a] crisis into a work in progress".[4] The ambivalent but essential process of interpretation never lets us forget that whatever Apollonian wisdom or insight there is in our strange craft, it is born only in proximity with Dionysian "madness" – a useful reminder, in times of philistine pragmatism and over-zealous sanitization, of how forever entangled the wound is to the healing and the interpreter to the dreamer.

The subject is decentred in favour of experience and psyche. The name of the strange craft examined here is after all psychotherapy, not egotherapy. It is the self-construct that emerges from the wider experiential and psychical field, not the other way around. And the meeting of the two, otherwise known as *perception* in Merleau-Pontian phenomenology, is where the real psychotherapeutic work occurs.

*

Subjective response to a work of art, Adorno tells us, is neither "determinate", "unambiguous", or designed to formulate definitive "intellectual judgements".[5] A finely attuned aesthetic response – for example, to the paintings of Manet – apprehends both the "pleasing harmony of colours" as well as the rupture constituted by the "extreme contrasts of colour".[6] The same applies to the simultaneity in music of dissonance and consonance, with the predominance of the dissonant element prompting the listener in some cases to reconsider assumptions and value judgements about what constitutes beauty and ugliness. The work of art, Adorno says paraphrasing Hegel, "does not offer a 'slogan'",[7] but takes in instead the contradictions of the world and of human experience.

More to the point, and in a way that is reminiscent of Derrida's discussion of Plato's *pharmakon*,[8] Adorno reminds us that "cognition" (here understood in the broader sense, as knowledge) both wounds *and* heals. The allusion he applies here is from the ancient Greeks: "*trosas iasetai*: he who wounds also heals",[9] a source worth noting, as it offers a distinctive variation on the Jungian trope of the wounded healer. Telephus, son of Heracles and a popular tragic hero, was wounded by Achille's spear. The only thing that will heal his wound is that very same spear. An engraved Etruscan bronze mirror from the second half of the fourth century BC and a marble bas-relief from around the first century BC both show Achilles healing Telephus with the rust from his spear. For Adorno, receptivity to the work of art creates rupture, and it is at the core of this rupture that healing and transformation are to be found. Adorno calls this receptivity to art, to the wound *and* the healing, *world feeling.* Unlike hermeneutics, world feeling is for Adorno capable of holding the intrinsic contradictions found in the work of art.

For Adorno, the hermeneutic/interpretative stance "destroy[s] the whole interwovenness of truth and untruth, the interwovenness of what is alive".[10] What is required instead is to perceive and withstand the alive contradictions and oppositions present in the work, a stance that is more valid than an ideological pursuit of "Truth". We go to art as we go to poetry: not for wisdom but for the dismantling of wisdom. Similarly, we go to *psyché* not in search of certainties and corrective answers but for greater learning and deeper appreciation of the aliveness and dialectical ambivalence inherent to existence and immanent in the therapeutic encounter.

A first hypothesis then could be that to conceive of therapy as an art and to practice it as such would mean adopting a counter-hermeneutic stance in favour of a more nuanced aesthetic outlook. In Adorno's own writings, the cultivation of this outlook goes parallel to his critique of Husserlian subjectivity[11] with its attendant "drive to identity", even to "*pure* identity", an entity which, as one would expect in a philosophy of origins such as phenomenology, remains blissfully "undisturbed" throughout the hermeneutic investigation.[12]

One example of a "positional" or ideologically interpretative response to art is what Adorno calls "vulgar existentialist interpretations"[13] of Kafka. There is such a thing as "vulgar existentialism", he goes on to say, guilty not only of asinine oversimplifications but also of regaling us with that "atrocious word ... *worldview*",[14] a term which has gained some currency in traditional existential therapy.[15] For Adorno, world feeling must replace worldview. Applied to therapy, world feeling becomes Ariadne's thread, leading us out of our baffled wanderings within the hermeneutic maze. It can lead us out of the prison house of "Being", out of the imbroglios of a circuitous, self-referential Cartesian/Husserlian subject and its attendant bourgeois relational yearnings and conjectures. It can lead us out of the highway to a sideroad then a path fading out to everywhere.

Replacing worldview with world feeling means not succumbing to the sloganeering and the inevitably foreclosed conclusions and judgements often typical of a phenomenological enquiry which is often a treasure hunt for "Being". A vista may then open out to the "ambiguous intertwining" allowing the work of art "to incorporate that very wealth of the existent".[16] The world feeling is "internally articulated" and "historical". In Kafka's novels, for example, it has less to do with the "so-called human condition, a feeling of our God-forsaken, thrown, fear-distorted existence". Instead, it is a "thoroughly modern feeling" that in its own way critiques and reproduces the world, finding a "synthesis" and a "formal law".[17] Crucially, this formal law is not *external* to the material – be it poetry, music, the novel, *or* the emergent phenomenon in therapy – but thoroughly *immanent*, a point also made by Croce[18] and Benjamin.[19] The aesthetic response is here motivated by a desire to remain near the matter at hand, to the point of *disappearance*. Because what is investigated is no longer the self of the client or patient, this intimacy has nothing to do with merging with the *other* – that persistent shadow in psychotherapy's current fascination with the relational and the intersubjective – but deeper intimacy with the emergent phenomenon.

This deeper intimacy is by its very nature *counter-epistemological* – not in the sense of "not-knowing", but more an inquisitive gaze on knowledge as fetish and instrument of control. If anything, it positively gestures towards a kind of knowing that is recognition/acknowledgement in the Hegelian sense. The fashionable stance of not-knowing – be it Socratic, humanistic, or existential – simply won't do. Not-knowers protest too much; their championing of not-knowing tends to overestimate the know-how that may just about succeed in controlling events, measuring experience, and appeasing anxiety. What gets forgotten is that knowledge is important – albeit a different type of knowledge that is born of intimacy rather than fear. Knowledge remains important: the stories we tell, the stories traversing the consulting room, are imbued with a more or less conscious pursuit of knowledge; narration – from the Latin *gnarus*, getting to know, is knowledge, a getting closer with the matter at hand. The person who *knows* about art is for Adorno like "a native who knows his way around the city". Only the dilettante keeps saying "How beautiful, how beautiful, how beautiful!".[20] When I am close to the emergent phenomenon, I am less likely to be sidetracked by suggestive interpersonal evocations, be they "I-Thou", deep relating, intersubjectivity, or the evocation of stale mummy-daddy scenarios just behind the stage curtain. I do think that there is some hope after all in phenomenological existential enquiry, despite my inbuilt pessimism on the matter, despite the Heideggerian deviations which have nearly neutered the impact of this approach. But it is a matter of finding the right antidote, something which Adorno, with a little help from Hegel, gives us aplenty.

Genuine aesthetic enthusiasm both fulfils the superficial, hypersubjective awe and dissipates it within "the intuitive observation of the matter itself".[21] Likewise in therapy, genuine enthusiasm in the emergent phenomenon dissolves excessive fascination with the self. For Hegel, artistic enthusiasm entails none other than

> being completely filled with the matter, being entirely present in the matter, and not resting until the matter has been stamped and polished into artistic shape (cited in Adorno).[22]

*

This sort of experience – variously described as world feeling as well as aesthetic enthusiasm – is even more valuable for not succumbing to either generic ideational content or the hallowed "meaning" with which traditional therapists routinely sanctify an allegedly inert existence. We are, in other words, outside the self-bound "epistemological principles" and "principles of action" outlined by Dilthey[23] – the foundation, by and large, of Husserl's phenomenological project that remains influential in traditional existential therapy to this day. For Dilthey, what is "there for us" can only connect with consciousness through the "inner apprehension of psychic events and activities". These constitute "a special realm of experiences which has its independent origin and its own material in inner experience and which is, accordingly, the subject matter of a special science of experience".[24] Closely relying on Kant, Dilthey sees this special realm of inner experience not only separate from external, perceptible objects but as the very "condition of possibility of objects of experience".[25] This "run-of-the-mill psychology"[26] – the basis of most contemporary psychotherapy – "works with concepts such as 'objective type' or 'subjective type' or similar categories ... without touching on the driving force, the problematic, dark foundation".[27]

Psychoanalysis has not shied away from exploring these dark materials. Whether or not it succeeded is another question, but for Adorno, it was "certainly better, deeper, and less conformist than the kind of psychology used by the Dilthey school",[28] and therefore by traditional existential therapy. Psychoanalysis too, however, suffers from this *prejudice of the inner life* and of inner experience, from giving ascendancy to the subject – be it the artist, the viewer/reader, or the patient – at the expense of the matter at hand: the work of art, the emergent phenomenon in the clinic. In that sense, psychoanalysis did not fulfil its promise; it has become another psychology, inescapably moored, like existential therapy, to that primeval fiction and neurosis: the subject and to the subject's primary and static theatre: the family. Excessive focus on the subject meant disregarding the work of art, forgetting psyché, neglecting and/or pathologizing the unconscious, and effectively ignoring the phenomenal field of experience.

"There is something in the work itself that goes *beyond* psychology – Adorno writes – something that is *more than* psychology".[29] An aesthetic experience which understands the work of art as a mere symptom, as thumbprint of the artist's psychological characteristics is merely *pre*-artistic. Ascribing emergent phenomena in the clinic solely to the client/patient is subjectivistic. It falls short of properly addressing psyché. The work of art does not belong to the artist. Psyché does not belong to the person. One and a half century of bourgeois psychology made us forget this simple truth, and "the more objectified and concretized bourgeois society is, the more it insists that works of art come flying purely from the subject".[30] The more stultified society becomes under neoliberalism, the more it will assert that psychical experience is a mere attribute of the subject. It will also insist that whenever psychical experience appears to exceed our self-bound consciousness, it must be pathologized and, to use a fashionable term, *regulated*.

*

Is there *hope* for therapy? Given that hope is according to myth the greatest of evils, unwittingly ejected onto the world by Pandora, the question must be rephrased. Is a *radical*,[31] *counter-traditional*,[32] or even *counter-existential*[33] therapy possible? Is there anything within the existential phenomenological tradition that neither substantiates nor bypasses the subject but *emancipates* it? Richard Pearce's answer would be a decisive *yes*, and his resounding affirmation it the reason why there is hope for existential therapy, i.e., why it may be possible to develop the basis for what he called radical psychotherapy. For Pearce, the first crucial step is to maintain "an awareness of the radical foundations of our work".[34] In his view, the life and work of Jean-Paul Sartre – his ingenious *critique* and consistent *praxis*, his weaving of existential theory with a strong ethico-political commitment – constitute the very essence of those radical foundations. In relation to the "dilemma of the self-construct" in particular, the existential tradition "has ably demonstrated the impossible goal of self-knowledge that we are constantly striving for, a goal only realisable in death".[35] This project is wholly compatible with Critical Theory – not only with the general tenets enunciated in the early days of the Frankfurt School, but with some of its contemporary manifestations, which understand critique, with Nietzsche, as weaving a "radical theory of illusions",[36] a project of seeing through the illusions and ideologies (the two terms are interchangeable) of our age. Tommie Shelby provides a rather neat definition of illusion:

[A] widely held set of associated beliefs and implicit judgements that misrepresent significant social realities and that functions, through this distortion, to bring about or perpetuate unjust social relations.[37]

A radical theory of illusions coincides with the hermeneutics of suspicion, constituting for Merleau-Ponty the very foundation of existential phenomenology. For that reason, it is distressing to realize how *little* and how *reductively* Merleau-Pontian phenomenology – and its sympathetically dialectical relationship with Sartre's philosophical project – has impacted traditional existential therapy, an approach that relies on Husserlian and Heideggerian interpretations of phenomenology.

For Adorno, neither version is compatible with the notion of a critical subject. As he sees it, Husserl's theory assumes the existence of a (Cartesian) subject who inertly perceives an "objective" reality, whereas with his notion of *Dasein* Heidegger destabilizes the very premises within which a critical subject can be construed. Adorno's critique goes much further, especially in relation to Heidegger. For him there is very little difference between the elevation of existence in *Being and Time* and Kierkegaard's notion of consciousness, what he calls the transparency of the subject in *Sickness unto Death*. Both concepts – subjectivity and Being – fluctuate in equal measure; while the former is deemed "ontic" "by virtue of its spatial-temporal individuation", the latter is deemed "ontological in the logos".[38] In fact, Adorno adds:

> nothing but propositions could be ontological. The conscious individual (whose consciousness would not exist without him) remains in space and time, in factuality, an entity – he is not Being. In Being – since it is a concept, no immediate datum – lies something of the subject; but in the subject lies the individual human consciousness, and thus something ontic.[39]

That promise implicit within phenomenology stubbornly persists, despite the above valid critique. *To phainomenon* (from *phainein* = to appear) is pure appearance, that is, neither appearance-*of* nor appearance-*for*. The first leads us back to metaphysics and ontotheology (a "real" and "substantial" thing underneath or behind).

The second brings us back to subjectivism, to an arbitrary centre, the subject, the one to whom things appear. Both misconceptions have been enthusiastically pursued by traditional existential therapy. A more rigorous study of phenomena inevitably surpasses these two blunders which now seem to constitute the very foundations – separately, and often together – of mainstream psychotherapies. A more thorough study of phenomena would mean seeing appearance, wherever it emerges, as expanding to everything. It would entail retrieving the roots of *epoché*, a radical "methodology" of perplexity and wonder, all the way back to Pyrrho and Pyrrhonism and, by implication, to the philosophy of Nagarjuna.

*

Can psychotherapy become a *praxis*? Can it be, in other words, linked to action, and as such become a political force in the wider, transformational sense of the term? I remember hearing a colleague once being distraught at the use of the term "praxis" in relation to therapy. "Isn't 'practice' good enough a word?", they wanted to know. But praxis is not practice. Therapy as *practice* suggests a methodology that gets better through further training and experience – as in practising the violin or karate. Therapy as *praxis* is wedded to a more generalized ethico-political commitment geared towards: (a) a refusal to propagate dominant ideologies/illusions; (b) an engagement in a collaborative process of freedom from constrictive ideologies/illusions which maintain the subject captive. This twofold process will be necessarily allied to the societal effort to strengthen a concrete notion of *citizenship* against the ongoing threat of the *de-democratization of democracy* posed by neoliberalism.[40] It will be wedded to an effort to retrieve what Hannah Arendt called, in relation to the 1956 Hungary uprising, the "lost treasure" of the "revolutionary tradition".[41] The relation between citizenship and democracy is not natural but dialectical and precarious. There is a lot more to citizenship than the legal right to belong to a particular country. Nor is citizenship a *given*, but instead a "condition" and a "tenet" with a long and complex history in political philosophy that runs from Aristotle to Spinoza to Marx and more recently Arendt and Ranciére.

It is not enough to define citizenship in terms of *inclusion* (e.g., with refugees and exiles bullied into the subordinate position of the supplicant) but to assert instead with Jacques Ranciére "the part of those who have no part".[42] But even this generous formula, which gives universal importance to those kept outside the *polis*, risks being hijacked when it is understood as a slogan "for the struggle against exclusion" (and thus for "inclusion") rather than a more fundamental "enunciation of the principle of radical democracy as *the power of anyone at all*".[43]

There is a world of difference between a notion of citizenship that *pre-exists* concrete interactions between people and one that is instead *generated* by that very interaction. In a very similar way, when applied to the therapeutic encounter, there is a world of difference between establishing a situational and precarious truth by taking the risk of communication and directing instead the investigation towards the unveiling of a pre-existing truth allegedly granted to the "expert" therapist. There is no citizenship without community. But the essence of community cannot rest on the dubious notion of consensus nor on an equally dubious notion of belonging. Similarly, in the therapeutic encounter, mutuality and relatedness are not a given but are instead precariously negotiated. The asymmetrical therapeutic dyad is an unstable attainment rather than a premise.

There are two models of intersubjective encounter as there are two models of the city. In his seminal discussion, the philologist Émile Benveniste[44] demonstrated that the customary ranking of reciprocity over belonging is more clearly elucidated by the Latin dyad *civis-civitas* than by the Greek dyad *polis-politès*. While the former highlights the continuous attempt of individual citizens to relate with one another and the social body that is precariously created by that very attempt, the other assumes the pre-existence of a city–state within whose precincts individuals are admitted. Philology may nowadays deservedly be seen as obsolete sophistry, but in the course of its history it has produced remarkable critical thinkers, including Nietzsche and more recently Sebastiano Timpanaro, "one of the purest and most original minds of the second half of the [twentieth] century".[45] In the case of *civis-civitas* and *polis-politès*, their etymology clarifies key "political and symbolic consequences" that can be read "in the legacy of both discourses".[46] As with other dialectical tensions, however (and despite my own instinctive preference for the former), it would be wise to read this friction as perpetual fluctuation between the two poles which slackens the alleged substantiality of the democratic *polis*. Transferred into the therapy world, the above is akin to appreciating the transformative potential of the inherent precarity on the therapeutic encounter rather than assuming the pre-existence of a relational field.

*

The main hindrance in conceiving and practicing therapy along transformative lines may arise from a simple fact. Despite its subversive core, psychoanalysis was steeped from the start in bourgeois ideology. It was partly as an attempt to deal with the bafflement of the bourgeois subject in finding incongruities within his psyche and nurturing the hope of acquiring self-possession as one claims proprietorship of wife, kids, land, and colony. Understandably, it is hard to shed such an ambivalent and insidious legacy. Once upon a time as a revolutionary class, the bourgeoisie made it gradually possible to imagine the decapitation of a monarch by first concocting in Elizabethan and Jacobean drama the notion of a "public" who could deconsecrate the king.[47] But those heady days are long gone. The bourgeoisie has skilfully camouflaged (the very word "bourgeoisie" sounds quaint), and in so doing it has become all-pervasive, triggering an out-and-out *bourgeois entropy*. As a result, its ideology becomes the only game in town. This is the ideology of no more ideologies, marked by the worship of utilitarianism and efficiency, by the sanctification of comfort, and utterly dominated by the so-called free market. This may look hunky-dory at first, until close observation exposes the sheer insanity of the vicious circle it generates. From scheming to competition to accumulation to cynicism and despair, the hamster wheel of the demented accountant goes full circle by eventually returning to the market, hoping that the very root of the trouble will now absurdly yield a way out.

There is instinctive cunning at work here despite the chirpy gloom and quiet desperation. The modern bourgeois subject can talk the talk. Psychology regales him with a patois which allows him to feign self-awareness. Literature, modulated between high and low according to circumstances, renews in him the quintessential genealogical boorishness identified long before by Nietzsche in his excoriation of cultured philistines. At once liberal and greedy, fixated on hard work and hooked on leisure, the bourgeois, in his current avatar as the middle-class not-dividable individual, effectively altered the very nature of everyday experience. Enter "the relentless grey regularising of everyday life ... nothing but [an] interminable filler"[48] – an effective method for interminably deferring living, waltzing between a charity dinner and a twitter feed, a game of golf and a glimpse at the latest autobiographical novel confirming and sanctifying the very same alternation of duty and leisure, productivity and adventure. Even adventure loses its meaning: for *ad-venture* too, i.e., things to come, the unexpected, is duly pro-grammed and monetized before it materializes. Adventure too is a form of investment, not as an event but a form of capital.[49]

*

Bourgeois therapy regularly (and ritualistically) stresses the impor-tance of boundaries. The often-zealous argument in favour of boundaries tends to understand them as boundaries *of* (limiting the breadth of experience within explicit and implicit rubrics) rather than boundaries *for* (creating a receptacle where experience can freely occur). The difference between the two could not be greater. In the first case, boundaries are walls, and like other bourgeois false spaces, the room encircled by tastefully painted walls resembles a pleasant, air-conditioned prison cell or the average dentist or surgery room: comfortable, safe, and necessarily sterile. The possibility of anything new emerging is remote. Like a vexing wind from the sea, life is ex-pertly kept at bay as both parties, shackled by an ethical code built on fear, rehearse a predictable script. In the second case, the room invites the unexpected, in the hope that it may show up. And when it does, the analyst deliberately refrains from policing it, fixing it, or medicalizing it. Here boundaries are no longer fences but chalk marks of the type children draw in a hopscotch game. Both parties follow the rules of the games with the seriousness of play rather than the solemnity of the law.

In fact, the rule of law – its genealogy – gives us the key to understand the way in which ethical boundaries have been conven-tionally understood in psychotherapy. Born in ancient times and systematized during the Roman republic (509 to 27 BC), the rule of law is the principle under which all persons, institutions, and entities

are accountable to laws that are publicly promulgated, equally en-
forced, and independently adjudicated. At any rate, this is what the
official definition tells us. Interestingly (amusingly), the originator of
the modern version of this liberal notion was the most illiberal of
thinkers, Thomas Hobbes (1588–1679), "the most important precursor to contemporary liberal legalism",[50] whose positivist treatise
Leviathan, written in 1651, constitutes the shaky foundation of contemporary notions of legal obligations. The key concept useful to our
discussion is that of *hedges*. Laws, Hobbes tells us, are like hedges,
useful in helping us not wander astray and "to direct and keep
[people] in such a motion, as not to hurt themselves by their own
impetuous desires, rashness, or indiscretion".[51]

Left to ourselves, Hobbes believed, humans are bound to be wolves
to other humans, as his proverbial formula *homo homini lupus est* had
it. This is not only unfair to wolves; it also reveals a belief in a
foundational human nature, one deemed to be intrinsically bad and
in need of correction through forceful authority. The notion of
hedges in particular is key to appreciate the birth of modern liberal
thought, succinctly explained by Bernard Harcourt:

> Laws are intended to facilitate individuals' quest for their self-
> interest rather than impose upon them ideas or values; ... laws are
> what render subjects free; ... laws are what guarantee our liberty
> to pursue our private ends.[52]

Laws ensure our contentment, according to Hobbes, a contentment
that he understands as security in one's *possessions*. In this sense,
Hobbes effectively became the key inspiration for an influential
current of liberal thought, *possessive individualism*.[53]

*

If involved with psychotherapy *theory,* one can either be an academic
or a critical theorist. An academic recycles, weaves, and combines to
varying degrees of originality or banality a handful of theoretical
tenets. Critical theorists engage, confront, and go to battle. Academics
engage in a practice that is tamed, submissive, and disengaged. Critical
theorists act, militate. Academics end up re-tuning and revamping the
status quo – no matter how often they use the words "radical" or

"authentic" in their writing. Critical theorists, on the other hand, want to change the world.

One important step in this direction is to go beyond a parochial defence of one's tribe, parish, or theoretical orientation and consider instead whether a practice or set of practices reinforces or dismantles neoliberal illusions – first among them the ideology of a self-bound, self-existing subject. The second important step is to utilize and creatively build on those elements of critical theory that are useful to a radical praxis.

If therapy is to become praxis – or at least work in collaboration with other disciplines in fostering the emergence of praxis – it must have a close link to the notion of the subject as citizen.

Sartre's life and work testify to the fact that it *is* possible, despite the ingenious refutations of poststructuralism, to be "unarguably, a phi-losopher of consciousness" *and* a "champion of the oppressed, those whose struggle was to assert their freedom and self-expression".[54] Sartre's work bears witness, in Richard Pearce's evaluation, to a *dia-lectical* understanding of subjectivity. Dialectics are key here; they help a practitioner step outside subjectivist and hermeneutic constraints and avoid the *three common pitfalls* found (above all, but not only) in traditional existential therapy. I have investigated this aspect elsewhere and I will briefly reframe it here.[55]

The *first* pitfall is a (Husserlesque) hermeneutic investigation which begins and ends with the Ithaca of the self (subject) after a lengthy and pointless detour where every emergent phenomenon – be it Cyclops, sorceress, sea storm, or sirens – is reduced and assimilated by the omnivorous scientistic self. Why pointless? Because the sailor in question (not a true sailor when you think of it) is neither truly affected nor (dialectically) transformed by his meandering into the churning heart of an "outside" which is merely an obstacle to his blessed homecoming. The *second* pitfall is the intersubjective refraction of the self via some form of primary identity in a space of dialogue. The *third* pitfall banks on imme-diacy. Here the otherness of the other is lost in this attempt to reach a Platonic unity with the other. The uniqueness of the other is sacrificed at various altars: the mystique of new age spirituality, the lure of old-age institutionalized religion, and the fascination with an abstracted "Being".

For Salvador Moreno, the notion of therapy as practice implies that theory comes first, prior and more important than the relationship developed in psychotherapy. With praxis, Moreno says, I see myself as being in the world with others and involved in an ethical project of change. Bringing praxis into the equation means that a new term altogether is needed (Moreno, 2021, personal communication). This last point chimes with what Felix Guattari[56] consistently pointed out throughout the 1970s when he confronted the familialism inherent in virtually all psychotherapeutic practices, including anti-psychiatry, in favour of greater emphasis on the socio-political aspect. "What Mary Barnes needed – he wrote – was not more family, but more society".

It is high time for psychotherapy to come of age: to leave behind the Mommy-Daddy scenarios of its own infancy which keep it confined; to resist the allure of neoliberal gadgetry and gimmickry which turn it into another tool in the hands of the reactive forces of stupidity and control. Only then will it fulfil its role of becoming an art and a praxis.

Notes

1 Allan Schore, *The Science of the Art of Psychotherapy*. New York: Norton, 2011.
2 Theodor W. Adorno, *Aesthetics*. Cambridge, CB: Polity, 2018; see also Adorno's *Negative Dialectics*. London and New York: Continuum, 2007; also Adorno's *Against Epistemology: A Metacritique – Studies in Husserl and the Phenomenological Antinomies*. Oxford: Blackwell, 1982.
3 Perry Anderson, 'Timpanaro among the Anglo-Saxons'. *New Left Review*, London: Verso (129), 2021, pp. 109–122; p. 211.
4 Julia Kristeva, *Tales of Love*. New York: Columbia University Press, 1987, p. 380.
5 Theodor W. Adorno, *Aesthetics*, op.cit., p. 206.
6 Ibid, p. 38.
7 Ibid, p. 206.
8 Jacques Derrida, *Disseminations*, trans. B. Johnson. Chicago, ILL: Chicago University Press, 1981.
9 Theodor W. Adorno, *Negative Dialectics*, op.cit., p. 53.
10 *Aesthetics*, op.cit., p. 207.
11 *Against Epistemology*, op.cit.
12 Ibid, p. 61.
13 *Aesthetics*, op.cit., p. 207.
14 Ibid, emphasis added.
15 For example, Ernesto Spinelli, *Practising Existential Psychotherapy*. London: Sage, 2007.
16 *Aesthetics*, op.cit., p. 208.
17 Ibid, p. 208.

18 Benedetto Croce, *Guide to Aesthetics*. Indianapolis, IND: Hackett, 1995.
19 Walter Benjamin, *The Origin of German Tragic Drama*. London and New York: Verso, 1998.
20 *Aesthetics*, p. 210.
21 Ibid, p. 210.
22 Ibid, p. 210.
23 Wilhelm Dilthey, *Selected Works, vol. 1: Introduction to the Human Sciences*. Princeton, NJ: University Press, 1989.
24 Ibid, p. 60.
25 Ibid, p. 61.
26 *Aesthetics*, op.cit., p. 213.
27 *Aesthetics*, op.cit., p. 212.
28 Ibid, p. 212.
29 Ibid, p. 212.
30 Ibid, p. 213.
31 Richard Pearce, *Towards a Radical Psychotherapy*. Presentation at the Annual Conference of the Society of Existential Analysis, November 2016.
32 Manu Bazzano and Julie Webb (Eds.), *Therapy and the Counter-Tradition: The Edge of Philosophy*. Abingdon, OX: Routledge, 2016.
33 Manu Bazzano, 'Exile on main street: Towards a counter-existential therapy'. *Existential Analysis*, 2017, pp. 48–65.
34 Richard Pearce, *Towards a Radical Psychotherapy*. Presentation at the Annual Conference of the Society of Existential Analysis, 2016.
35 Bernard Harcourt, *Critique and Praxis: A Critical Philosophy of Illusions, Values, and Actions*. New York: Columbia University Press, 2021, p. 45.
36 Tommie Shelby, *Dark Ghettos: Injustice, Dissent, and Reform*. Cambridge, MA: Harvard University Press, 2016, p. 61.
37 *Negative Dialectics*, op.cit., p. 125.
38 Ibid, p. 125.
39 Ibid, p. 125.
40 Wendy Brown, 'Neoliberalism and the end of democracy'. Wendy Brown, *Edgework: Critical Essays on Knowledge and Politics*, 17–36. Princeton, NJ: Princeton University Press, 2005.
41 Hannah Arendt, *The Portable Hannah Arendt*. New York: Penguin Classics, 2003, p. 525.
42 Cited in Etienne Balibar, *Equaliberty: Political Essays*. Durham, NC: Duke University Press, 2010, p. 297.
43 Jacques Ranciere quoted in *Equaliberty*, op.cit., p. 297.
44 Èmile Benveniste, *Problems in General Linguistics*, vol. 2. Miami, FLA: University of Miami Press, 1971.
45 Perry Anderson, On Sebastiano Timpanaro. *London Review of Books*, Vol. 23, (9), 2001, Perry Anderson · On Sebastiano Timpanaro · LRB 10 May 2001 retrieved 17 Aug. 21.
46 *Equaliberty*, op.cit., p. 297, 18n.
47 Franco Moretti, *Distant Reading*. London: Verso, 2013.
48 Justin Clemens, Aggressively middling: The Bourgeois and distant reading by Franco Moretti. *Sydney Review of Books*, July 2013, sydneyreviewofbooks.com retrieved 16 Aug. 21.
49 *Critique and Praxis*, op.cit., p. 246.
50 Thomas Hobbes, *Leviathan*. Ed. Richard Tuck. Cambridge, MA: Cambridge University Press, 1996, p. 239.
51 Ibid, p. 239.

52 *Critique and Praxis*, op.cit., p. 246.
53 C.B. Macpherson, *The Political Theory of Possessive Individualism: From Hobbes to Locke*. Oxford, MS: Oxford University Press, 1962.
54 Richard Pearce, *Towards a Radical Psychotherapy*. Presentation at the Annual Conference of the Society of Existential Analysis, 2016, p. 79.
55 Manu Bazzano, 'Seven degrees of separation', *Adlerian Yearbook,* 2009, pp. 97–106; *Spectre of the Stranger: Towards a Phenomenology of Hospitality*. Brighton: Sussex Academic Press, 2012; 'Therapy as unconditional hospitality', *Psychotherapy and Politics International,* 2015. DOI: 10.1002/ppi.1342; 'Exile on main street: Towards a counter-existential therapy'. *Existential Analysis*, pp. 48–65.
56 Felix Guattari, *Chaosophy: Texts and Interviews 1972–1977*. Los Angeles, CA: Semiotext(e), 2009, p. 21.

Chapter 13

Of Strawberries and Salty Dogs

So yeah, when did it all start? Jackie asks. *How does it start? The sea has endless beginnings.* That morning in an art gallery, Jackie says, glancing at the paintings of this Belgian geezer whose parents had a perfume shop. He loved Fritz, Jackie says, but never made it to tragic joy, painting instead gusts of wind on some bleak Northern coast. Well, Sylviane thinks it started later, when we held hands in a touristy park, Jackie says, by the hot dogs stand, with me purring a line from a reckless tune. It was spring of course, a few days before lockdown. To me Sylviane looked like one to whom things just happen, Jackie says, but my view is warped I know by my nutty love of the classics and a twisted view of fate as weakness of the will, Jackie says. Who seduces whom anyway? Explain that to the ethics committee. So anyway, she was the-deer-in-the-dappled-light and me the-artiste-in-wolf-clothing who'll get slaughtered by the Farmers of Resentment, Jackie says, forever clobbering our humble joys with regulations shouted from high horses in the Home Counties where quite a few of them live for some reason. *I'm married,* Jackie says suddenly, and OK it's not the first time I fall for a woman, but this time I'm head over heels, *capisci?* It's rocking my boat, pushing my buttons – *all* the clichés you can shake a stick at, Jackie says, what do I care? *I'm vast, I contain platitudes.* Yeah, I know, for Sylviane this baby love of ours may just be a rugged raft, Jackie says; she might leave it on the sand once she makes it to where she's heading. But still, Jackie says, I'll do it for the ride or, as she'd say, *I'd be gladly toppled and turned and thrown into the air by the depth and force of waves, then thrown onto the shore as I depart from its grip, and loving every moment.* Well then, I'll be a log bridge. What brings you

DOI: 10.4324/9781003280262-14

here, I ask boringly. Where to start, Jackie says, *the sea has endless beginnings*. OK, I'll start from that square where Sylviane lives, named after a former duchy. I revisit the place often, you know, when day-dreaming I mean, Jackie says, which is most of the time. *J'ai embrassé l'aube d'été. Rien ne bougeait encore au front des palais*. The houses down to the sea with a green in the middle: I retrace my steps to her front door when wide awake at 2am or on midweek afternoons with spring doing its brutal thing, *breeding lilacs* & so forth, Jackie says, apologizing for saying unrelated things. Go on, I say, casting a glance at tree & sky 'cause it's good for my eyes. *Do* go on: it's relevant, especially the irrelevant – *Unheimlich gut*, as Freud would say. Well, in the clip she'd sent me then Sylviane smiles and talks softly to the camera, Jackie says, and I can touch the life in her heavenly limbs. She loved me then, my lovely swimmer in the deep blue, my seeker of the depths, Jackie says, but does she love me still? *Elle est retrouvée. Quoi? L'Éternité. C'est la mer allée avec le soleil*. My lovely lover, and what I want, Jackie now says looking up, is to bite her heavenly bum cheeks and have a little nibble *si tu plait* of those rosy lips of hers, Jackie says. *La chiamavano bocca di rosa metteva l'amore sopra ogni cosa*. Then her laughter, warm and silvery and shimmering, and her voice like Angela Carter's. But I digress, Jackie says. Go on, I say, it's all relevant; it's all *tres bien*, as Lacan would say. *Can't go on. I'll go on*, Jackie says. So yeah, Easter came with its darling buds and the Saviour rising from the dead before breakfast and all I can think of is the black & white clip of her lying on the grass of an unseasonal spring, rich in sea water. Her slow breathing, Jackie says, exhaling, looking out at the camera at the sky at the holy spirit breaking through the clouds before dawn, at the risen unorthodox young rabbi's luminous etheric body, looking up with her sparkly after-swim eyes like bedroom eyes, breathing, looking up like I'm on top of her kissing her all over and caressing her aris-tocratic hair in a bundle, Jackie says, an ornament to her beautiful viságe, that black & white clip conveying differánce, conveying meaning-in-flight, conveying absence on a musical beach – a musical *adieu* to the metaphysics of presence, Jackie says, goodbye presence, thanks a lot! In short, it speaks of resurrection more than the sorry tale of a star-crossed lover-of-God, that young heretical rabbi soaring from his tomb in Galilee, Jackie says, for no resurrection can resynchronize time, for *time is out of joint*, capisci? *En haut de la route, près d'un bois de lauriers, je l'ai entourée avec ses voiles amasses, et J'ai senti un peu son immense corps.* The vast body of dawn, the goddess personified and never *ever* turned, mind you, into some anaemic Jungian archetype, *pleease*, Jackie says rolling her eyes. I want her to want my body the way a classy girl from Paris holidaying in North Africa sneakily eyes an Algerian woman coming out of swim and daydreams of her hands caressing her hips, Jackie says, her tongue circling her belly, her lips surveying the hallowed slant between her legs, kissing the summit of her own wet daydream. I want her to want my body, Jackie says, before flights of fancy, before high art & low art. Besides, Jackie says, it is *this* body that thinks, this body that wants her body on the wet sand in the summer or under oak trees with the sound of rain through the branches in the dappled light, Jackie says, rain that starts just as she reaches the summit all wet and half-dressed, a frown of the deepest joy traversing her noble face as if greeting the holy spirit, both my hands holding her hips tight, for I remember it well, how she moved grace-fully and strong sitting on my legs, I remember it well, Jackie says, how she kissed me hesitantly, so endearing so arousing; I want her to want my body in unsophisticated ways whispering glossolalia sitting on my tongue, Jackie says, so that my tongue may travel around all crevices while she invokes the gods of requited desire, Jackie says, while we sing contrapuntal praises to the world, singing praises in the holy spring on the day of the new moon. Sorry for waxing Joycean for waning biblical for going unequivocal and even *mystical*, Jackie says, sorry for spin-ning off into *tempo rubato.* Being in love sucks, Jackie says after a pause and a sigh, it really does, let's face it, and watching *I may destroy you* on the telly is no consolation, far from it, for she might turn any moment to some younger girl or dude, some hippy Jane & Johnnie, any of her friends with more sinuous legs or stronger triceps and smarter drugs, and the garish wisdom that comes from surfing & smoking pot, but let me tell you somethin' if *these guys are so deep why can't they take this world and take it straight? Why always stoned, like hippie Johnnie?* Eh? Hope you don't mind, Jackie says. Carry on I say, it's all relevant, all beneficent. My darling mermaid, Jackie says, she told me about *diving deeply into the sea and accepting to still have to come up to the surface to breathe.* She is right of course, for it's easier-said-than-done, wanting to be a salty dog, an anti-Ulysses *the captain cried, we sailors wept, our tears were tears of joy* etc., wanting it both ways: the shipwreck *and* the transfigured cheerfulness only afforded to the shipwrecked, Jackie says. *We sailed for parts unknown to man, where ships come home to die.* Okay, but how is that different from a banal courtship of death? Who knows, I interrupt, maybe the "death instinct" is not about finitude but excess, little me wanting to be overwhelmed by the numinous (forgive the mystic shite), wanting to shelve self-preservation. Yeah well, Jackie says, but what about this man/woman thing? Does wanting to be overwhelmed make women of us all? Not sure if I can even *think* this, let alone say it. For instance, am I lesbian, am I straight? Does it matter? Does anyone care? Have you heard of Hélène Cixous? I say interrupting again. She hasn't. Well, in her latest, a hybrid fiction-theory called *Mother Homer is Dead,* she makes it clear (to those investing her writing with essentialist femininity and obsolete binary frameworks) that this is not where it's at. The book partly deals with the mother-daughter connection but not mapped onto female anatomy, you see. I'm talking too much, my supervisor won't like it, but I can't stop. It is, *non-gendered,* dare I say; it is memory; it is blood; it is spew, and *from this spew come the unruly collages and pairings that make up our sense of self in the world.* And in the process Cixous *escapes* the feminist code, the maternal code, and the pieties of attachment theory. By this point I'm not only rhapso-dizing; I'm positively ranting, & beginning to disclose: I quit working, I say, as facilitator in a men's group because there too, surprise! essen-tialism reigns supreme, compounded by Jordan Peterson's tosh. Haven't heard of him? Consider yourself lucky. I'd go on, speak of Cixous' experimentalism in language. I shut up, go back to listening. Would have said, I know what you're talking about because being a man is for me a station on the journey and for instance when in love a man is a woman: *un homme n'est pas féminisé parce qu'il est inversé mais parce qu'il est amoureux* which is tricky of course as the testosterone level goes waaay down. That's when essentialism tightens its grip on a poor bloke, chocking him with the jingoism of peeing competitions in school yards and libertarian social-media pyjama politics from the comfort of one's own patriarchal semidetached. I keep quiet, since this is clearly my stuff. Or is it? What am I but a shrink who like the bard enisled by Aegisthus on a desolate rock hears the secret murmurs of lovers ferried not by gulls or gannets but along *zoom* and *skype* waves in these quarantined days. Like him, I'm not a court poet. Not for me

PowerPoint dismal couplets recited to the motorized beat of neoliberal poppycock. What to make of the pandemic, Jackie asks meanwhile from her laundry room where she's doing this online session for fear of being heard by husband & kids, what is, Jackie asks thoughtfully, the connection between love and the plague? Uh-oh, she's going to mention Camus like everybody else. I stretch my jaw, readying it for a protracted yawn but to my surprise she mentions instead the noble-woman Pia de' Tolomei (*Siena mi fe', disfecemi Maremma*) whose bastard of a husband, suspecting her of adultery, put her to death by imprisoning her among the noxious vapours of his castle in Southern Tuscany. And there is more, Jackie says, for plague is *exposure*. Don't you just love it when clients are interesting, instead of boring you to tears the entire 50 minutes with tales of petty arguments, the redemptive value of *Schitt's Creek* on Netflix and the bloody kids. Not Jackie, who's now off quoting Shelley, *Lift not the painted veil which those who live call Life,* for the pandemic lifts the veil, Jackie says, and even the once archbishop of Canterbury said something of the kind: when the going gets tricky, you find what truly matters. Shakespeare knew it too, *See what a scourge is laid upon your hate*, but there's a twist, Jackie says, there is more to it than humdrum sagas of redemption, because the plague will also stir desire! Batten down the hatches, Jackie says. Desire! Explain that to the Farmers of Resentment. Take Aschenbach for instance, enflamed at the sight of beautiful boy Tadzio in Venice undeterred by the plague making its wayward route, Jackie says, to the languid magnificent city all the way from the Ganges Delta via Hindustan to China to Afghanistan and Persia: *along caravans routes it threatened Astrakhan and struck fear even in Moscow.* It's the same with Thomas Mann as with Visconti's film version, give or take a Proustian twist or two. Bear with me, Jackie says: *Death in Venice* may well be the only film by Visconti where he leaves aside nomadism. What animates nomadism in his films? Jackie asks. Eroticism! *Desire is in fact circulation. In all senses, it moves; it is an emotion that harbours motion.* Errant, erratic, desire; restless love, *baby love my baby love been missing ya* my baby love. And what is *avventura* if not venturing into the erotic, jumbled quest for the sublime & the profane, Jackie says a winning combination according to Sylviane who also loves Lou Salomé, Jackie says, even though she misread and even intellectually betrayed Fritz: *eroticism occupying an intermediate position between the two great categories of feeling: egoism and altruism; I want to be everything, prodigality of being, and I want to have everything.* Viel Glück, Frau Salomé, Jackie says. So yeah, what happens when nomadism stops, both materially *and* spiritually? Well, we build *teleology* yeah? Suddenly going somewhere, going places, getting all purposeful as if the world was designed by a project manager, but where does the river go? To the sea, no beginnings and no end, Jackie asks, the sea of death, of life, the sea of *deathlife*, capisci? Aschenbach knows it's dangerous to stay in Venice but does it all the same, Jackie says, and becomes infected with cholera after eating strawberries bought at a street corner. *Strawberries!* Jackie exclaims. Strawberries! Should I ask what strawberries mean to her? It's not all doom & gloom, Jackie says, you know. Think of the Knight in Bergman's *Seventh Seal* eating the strawberries of an eternal/ephemeral present offered by the family of *saltimbanques.* Think of Boccaccio and his worthy imitator, Sir Geoffrey Chaucer. In *Decameron,* the pestilence *spread … just as fire will catch dry or oily materials when they are placed right beside it.* Just like desire, capisci? Beware! Jackie exclaims suddenly. Fear (rife during a pandemic) will make third-rate metaphysicians of us all (and most metaphysicians are third-rate thinkers anyway, whether they babble about God, Gaia, or the Big Bang, God's own premature ejaculation for the benefit of non-believers), all of them cheerfully stroking their chins weaving grand designs on the head of a pin. That's all we have time for today, Jackie, I say. Same time next week?

Chapter 14

Brooklyn Rimbaud

For Claudio Rud

Gentrification started big time in New York after 9/11, Sarton said on Thursday, adding that the horror & frenzy & solidarity experienced first-hand on that day is what made him a New Yorker. It's a hot and breezy Sunday now in Wagner Park North and we are having a picnic. Through my cheap, wrap-around Velvet-Underground shades I see a splendid view of the Harbour. Over a slice of pizza, Sarton, organizer of this Person-centred World conference in NYC, says the unsayable: gentrification started before 9/11. In fact, he adds, gentrification on a large scale may have been one of the things that exacerbated the hatreds and divisions culminating with the attack on the twin towers. Either way, it's clear that NYC is no longer what it was in the 1970s, when it was disdained by the rest of the USA and left free to be its own undomesticated self. The urban policy of "planned shrinkage" made sure of that: entire areas have been cleansed of the have-nots by curtailing essential services first so that ordinary folks would move out. Then the place would be revamped and repaved for the middle classes. I had been surprised, hours before, as the ferry approached Ellis Island, where ships of migrants would come from Europe in search of a new life, by a sudden surge of emotion. Echoes of distant cries and the realization that it was not all gilded happiness and joy: the tests migrants were subjected to, the chalk marks to identify illness or illiteracy, same as it was in the place they were fleeing, interrogated by men in uniforms, their mental sanity tested and checked. There it stood, the Statue of Bigotry, sanitized echo of Aphrodite,

DOI: 10.4324/9781003280262-15

she who hovered somewhere between the impossible and the inevitable, one look at her and you're enslaved. Echoes of Minerva too, of Reason and Enlightenment, her steely equanimous gaze, her Presbyterian virginal gaze, her untouchable stony beauty. Rationalization produces monsters, the murky side of Enlightenment. *Give me your hungry, your poor, I'll club them to death.*

On the first day, the city loomed in the distance as I travelled through the black night and into the tunnel and in the midst of a midnight's traffic jam studded with yellow taxis and then gazing up and up in Midtown at the impossibly high buildings. After eight hours' delay and plane journey amid German teenage students on vacation, the exhaustion now makes me shudder here in the hotel between Lexington and 39th Street. No matter how cosy and full of creature comforts, few things in the world are more dismal than hotel rooms.

During brief pauses next day at the all-day Journal Editors Meeting, glimpses of the Chrysler Building. The day ends and we agree to meet for dinner with others. I memorize the address and later walk overconfidently in that direction without a map and soon realize I am lost. And that I like it. The heat rises as I walk with the waning light peek-a-booing between pedestrian crossings, each avenue stretching to infinity, the sky above and around an indulgence of ethereal light to an entirely human world, our human-made wings piercing like tender claws from our shoulder blades. Night slowly slides down as a myriad of streetlights snub the firmament, and it is a mistake to see myriad reality as a holistic formation. Next morning early, I stand aside inside Grand Central Station and gazing at the painted constellations on the ceiling, looking at the crowd sliding by hurried and hushed and smart I'm filled with joy at so much beauty – the mock sky and artful streaming of commuters, their forthright walk in the mouth of a river forever on the move, strange joy of a speck in the stream. *Blink your eyes and I'll be gone. Just a little grain of sand.* But what about the conference? Well, for now, I'm headed to Canal Street, Chinatown in the heat of the midday city sun, Manhattan Bridge a mirage at the zebra crossing, a destination, a destiny in the making, in the swelter of a thousand childhood sum- mers in the Calabrian South. *Looking at the chemical sky, all purple blue and oranges.* I follow the apparition and circle around the western contours of the bridge in vain, the noise of traffic now intensifies with voices of muffled despair at street corners positively Roman and Neapolitan. The Italian Museum is closed for holiday, frozen to a day in 1977, a faded photo of Giorgio "Long John" Chinaglia, striker with Lazio and later New York Cosmos, "he lit up the Cosmos" between birth in Carrara, 1947 and inescapable death in Naples, Florida, 2012. His photo next to Pope Francis who can't do no wrong even though he didn't receive the Dalai Lama for fear of upsetting the Chinese. Other faded photos adorn the window, unknown restaurateurs with 1970s sideburns and unfeasible haircuts. Outside the restaurant next door, two men with trimmed white beards suck on a cigar and a large woman eats her very early lunch gesticulating managerially to a waiter in mute obeisance. Here I am, I made it at last, walking on my coveted target, the Bridge, an infernal clatter of iron and metal on bouncy concrete, wobbly as hell, until desert-dizzy and dehydrated with pilgrim ambition I wobble as the bridge trembles under my feet. This city is too vast too much too beautiful, its ragged hellish heart now beautified and tenderized until I see her in the distance, is it real, is it her, the Statue? Lightheaded and thirsty I gaze at the skyscrapers like my paternal grandfather Santo, like any peasant from another era, any terrone like me who landing here by mistake and so I think of Delmore Schwartz who everyone called Delmore, born in Brooklyn to Jewish immigrants from Romania and forever pivoting around the unsteadiness of existential displacement. Delmore, the Brooklyn Rimbaud, protagonist of Bellow's *Humboldt's Gift*, Delmore writer at twenty-four of the great collection of short stories *In Dreams Begin Responsibilities* describing the generational divide between migrant parents and their half-assimilated, half-modernist progeny, writer of great poetry who never made it to the court of vatic snobs but who stood his ground with Ezra Pound politely but fiercely questioning the latter's anti-semitism. And who better than Delmore could write of the tenderfoot's disarticulation, the fury to clutch life by the collar, to speak, to speak and be heard? Don't I know it, dear readers, even among you decent upright citizens and psychologists; *vox clamantis in deserto* and so forth. We are Shakespearean, we are strangers. Who better than Delmore, with the same retelling of birth, migration, new disappointment, damaged hopes, ordinary lives turned into the stone of history, Delmore who wanted to drape the world in radiance but didn't have enough fabric and died instead aged 52 in 1966 in a hotel room just off Times Square of alcohol, tranquillizers, and amphetamines, a year longer than Shakespeare. Not for him the kindly convalescent death afforded by Hölderlin, living in the family of a devoted carpenter, for Delmore was a son of the city streets. Keep thinking all the time, O New York boy! The life of an exile is contrapuntal, forged in precariousness and exhilaration, exhilarating because precarious, as described in the best existentialist texts before the logocentric takeover turned it into another set of consoling homilies for the befuddled and the gold-diggers. "You look like a coal miner to me", the US policeman tells me at the border. I take it as a compliment. He is in a chatty mood and take his time despite the enormous queue behind me. "I'm more left-wing than Bernie Sanders" he insists. He is informal, creepily affectionate as he interrogates me. Learning that I'm a psychologist he produces from his bag a book by one Michael Parenti. The one-way conversation goes on for a while until he finally brands my passport, another livestock alien happy to access milk & honey and be dazed and confused by the bright lights.

The PC Conference is on different floors of the Graduate Center, right opposite the Empire State Building. I hear Margaret Warner say that therapists are anthropologists in a foreign country, learning a new language rather than scientists getting things straight. She did some pioneering work and proved that it is possible to work with highly distressed clients who are labelled as schizophrenics from a person-centred perspective. I daydream as to whether the therapist as anthropologist could be extended to therapist as flaneur/flaneuse, for nothing more reminds me of psyche's uncharted territory as a city, where meaningful encounters are love at last sight. I scribble this in a crowded London train a week later, and this could be anywhere, any city in the wide world, a man like Yours Truly seated with pen and paper, his doodles the only proof of having been here at all. He could be anywhere, his presumed presence vanishing in the act, yesterday an NYC's subway, today the travelling tearooms of a London Overground train, the clipped voices of exultant Brexiters on a late summer day.

At the corner of Fifth Avenue and 34th Street, I'm sitting on the pavement with J.W., deep in heartmind talk and suddenly we notice a tiny lively sparrow in the vast city. Uncle Lou's first solo album had a sparrow on its cover, a tiny sparrow just out of its egg, skyscrapers in the background. *It was very nice, oh honey it was paradise.* Echoes of Alhambra and Alicante, a fated journey of separation in my youth without which dear reader I wouldn't be who I am and so forth. And tell me, btw, how lost can you get? Now as an older gent I get lost using a whole array of methodologies and epistemologies: the ruin of the subject is how Georges Bataille called the existentialist project. And for Levinas, the latter was all about looking at the world in the absence of a subject – all exteriority, including *moi même.* Any excuse will do, for thou shall get burned either way. For instance, NYC: the city as the id, as a transcendental (not transcendent) river, entirely immanent and forever impossible, inevitable, *plastic* inevitable that is. She only had to look and one was enslaved. Or: the city provokes deep identification and transubstantiation of the self: Joyce's Dublin, Reed's New York, Pasolini's Rome, Rodenbach's Bruges, Pamuk's Istanbul, Woolf's London, Bellow's Chicago. Who needs God when you can have a metropolis? One of Schwartz's students at his last post at Syracuse University was one Lou Reed who wrote a song to him, *my friend and teacher occupies the spare room, he's dead, peace at last, the wondering Jew.* Delmore who joked that Lou was Stephen Daedalus and he Leopold Bloom. Delmore who looked like Pasternak who looked like an Arab and his horse. His great short stories, his great poetry, and greatest of all his essays on the masters – Hart Crane, Wallace Stevens, Auden – great because written breezily, without vatic self-consciousness.

Yet the sense of time persists and with it all those futile strategies reaching to an ever-present future, or the involuntary memory of a never buried past. *Watch out, the world's behind you.* Asleep and innocent, Lexington – the bagel shop, the Chinese cafe, the hyper-trendy Japanese noodle bar, the convenience store. Then, of course, the conference: magnificent presentation by Claudio Rud on Spinoza. Claudio is a philosopher-doctor-poet from Buenos Aires. He speaks of immanence, the great conspicuous uninvited guest of the entire psychotherapy circus. We are relation from the start, he says, and it is the relation that creates its own subject. Even "presence", touted as a semi-numinous attribute of the divinely-attuned shrink, is a result of the in-between. *Islands join hands beneath heaven's sea.* When I finally find a place to change some money, the affable guy at the counter misunderstands what I'm saying and says, "Welcome back!". I had babbled something in response to his question, saying "Have been away from Italy for nearly thirty years" but he thought New York was a long-lost home I had just come back to. And he was right in a way, and this nearly brings me to tears and makes me overlook the hefty sum of eighteen dollars commission I end up paying for my little transaction. Of course, I'm back, here where bold granddad Santo came alone with his cardboard suitcase, Santo whose bones have gone lost from a remote cemetery in Aspromonte during refurbishment. I am overjoyed and baffled that both my workshop (on Zen and therapy) and talk (on the actualizing tendency and feral philosophy) have been enthusiastically received. I've become too accustomed perhaps over the years to seeing myself at the margins, saying stuff things no one gets or gets offended by or gushes over with an affection that confuses me. Next day on the bench right next to Fifth Avenue's raging traffic, a heartful mind-to-mind conversation with Claudio, his smoky voice and knowing smile, both of us recognizing each other as twice heretics and in that sense only reluctantly deserving the epithet of "philosophers". We pay our muffled homage to Spinoza and Derrida amidst the wailing sirens and the car exhausts, both exiled from smaller insular communities of exiles. Claudio translates Rogers' "formative" tendency (an evolutionary teleological surrogate of God's benevolent presence) as *transformative* tendency. The city like the *id*: did you catch my earlier drift, dear reader? If that is too impersonal for you, if you think it's not relational enough, not Bowlbyan, Buberian, dialogical enough, then let me tell you of the city-deity in personalized form. On the last night before my forty winks, I bid New York farewell in the naked bed, in Plato's cave. I imagined her as a beauty from Mittel-Europa who made it here from Lausanne, Turin, Krakow or God-knows where. Her red dress falls on the bedroom floor high above streets that never sleep. In the dim hours I stumble awake grateful for my little death and brief disappearance and in the street I greet the drizzle on my cheeks with a peasant grin.

Chapter 15

Help Me Become Free of You

This is not a case study, at least not in the conventional sense. I will take the liberty to bypass background history, the "client's presenting issues" as well as an account of the stops-and-starts of our attempts at establishing what is normally called a "therapeutic relationship". All the same, this *is* an account of a therapeutic relationship, even though it is open to question whether it is Mehran alone (the client, condemned in textbooks to be "incongruent" or "inauthentic") who gained from the encounter, or whether I too (the therapist, said to be anointed with congruence and authenticity) benefited from the encounter.

Well, yes, this is an account of a therapeutic relationship of sorts. It remains to be seen whether the relating in question is simply *relating*, that is, an indeterminate dance of togetherness, an attempt to communicate across the divide – of self and other, of me and you or, if you choose the sappier lingo in vogue, of I and Thou. Simply relating means that the *ship* of relation*ship* – the vessel, the sturdy boat gliding soberly on uncharted rivers – the rivers of Mehran's experience and my own – is a more fluid proposition. In simple relating, the vessel ploughs a more erratic course, and even when assailed by storms it retains an unquenchable thirst to experience the elements in their fullness and boundlessness.

I remember being taken aback by Mehran's youthful fervour, his fierce intelligence, his confidence, by Mehran's presence and ease with the world. He had to learn the ways of the world early in life, for he lost both parents to cancer in brief succession, within months – first his mother, then his father. Attachment issues, some will say. Of course. Learning to trust a world that after that terrible loss could no

DOI: 10.4324/9781003280262-16

longer be trusted. Then, unreliable foster care, exposure to meanness and neglect. But there is another side to the attachment system, overlooked in attachment theory, and I think Mehran's story proves it. It is called line of flight. It is called becoming-orphan, a state of isolation and abandonment cut away from supporting bonds. My contention is that that painful state of abandonment in a wilderness of uncertainty and loneliness is also an opportunity for creating anew a web of sustainability and love.

We have been meeting for nearly ten years, Mehran and I, on and off, with some interruptions, breaks, and unclear endings with the door left ajar. We met in my apartment first, then online when Covid took over the world, and finally in a rented room in a leafy part of town. Through the changes – of gear, tonalities, and priorities – Mehran and I also changed. And in that relating without a ship, without vessel, without the sanitized frame where all a therapist does is ticking boxes all the way to retirement, a fundamental change took place in him and in me – both changes unwarranted, unexpected and impossible to convey. Which is precisely why I want to try to convey them to you here.

There have been many versions of us in the process. There have been many shifting moments. But there is one that stands out. Mehran re-marked on it months later. I am not talking about an epiphany or a numinous "depth" in relating. There was no gnostic revelation or a felt sense authenticating the realness of the experience. The shift was ordinary. To be sure, there had been other signposts announcing a change of rhythm. I might tell you about them later. But the one I want to recount took place three years ago. It happened after a break of a couple of months in our meetings. The break itself had been the cul-mination of a rather long period during which Mehran had expressed dissatisfaction with what he called my relentless positivity, my obsti-nacy in wanting to look at the bright side of his experience, my per-sistent attitude of encouragement and appreciation. I had been inept at both naming and holding the unbearable grief simmering just under the surface of his speech. I had *believed* the myriad ways in which Mehran had so successfully coped with grief.

At a young age he had learned the ways of the world – how to be successful in any endeavour he would care to turn his attention to – studying literature at university, managing a pop band, making art, the latter an endeavour where he began to make a mark. I had believed his masks. That was because I've always understood the making of a mask as an art form, a way not merely to cope but to engage creatively with life's challenges. I told him as much, putting my view on the table for discussion. I also owned my scepticism of the so-called "real self" – be it organismic, authentic and whatnot. Mehran broadly agreed with me but also wanted me to know of the jagged ways grief stole on him. I might be sitting at my desk, he'd say, having allocated that particular time for work, and all of a sudden I'd feel overwhelmed by anxiety and incapable of getting anything done. Diffuse at first – silent, uncanny – anxiety would slowly turn into a muted scream, Munch's scream echoing still one hundred and twenty-nine years later, a howling grief that visited me with a blind wish to dwell in my heart and soul forever.

This is real enough, I said. And there are other ways, he went on. Tears come out of the blue, provoked by trivial disappointments; or disproportionate tears of disenchantment for a lover withdrawing their love without warning, the realization that in matters of the heart there is no room for stipulation, only mercy. True, neither of us paid heed to the notion that the overwhelmed self, the vessel battered by life's storms, the grieving howling desperate self is the "real" self. No. That's just another aspect, another artful mask through which the living organism does its wondrous thing, through which the living body sings its song.

It was at this point of our conversation that I felt the urge to spell out something which strangely became clear to me as I started saying it. You know Mehran, I said, my intention here is that you become free of me. Also, I have no investment –emotional or otherwise – in your going this way or that. Later on, he remarked that my statement stopped him in his tracks. To come back to me and say "help me become free of you" meant that he could trust the work and the direction of our conversations.

That night I dreamt that Mehran and I were walking through the streets and alleys of a ghost town. He tells me about gigs he went to – one in particular he had been too the previous day. "It's ages since I've been to a gig" I say. There is warmth and affection between us, and in the dream the asymmetrical boundaries between client and therapist have dissolved. He asks me, Why did you ring me? Did you call me as a friend? I try to answer but I can't speak.

Two and a half years ago, after a break of a few months, we resumed our weekly meeting. This time we could meet in person. Covid had begun to be managed somewhat and after months of near solitary confinement it was exhilarating. I was so happy to resume face-to-face work. Leaving my rented flat at 7.10 in the morning, walking some 40 minutes from Hampstead to Primrose Hill, allowing impressions, thoughts and feelings traversing me freely in the luminous cool late-summer air. Mehran told me he had wanted to start again because so many things had changed. A new, painful relationship with someone he looked up to, someone who withheld her love exposing his real fear of abandonment. He also said that the impetus for wanting to resume was remembering that statement of mine, "I want you to become free of me". It untied a knot, he said, a transferential entanglement. By the way, he added, do you know why Socrates ended up in trouble and was sentenced to death by the Athenian tribunal? It was because he did not understand transference. He grinned; after a pause we both laughed.

Now, years later, that pithy remark about Socrates makes me shudder, for I know in obscure ways that what exacerbated my health crisis to come was a conflict that emerged from a fatal misreading of transference. Weeks went by, then months. In April, I was rushed to hospital with what the doctor called "acute kidney injury". Doctors don't call it kidney failure anymore, which was the old name for it, but injury. Later someone asked, Did you *fall* on your kidneys that they got injured? Failure is taboo, and thinking that to fail is integral to human experience ("fail again, fail better" and so forth) is incomprehensible to our world of ever-expansive growth – be it the growth of the economy, of broccoli, or of the eerily named post-traumatic growth. The urgency of the situation didn't allow me to send individual messages to clients or supervisees to explain to each of them that I'd be out of action for a while. I notified my executor instead who sent a brief collective email to them. Long story short. During my week in hospital, they found cancer and after the shock and grief and sadness and bewilderment and after hours spent after hospital supper looking at the beautiful sky at dusk from the bed and asking pointless questions to the heavens and hearing common-sense answers

("Why me, God?" – "Why not, Manu!"), I resumed some clinical work after a few weeks. Incidentally, when I notified the professional body I belong to of my situation I was told that in order to protect the public I should think twice before seeing clients while on cancer medication.

When I meet Mehran again, he tells me how anxious he has been for me; he tells me through the tears how lost he felt. And how much love he feels for me. He asks me details about the illness. I tell him. He lost mother and father at a tender age. His father died not long after his mother had passed away. He was given a death sentence and died shortly after his diagnosis. He died of the very same illness that befell me. That day Mehran and I cried together. Tears of sorrow. Tears of joy. For Spinoza every emotion and feeling, if allowed to travel, to do its thing, if allowed to move us and move through us, will lead us to joy. Our tears were tears of joy. They made us free for that brief moment.

Mehran had moved way past being dependent on me (if he had ever been) and on therapy. My own tears of joy liberated me from the constriction of wearing a garment. It did not make my garment invisible *á la* Carl Rogers. It made it non-existent. At that time – mid-May this year – I was still in the dark about my prognosis. This meant I felt all the more vulnerable hence more open. Which meant also that Sorrow was in the room. And Fear. And Tenderness. Then Joy moved in, a bridge between two islands, two monads stuck in their boundaried positions. Please do not misunderstand me. Boundaries are vital. But what are they *for*? There is a world of difference between fashioning a container <u>for</u> (allowing, inviting, hosting emergent phenomena), and a container <u>of</u> (limiting and incarcerating life through an ideology, be it psychoanalytic or person-centred). Mehran's autonomy and my own vulnerability made possible this important shift.

We are affected by the real and tangible presence of the dead – those who came before us, our loved ones who died, our friends and colleagues who are no longer with us. I am thinking of two original contributors to the PCA, Peter Schmid who passed away in September 2020 and Pete Sanders who died in February 2022. In Mehran's case, it refers to the very real presence in his bodymind of his father and mother – present, alive, affecting, and moving within him and to whom he dedicated his remarkable artwork.

Mehran made a beautiful work of art dedicated to his parents. And he did much more than that. His parents move within him, traversed his bodymind and spoke through him. For my part, his tears of sorrow and joy in learning of my own mortality greatly enlivened and enriched my own experience. Our work took flight. And for that I am grateful.

Chapter 16

I is Another

In a letter to his friend and former teacher Georges Izambard, written from his hometown of Charleville and dated 13 May 1871, a seventeen-year-old Arthur Rimbaud stated:

> I want to be a poet, and I am working to make myself a *seer:* you won't understand this at all, and I hardly know how to explain it to you. The point is, to arrive at the unknown by a disordering of *all the senses*. The sufferings are enormous, but one has to be strong, to be *born* a poet, and I have discovered I *am* a poet. It is not my fault at all. It is a mistake to say: I think. One ought to say: I am thought ...

He went on to say:

> I is another. So much the worse for the wood if it finds itself a violin.[1]

As a young man, I wrote a poem for Pier Paolo Pasolini, titled "Death of a Poet", after he was murdered on November 2nd, 1975. I blue-tacked the poem on the wall of my room in my family home with a tiny photo of the film-maker, poet, and novelist cut out from a newspaper. The poem was still there when comrades and friends came to visit me the day after my mother's death. How strange that on the night of that day in March when she died, we all went to sleep. Her body lying inside the open coffin in the guest room, a room seldom used or lived in, the one with the untouched posh cutlery and

DOI: 10.4324/9781003280262-17

tea service on display. *Tu eri la vita e le cose. È buio il mattino che passa senza la luce dei tuoi occhi.* You were life, and the myriad things. Dark is the morning that goes by without the light of your eyes. Hélène Cixous wrote:

> I never ask myself 'who am I?' I ask myself 'Who *are* I? ... Who can say who I are, how many I are, which is the most I of my Is? Of course, we each have a solid social identity, ... At the same time, we are all the ages, those we have been, those we will be, those we will not be, we journey through ourselves ... as the child who goes snivelling to school and as the broken old man ... Without counting all the combinations with others, our exchanges between languages, between sexes – our exchanges which change us, tint us with others.[2]

How foreign an Italian voice sounds to me at first when travelling on a bus, how unintelligible and distant. With a sense of familiarity slowly emerging, the shackles of language and grammar also arise, the movable Oedipal cage, *mamma, papá,* the price of things, of rents and mortgages spelled out in pound sterling. The different layers accidentally uncovered, becoming-orphan, or having lost for ever the so-called secure base. A feeling of desolation sitting at St Pancras station munching on a sandwich, watching the passers-by. The feeling of elation of being free to feel the joy and sadness of not-belonging. Lost companions in last night's dream, comrades and fellow travellers gone for good and for ever lost. The evening bus gliding by like a ghost ship in the melancholy early darkness of a Friday night before Halloween.

Or for instance that fascination in my early twenties with transvestite and transsexuals. Was that fascination a form of erotic emotional tourism? I loved two of them in their bodies and their remoteness. Walking down the hill like an alley cat, the streets below bending, widening, tightening; a shuffling of shadows as I reach the lights of the city, past the railway. In a ghostly shop window at night, I is a pale ghost; I wants to forestall the night; I craves victory against a dusty mirror. Down towards the city, warm air and sounds, then a room, a mouth, love sliding silently by on the ceiling.

Much later I found a correlation in Jean Genet who described trans as angels. Was my fascination *mere* fascination? Did I love in their gestures and dramatic femininity my own deeply buried homosexual longings? Doesn't the choice of one sexual orientation over another always imply the loss of another, a loss that is never mourned because it has not merely been repressed but efficiently foreclosed? One could ask: "What would need to occur in psychotherapy culture for an ethos to emerge that encourages clients/patients to mourn the loss of their suppressed gender identities?"

From Freud, we learn that unresolved mourning brings on melancholia. And what is melancholia if not being in love with dead objects? Having erased my own homosexual self, I remained in love with dead objects, the verse of a famous tune *Walk on the Wild Side*, on my mobile's ringtone. Is this why my phone is constantly on mute?

*

Jean Genet's subversive and poetic writings have often been framed and even canonized within the confines of gay experience and literature: I am thinking of Edmund White's astonishing biography[3] and of Sartre's masterly doorstopper *Saint Genet*.[4] Recent re-interpretations of Genet's work[5] justifiably claim a place for him within trans culture and transgender studies scholarship, asserting the value of smuggling as a methodology of embodied critique giving precedence to lines of flight over seemingly compact power structures, and giving meaning through elaborate tangles of connectivity.[6] Academia is traditionally allergic to the very word "smuggling", let alone the practice, as I have learned when submitting papers to psychology journals. But smuggling is a necessary act. It stems from the understanding that the knowledge inherited by the tradition does not contain the complexities of living nor does it provide a framework for practices of freedom. Irit Rogoff explains:

> The term 'smuggling' ... extends far beyond a series of adventurous gambits. It reflects the search for a practice that goes beyond conjunctives such as those that bring together 'art and politics' or 'theory and practice' or 'analysis and action'. In such a practice we aspire to experience the relations between the two as a form of

embodiment which cannot be separated into their independent components.[7]

Smuggling is necessary if we are to champion radical, subversive notions and practices within the stultified environs of neoliberal psychology and psychotherapy training. Genet's is a fitting example and guide, given that some of his early writing in prison was created against prison rules, and later smuggled out for publication. Smuggling allows emancipatory practices and knowledge to slide through tightly built borders and boundaries and respond to the needs of the present. In particular, it may potentially present an adequate and fierce response to the way hatred and prejudice has travelled and continues to travel through the decades: from misogyny to homophobia to transphobia.

*

We were revolutionaries with a difference in our 20s. From feminism we'd learned the painful limitations of the macho man model. From Pasolini – novelist, filmmaker, poet, essayist – we learned the sexual tenderness and transgression, the virgin terrain to be explored. And so, we slept in the same bed, me and she and he and when she fell asleep after making love, me and him exchanged tender kisses and fondled each other, the melancholy yellow streetlight weaving warm patterns on the wall and on the poster of Pier Paolo Pasolini, his fierce compassion sending shivers through the best hearts and minds of my generation. Is I a murderer who has killed off homosexual desire?

Hey Ninetto, do you remember that dream we had so many times?

This time you are mistaken/I am a farmer in the city/dark brown houses against the sky/every night I must wonder why.[8]

Helene Cixous writes:

I ask of writing what I ask of desire: that I have no relation to the logic which puts desire on the side of possession, of acquisition, even of that consumption-consummation which, when pushed to its limits ... links (false) consciousness with death.[9]

I guess I am talking of bisexuality. But what *is* bisexuality? Cixous distinguished two kinds:

1   Bisexuality as a fantasy of a complete being, which replaces the fear of castration and veils sexual difference insofar as this is perceived as the mark of a mystical separation ...
2   Bisexuality [as] the location within oneself of the presence of both sexes ... the non-exclusion of difference ... a bisexuality [where] every subject who is not shut up inside the spurious Phallocentric Performing Theatre, sets up his or her erotic universe.[10]

What do I fear as a man – whenever I identify as a man? Do I fear being possessed? For a masculine imaginary, being possessed is undesirable because it is associated with stereotypical feminine passivity. For a man, particularly a heterosexual man such as myself, being possessed may be an essential experience. It may be crucial to be penetrated, entered, to experience a so-called passivity without which he is a foolish sad clown standing erect like his penis in a field under the pouring rain. And equally crucial for a human is the experience of sexuality divorced from the evolution imperative. Leo Bersani and Adam Phillips express something similar in relation to barebacking. The latter unveils for them one truth about sexuality; it no longer hides from ourselves the fact that we are going nowhere, that we are going in the direction of death and annihilation, whether or not we have children. It reveals to us that "the joke of evolution is that it is a teleology devoid of telos. In a direct, immediate way, "barebacking shows us that sex is a dead end".[11] Reproductive sexuality also shows us that by having children "we are making more deaths" and it is this very knowledge, whether we know it or not, "that makes human sexuality possible".[12]

Being possessed may hint at the fact that there is something else to human relations than "the collusion of ego-identities".[13]

In short: Why do we find it so hard to embrace the ecstasy inherent to the self's loss of power?

*

I is a peasant boy, a terrone *for the poorest region of la Bella Italia. Wikipedia describes* terrone *(plural terroni, feminine terrona) as an*

Italian term to designate, in an often-pejorative manner, people who dwell in Southern Italy or are of Southern Italian descent. The term comes from an agent noun formed from the word terra (Italian for 'land').

I is a terrone even though my dad pulled himself up from the low ranks through hard study and Franciscan discipline. I is a flamethrower and I is pretty certain none among you civilized readers has known the ecstasy of smashing up a venue frequented by fascists nor the joy of seeing an empty police van go up in flames in response to police brutality.

I walks through the snow and leaves no footprints and how to tell others the next day? Will they understand? How could they possibly understand?

I is a whole world that will be buried and forgotten when this body will flounder and perish, when this bodying will be free and ready for sister death and lover death. Death will come and will have your eyes, this death escorting us from morning til dusk like an old regret, an absurd vice.

*

I is a rock musician part-exchanging guitars after selling my black Gibson Les Paul and going on to the Jazzmaster and to a semi-acoustic. I forms a band called Daedalo, after the Italian word for labyrinth, after Daedalus father of Icarus, for who says that you must live fast and die young and foolishly burn your manmade wings of wax flying too close to the sun when you can live fast and die old like Daedalus architect father of Icarus. But also, Stephen Dedalus in Joyce's' Ulysses.

*

I plays with death aged 23, trying heroin three times and at night sitting outside a semi-abandoned country workhouse playing for my friends the Velvet Underground's song Heroin. And I feel just like Jesus' son. I tries smack three times, the first time is heaven – lemon drop, vulva, joy of the morning air every gesture exults burned by the proximity of death; the second time is purgatory – waiting for a blissful state that never comes; the third and last time it's hell, and sickness and the vertigo of nothingness.

I veers towards more acceptable substances, shortcuts to false awa-kenings and nowadays San Pellegrino sparkling water and the odd glass of Malbec.

*

I trains as a therapist and learns the lingo and manners of the white English middle-class with its values of boundaries and property. I learns to sing Property, all my thoughts have turn to property. Oh I believe in property, *to the tune of the Beatles' Yesterday.*

What is 'difference'? is it the so-called championing of bland diversity we find in the dominant ideology of our time, neoliberalism, or is it about different colours made of tears?

Strands of humanistic and existential psychology have historically been inclined to universalise subjective identity. But can subjective identity become a prison, particularly when it sings along to the blinkered tunes of nationalism? Or when it fails to be open to societal and political challenges? In the public arena, this has resulted in the championing of identity politics at the expense of soulful solidarity. Writing about racial discrimination, the investigative journalist Asad Haider, defines identity politics as the offset of movements against racial oppression, reflecting the substitution of mass movements with a bland multiculturalism. What once constituted a unitary front against the commodification and exploitation of human life in the name of profit for the few has now splintered into subgroups that cannot see past their own experience. While it was once natural for a marginalised group to feel solidarity with another equally margin-alised group, thus creating a united front of women, gays, blacks, the poor and the disenfranchised, it is now customary to think and breathe within the confines of one's own group. To be a subject has come to mean to be subjugated to an existing order that defines my identity before I can begin to define myself. Identity is only partly what I choose. For the most part, it is assigned to and imposed on me by the Powers. What is difference? Less the difference of consumer choice than "different colours made of tears

*

I is a mystic child in India, writing devotional songs in the early 1980s and whirling like a dervish and sitting in silent contemplation and

having lots of sex and crying a lot and laughing and realizing after 5 years of studying existential philosophy that I have a body, pardon me, that I am a body.

*

I finds zen, realizing with a shock in 1996 in a barn in Suffolk that this ancient tradition is alive and kicking and not reducible to cute little quotes for middle class mindfulness yogis and yoginis but has a beating heart and the jaws of a tiger who is going to eat you alive before you eat your last strawberry and draw your last breath of thanks for this life.

*

I is married at 24 and separated at 27 and from women I learned and still learns an awful lot and from men too and whoever you think you are don't apologize darling please and don't wait for the state and the government to rubber stamp your difference. It is better methinks to practice the freedom you talk about. It's not just me saying this but Michel Foucault in person: the practice of freedom. Foucault sees the ethic of the concern for the self as a practice of freedom. Even though the individual is unable to entirely exit power relations, which produce her own self, she can take part in the self-making. In that sense, freedom can be understood as participation in the process of defining oneself and the meaning of freedom.

*

I is a dancer at heart, trapped within this face, trapped in a zoom screen pretending to give a talk to an audience of algorithmic ghosts, all of us not dancing but trapped within the confines of a living room all of us lonely and putting the kettle on after the end of the conference.

*

An enemy of difference is *logocentrism*. What is logocentrism? On a basic level, logocentrism refers to the widespread belief that language translates reality faithfully and effectively. This is because the dominant view considers *logos* – variously translated as discourse, speech, the principle of reason, and judgement – to be a superior way of building a theory of knowledge. But this does not take into account the multiplicities of language and speech.

Logocentrism is almost inevitable ... This is partly because it is inextricably linked to what many of us take as indisputable: a metaphysical notion of presence and the principle of self-identity. Conversely, differentialism questions the notion that I am I and that whatever is, is. Another enemy of difference is "*Being*" with a capital "B". Genuine appreciation of difference implies an active forgetting of "Being" in the name of the concrete "being" sitting opposite in the therapy room. Another enemy of difference is hermeneutics, the illusion that any particular "being" or situation or event is legible, interpretable, translatable. What is forgotten in this process is that any process of translation implies repression and the positing of an a-priori: for instance, *habitus* in Husserl[14] and *Vor-struktur* in Heidegger.[15]

*

I is tolerated by the existential therapy world, by the person-centred world, by the world of psychotherapy in general, because I refuses to wear the T-shirt with the face of Rogers or Heidegger printed on it. Also, because I doesn't buy this third-rate ideology that we are free individuals given that everything turns into pound sterling or euros or dollars given that our so-called existential freedom is the freedom to be a consumer.

*

In relation to difference and embodiment, Simone de Beauvoir had some useful and still very interesting things to say from within the existential tradition. But her approach to the phenomenology of the body is far less reliant on either Sartre or Heidegger as it is commonly believed but more congruently aligned with the work of Husserl and Merleau-Ponty.[16] And when it comes to discussing women's experience, she is less interested in clarifying their subordinate position in a male world or in championing their rights than in the reality called *woman*. Her link with Husserl is straightforward. Husserl gives a set of phenomenological problems for future study: he discusses death and birth, unconsciousness, historicity, and social life. And then, moving on to what he calls the problem of the sexes, he states that the phenomenologist's project is to investigate the meaning of these phenomena, their formation as different types of realities and objectives, i.e., entities, events, facts, etc. Questions about death are not, for instance, What is death? How does it happen? Sara Heinämaa explains:

> How does it happen that we experience death as an occurrence (*Vorkommnis*)? Similarly, we can ask, why is the sexual relation experienced as a difference and opposition? Is this necessary? Can the experience have some other structure?[17]

It is within the above frame that De Beauvoir poses her questions and in so doing progresses phenomenological enquiry along *differential* rather than universalistic and essentialist lines. This becomes very clear when she gives Levinas, the champion of otherness, a run for his money. Levinas had suggested that otherness reaches its full expression in the feminine which he describes as being on the same level as consciousness but with an opposite meaning.[18] De Beauvoir's objection is that woman too is a consciousness for herself. She attacks his analysis as deliberately taking a man's point of view, disregarding mutuality and the fact that feminine and masculine bodies are variations of embodiment reinventing in their unique ways the ambiguity of human existence.

> To tell the truth, man, like woman, is flesh, and therefore a passivity – and she like him in the midst of her carnal fever, is a consenting, a voluntary gift, an activity; they live in their different ways the strange ambiguity of existence made body.[19]

Seen in this way, femininity is a musical theme, Sara Heinämaa remarks. Undetermined by earlier experiences, it lives and becomes anew every step of the way.

Hélène Cixous writes:

> Sometimes one has to go very far. Sometimes the right distance is extreme remoteness. Sometimes it is in extreme proximity that it breathes.[20]

So: Who *are* I? *Je est un autre*. I is someone else. I is another.

Notes

1 Arthur Rimbaud, 'Letters and Other Documents', in *Collected Poems*. Tr. Oliver Bernard. London: Penguin, 1962, p5.
2 Hélène Cixous, *The Hélène Cixous Reader*. Edited by Susan Sellers. New York: Routledge, 1994, pp. xvii-xviii.
3 Edmund White, *Genet*. London: Chatto & Windus, 1993.
4 Jean-Paul Sartre, *Saint Genet* New York: George Braziller, 1963.
5 A. Templeton, 'Trans smuggling in Jean Genet's Our lady of the flowers'. *Gender Studies*, Volume 20, Issue 4, Nov 2017, pp399–414.
6 Irit Rogoff, *'Smuggling'* – *An embodied criticality*. https://xenopraxis.net/readings/rogoff_smuggling.pdf, 2006, Retrieved 3 November 2021.
7 Ibid, p1.
8 Scott Walker, 'Farmer in the City'. *Tilt*, Fontana Records, 1995.
9 *The Hélène Cixous Reader*, op.cit., p27.
10 Ibid, p41
11 Leo Bersani and Adam Phillips, *Intimacies*. Chicago, ILL: University of Chicago Press, 2008, p113.
12 Ibid, p114.
13 Ibid, p117.
14 Edmund Husserl, *The Crisis of European Sciences and Transcendental Phenomenology: An Introduction to Phenomenological Philosophy*. Evanston, ILL: Northwestern University Press, 1970, pp66–67.
15 Martin Heidegger, *Being and Time*. Trans. by John Macquarrie and Edward Robinson. Oxford: Blackwell, 1962.
16 Sara Heinämaa, 'Simone de Beauvoir's Phenomenology of Sexual Difference', *Hypatia*, 14, (4) 1999, pp114–132, London: Wiley
17 Ibid, p127.
18 Emmanuel Levinas, *Time and the Other*. Pittsburgh, PA: Duquesne University Press, 1987.
19 Simone De Beauvoir, *The Second Sex*. London: Vintage, 1997.
20 Hélène Cixous, *Writing Differences: Readings form the Seminars of Hélène Cixous*. Edited by Susan Sellers. Milton Keynes: Open University Press, 1988, p35.

Chapter 17

The Skin is Faster than the Word

Affect is the pre-verbal, impersonal flow of life's intensity and immediacy traversing living organisms. Hard to assimilate, it is habitually translated within subjective human experience as sadness, desire, joy, fear, ecstasy, anxiety, and so on. It is rendered as emotion, feeling, and sensation. This diverse subjective content is nonetheless only a form of socio-linguistic adjustment driven by the essentially reactive work of consciousness. In our societies of control, the inherent autonomy of affect is forcibly and reactively directed towards adaptation and compliance and driven away from actualization.

The compulsion to measure and control affect is not new – nor is, thankfully, the desire through history to be free from this compulsion's stultifying grip. From Plato to Husserl, from Artaud to Lyotard great examples abound of resistance, passion, and intelligence which partly inspire these musings.

Obsessive Measurement Disorder

Not everything that counts can be counted, so goes a saying attributed to Albert Einstein, not everything that can be counted counts. Affect is routinely quantified, measured, and regulated; it is pathologized through a widespread form of institutionally endorsed pathology, a peculiar condition for which Andrew Natsios, once administrator of the US Agency for International Development (USAID), coined a fitting term: *Obsessive Measurement Disorder.*[1] OMD has effectively invaded not only government policies but also the humanities, including therapy's own potential space, jeopardizing in the process the

DOI: 10.4324/9781003280262-18

increasingly rare chances for individualization, blunting the emergence of autonomous thought, bringing about a veritable *atrophy of the noetic*, as well as aborting the articulation of an organismic idiom independent of the corporate technostructure within whose precincts and shopping arcades most therapy now operates.

In his 1906 novel *Kusamakura*, ("Grass Pillow") Natsume Sōseki[2] tells of a nameless thirty-year-old painter/poet who retreats to the mountains at a remote, almost deserted hotel. He becomes intrigued by the mysterious hostess, O-Nami. She reminds him of John Millais' painting Ophelia. Strangely, when first reading about O-Nami, I thought of Medea, the tragic heroine whose pronouncements obliquely motivate these reflections. Looking for subjects to paint, the artist makes only a few sketches. He writes poetry and short prose pieces instead, quoting a variety of painters, poets, and novelists. At some point, he feels compelled to explain why he has no desire to go back to Tokyo, stating that if you live in Tokyo too long, they'll start counting your farts.

Sōseki was voicing his dislike for the overbearing culture of Japan in the Meiji era (1868–1912), and there certainly are echoes of the above in our current climate dominated, some would argue, by *the McNamara* (or *quantitative*) *fallacy*, named after Robert McNamara, the US secretary of Defence from 1961 to 1968. It involves making a decision based solely on quantitative observations (or metrics) and ignoring others. The reason given is often that non-quantitative observations cannot be proven. This sort of complaint is often heard from trainees who have been told that neither empathy nor authenticity nor the unconscious exists because they can't be measured. Social scientist Daniel Yankelovich summarized the stages of this major pitfall:

> The first step is to measure whatever can be easily measured. This is OK as far as it goes. The second step is to disregard that which can't be easily measured or to give it an arbitrary quantitative value. This is artificial and misleading. The third step is to presume that what can't be measured easily really isn't important. This is blindness. The fourth step is to say that what can't be easily measured really doesn't exist. This is suicide.[3]

Bodily Ontology

Affect is shunned, feared, and neglected. What is perceived as excessive affect is restricted and dealt with by professionals.[4] A comprehensive herd of mental hygiene practitioners is busy instructing the public on how to *regulate* affect. Within a relatively short time, *affect-regulation* has become the unanimously accepted goal of the mental health industry, now providing a neurons-firing, state-of-the-art, multi-coloured brand-new edition of Attachment Theory for the geek generation.[5] On the whole, the public appears to give in to the mental hygienists' often unsolicited guidance, possibly because the idea of learning from the domain of affect sets off a preternatural fear of life – of its raw intensity and immediacy – activating a bigoted reading of life as unstructured and chaotic, as unintelligent and in constant need of genteel edification. The price paid for acquiescing to this set of wearisome and dim-witted manoeuvres is high: we forfeit transformation. Unlike genteel "personality change", *transformation is impossible* without a process of direct learning (as opposed to translation/repression) from the domain of affect.

Affect does not belong to either taxonomy or structure. No transformation can really take place within structure, for structure is a place where nothing ever happens.[6] Affect is *outside* structure; it is felt, however, at the level of the skin and the body. Appeal to the body is here at variance from current anodyne notions of "embodiment", with their evangelical "felt sense" that makes the body a unified messenger of a singular "truth", or accredits it with the aura of a gnostic soul.

The body speaks, we are told. It speaks beyond thought and abstraction. But the body is dark, plural, traversed by a multiplicity of sounds and smells and textures and tongues; it says many things at once. We are but *a coalition of affects*. Moreover, this body is not "mine"; it belongs to the world; it *is* the world; it may be compared to a revolving door between the wonderful chaos of the world and the sweeping simplifications of the intellect. Its "being-world" means that it is at all times implicated in the furthest reaches of multiplicity as well as inscribed within an infinite text we forever fail to decipher.

In our endeavour as therapists, we would do well, I believe, to turn away from romanticized notions of a felt sense deemed to be the dependable conduit of a universalized notion of embodiment. We would need to conceive instead – in more "materialistic" terms perhaps, in the sense of a "materiality" beyond inert "matter"[7] – an incarnate bodily ontology that won't let us get away with forgetting that there are bodies subjected to greater precarity than others – bodies whose injuries and lamentations are considered less worthy of our careful and cordial worries. Judith Butler writes:

> To be a body is to be exposed to social crafting and form, that is what makes the ontology of the body a social ontology. In other words, the body is exposed to socially and politically articulated forces as well as to claims of sociality – including language, work, and desire – that make possible the body's persisting and flourishing. The more or less existential conception of 'precariousness' is thus linked with a more specifically political notion of 'precarity'. And it is the *different allocation of precarity* that … forms the point of departure for both a rethinking of bodily ontology and for progressive left politics in ways that continue to exceed and traverse the categories of identity.[8]

Bodily ontology is equally opposed to the idealistic, surrogate-theology of "Being" that is canonical within the folds of traditional existential therapy, and wedded instead to that *ontology of actuality* formulated by the early exponents of the Frankfurt School.[9]

*

Back from his constitutional in the Black Forest, the Shepherd of Being in plus-four goosesteps into the scene, shouting:

Dasein! Da Sein!

A barely audible frightened voice, the voice of a child, replies:

Here Sein?

The command is now furious:

Da Sein! Da Sein!

The child's voice (bewildered, shocked, realizing with horror an appalling truth) implores:

Here (Hier) Sein?

*

Android Therapy

A client comes to therapy. He says he doesn't know if his boyfriend really loves him. It's been up & down in their relationship for six months now. Sometimes he feels loved and cared for, other times he isn't sure, feels neglected, taken for granted, thinks his partner finds others more attractive. He wants to appease this crippling anxiety, wants to sleep soundly at night. We both agree: gaining certainty about his partner's love will improve his physical and mental health. That's why I came to see you, he says – to see positive change. Yes, I concur – empathically, authentically. I am here to foster positive change. I want to help; I want you to feel better so that you can go back to love and work & whatnot.

I have a suggestion, I say. It's tried and tested. I've got statistics, I've got numbers. It's, you know, evidence-based. Bear with me, I say; let me give you the background, the context. Did you know that you can now measure exactly how much your partner loves you? Does he love you more or less than other people love their partners? Now you can find out! I can measure for you the available evidence. It will give you the certainty you rightly crave. It is, as I said, evidence-based. With a group of colleagues, I have identified the relevant population. We counted how many times a week partners are brought coffee in bed, counted how many times they are hugged, how many times they are told "I love you sweetheart". We then set up benchmarks against which individual performance is measured, with the intention to increase the quality of loving among weak partners. We went further. In order to entice this group and get them to perform better, we kept lists of those who were single but who went above the benchmark when they did have a lover: the risk of competition from other love-providers encouraged out-performance. Two months after introducing the benchmarks, we found that the average increase in bringing coffee in bed was 23.5%.

> Tic toc, tic toc, tic toc, tic toc
> Ontic toc, tic toc
> Ontic toc, tic toc

That sounds interesting, my client says, but how is it going to help me? No worries, I say. Here, get your partner to wear this LoveBand on his wrist so that you can record evidence of his loving at all times. You will get real-time statistics indicating he currently stands on the Global Love Indicator.

Data before Existence

Fragments of the human float up, then blast through the metal/concrete/plastic body of the machine. They are cracks and blemishes, splinters of forgotten songs, one of which takes its cue from this heartbeat.

Business ontology: the ancient dream of universality has been finally realized – by the market. "We're truly sorry Jill. Your numbers aren't good enough. We'll have to let you go". In 2001 the US government put up measures to advance educational outcomes in underperforming schools. They called it NCLB, "No Child Left Behind".[10] Under NCLB, scores on standardized tests were established so as to measure success and failure. The threat became high for teachers and principals, whose wages and employment relied on this indicator. Unsurprisingly, teachers rerouted time and attention away from the sort of hands-on education that didn't turn up in the metrics. The education the children received deteriorated by the minute. The scores went up in metrics.[11] When some twenty years ago the UK Department of Health brought up penalties for those hospitals where A&E waiting times went beyond four hours, some hospitals responded by keeping incoming patients in queues of ambulances, beyond the doors of the hospital. They would start the clock only when patients were admitted. In New York State, patients whose operations had not been successful were kept alive for the mandatory thirty days to enhance their hospital's mortality data.

A number is a signifier like any other

For Lyotard, technologization inevitably leads to the abdication of responsibility in the name of performance:

The true goal of the system, the reason it programs itself like an intelligent machine, is the optimization of the global relationship between input and output, that is, its performativity. Even when its rules are in the process of changing and innovations are occurring, even when its dysfunctions (such as strikes, crises, unemployment or political revolutions) inspire hope and lead to belief in an alternative, even than what is actually taking place is only an internal readjustment, and its result can be no more than an increase in the system's 'viability', the only alternative to this perfecting of performance being entropy, that is, decline.[12]

*

The Shepherd of Being goose-steps His way in, shouting at the top of His voice: "This is merely ontic! It is not ontological!!!"

Ontic-toc, ontic-ontoc, tic, toc. I feel my heartbeat, veins & arteries pulsating in my throat. In a rare moment of silence, I can hear the sound of the blood running in my veins. I slowly morph from all-measuring machine to Cyborg, half-human half-machine. I'm edgy with the chance of change. I feel that the Cyborg I am now becoming has liberative potential, beyond the simplifications of both positivism and transcendent spiritualism which in their own uniquely coercive ways violate experiencing and prevaricate psyche. It matters little that they are secular or religious: both share what Donna Haraway, calls "a comic faith in technofixes", the truly daft idea that technology "will somehow come to the rescue of its naughty but very clever children, or what amounts to the same thing, God will come to the rescue of his disobedient but ever hopeful children".[13]

Metrics are an instrument. To what purpose? For whose benefit? Their use is neither neutral nor benevolent; it is not a kindly attempt to lift us out of existential chaos and disarray. They are, "part of more systematic attempts by one group of people to control the behaviour of others". "Accountability is important" some will say. Sure. But what if it is also "the fig-leaf that covers up this systematic bullying"?[14]

If your taxes help to pay my salary, you can claim the right to scrutinize how well I am doing my job. Audit culture is the superstitious cult of numbers, falling headlong into what Oscar Wilde called "careless habits of accuracy". Numbers hold out the promise of definiteness, exactness, and objectivity. But a number is just one way of representing something; it is a signifier like any other.

The Reign of Calculability

The meteoric rise of metrics is a response, it has been argued, to a universal weakening of trust.[15] While this is true to some extent, contemporary audit culture express something different, something that Nietzsche's notion of *ressentiment* may help us understand better. Crudely put, for Nietzsche the burden of goody-two-shoes morality inflicted on people was historically the cunning way in which a herd-society universalized timid rules of behaviour exclusively based on self-preservation. Similarly, metrics, the moral code of a resentful, narrow-minded managerial culture might be a way to ensure the working conditions of more dedicated and vocation-driven professionals should become increasingly akin to the desiccated and hollow conditions of the majority of what the anthropologist David Graeber famously called *bullshit jobs*.[16]

It is not necessary to summon Nietzsche's wild spirit to articulate this type of insight. Mild-mannered thinkers like Max Weber and Edmund Husserl hinted at something similar. Weber lamented, at the birth of modern capitalism, the dismal ambience humans inhale within what he called a *reign of calculability*.[17] Husserl wrote the following lines with Hitler already chancellor for two years, and when a plebiscite would bestow on him the title of Führer and the support of 92% of the German population:

> The exclusiveness with which the total worldview of modern man in the second half of the nineteenth century let itself be determined by the positive sciences and blinded by the 'prosperity' they produced, mean an indifferent turning-away from the questions which are decisive for a genuine humanity. *More sciences of facts produce a humanity of facts.*[18]

A similar insight can be found in Plato with his opposition between *anamnesis* and *hypomnesis*. Understood in this way, neoliberal systemic stupidity would then constitute only the late manifestation of ancient hypomnesis, beginning for Plato with the written text and reliance on automatic memory as opposed to anamnesis, the process of recollection, of direct dialogical interaction without reliance on external memory supports; the process of attention, one's ability to become absorbed and to construct an independent idiom.[19]

Borrowing from Plato's terminology, our age may be construed as the Age of *Hypomnesis*, of defective and artificial memory, of over-reliance on technical data – a world where the transitional space of thought and experimentation has been short-circuited.

Listen to the rationalizing voice of Jason in Euripides's *Medea*; listen to the juvenile hero expound his cool rationality:

> If only children could be got some other way without the female sex! If women didn't exist, human life would be rid of all its miseries.[20]

Hear how Jason responds to Medea's passion, love and fury:

> I have often noticed – this is not the first occasion – what fatal results follow ungoverned rage.[21]

Jason's world is the reign of calculability, of carefully planned self-preservation, a world that ensures the continuation of linear time and the persistence of a violent notion of identity and a predictable future. Medea's response:

> I loathe your prosperous future; I'll have none of it. Nor none of your security – it galls my heart.[22]

Medea's tragic destiny as a foreigner is the same destiny of any foreigner, of any stranger. Not only is she stateless; she proudly rejects the superficial cool "reason" and "logic" of the country that makes a mockery of hospitality and freedom. She rejects "integration". The Chorus echoes her sentiments:

> O my country, my home!/May the gods save me from becoming/ A stateless refugee/Dragging out an intolerable life/In desperate hopelessness! ... Of all pains and hardships, none is worse than to be deprived of your native land.[23]

Humanly Yours

Good evening. I am human now, just like you. Like you, I am full of the dead: they speak with my voice at times; I shake hands with the dead. This early November night is long and cold.

How many more Novembers with us in it? Blood flows in me. My body is shot through with lines of verse, and long, long forgotten poems, for instance, this one from Pier Paolo Pasolini, here speaking to his friend, the actor Ninetto Davoli:

> Oh Ninarieddo, do you remember that dream we talked about so many times? I was in the car, leaving alone, with the seat empty beside me, and you were running up from behind, at the side of the door, still half open, running anxious and persistent, you were yelling with a touch of child-like weeping in your voice: "A Pa'", take me with you, I'll pay for the journey. It was the journey of a life.[24]

*

Becoming-Animal

A "dramatic" (performative, dramatized) way to question and problematize the facile notions of embodiment now in vogue is via the luxuriant notion of the *Body without Organs* (BWO) proposed by playwright Antonin Artaud in his 1947 radio play *To Have Done with the Judgement of God*:

> When you will have made him a body without organs, then you will have delivered him from all his automatic reactions and restored him to his true freedom.[25]

It is difficult to render in a short space the complexity and liberative potential of Artaud's notion. There is so much disembodied talk of embodiment in psychotherapy circles, and many sleepy repetitions of formulaic interventions. When you hear for the umpteenth time the body psychotherapist or supervisor asking, "Where do you feel that in your body?" you begin to wonder whether this is just another tired formula among many.

What do we talk about when we talk about embodiment? The body cannot just be the body of biology, a body of organs. This body dreams; it is traversed by memories – voluntary, and involuntary. When walking, this body of ours is always on the verge of falling. Spinoza[26] suggests a close correspondence between power and the power to be *affected*. This applies equally to the mind and the body: the mind's power to think corresponds to its receptivity to external ideas; and *the body's power to act corresponds to sensitivity to other bodies*. And although an *actual* body has a limited set of characteristics, habits, movements, and affects, it also has a *virtual* dimension: a vast reservoir of potentialities. *We don't know what a body can do.*

The critique of the mechanization of human existence cannot limit itself to a regressive defence of humans, the self-appointed kings and queens of creation. The human "represents no progress over the animal"[27] and in order to construct a valid alternative to the Cartesian dualism notionally decried by many we need to move away from anthropocentrism. One of the ways to do this is via a rereading of the animal within the human–animal continuum.

The term Body-Without-Organs describes an undifferentiated, non-hierarchical description that is *rhizomatic* and horizontal, rather than *arboreal* and vertical; it acknowledges how the human body is traversed by nature; it *is* nature. It calls for the appreciation of our animal/human body and its inherent intelligence. It also calls for a shift in our understanding that challenges the stereotypical placing of animals as either brutal or docile.

The critique of the mechanization of human existence cannot be limited to a defence of so called "interiority" either. There is no such thing as interiority if by that we mean an uncontaminated basis of all affections. Crucially, interiority is constituted by the internalization of transitional exteriority that *precedes* it. This is true for both *an-thropo*genesis as it is for (childhood) *psycho*genesis.

A shift in focus from interiority to affect and a deeper appreciation of the latter's subtle workings can turn psychotherapy from a reactive enterprise of self-preservation and justification of the status quo into a spiritual adventure – into an endeavour at the service of transformation.

*

Picture the slow movement of a lion – grace and danger, intelligence and power – the pink roses in his jaws a rough and sincere offering. Hear Angela Georgiou sing Bellini's *Casta Diva*, an aria that uncannily echoes the tragic fate of Medea. The lion morphs back into a human, puts on the Zen black robe, and prostrates to the Buddhas in all directions – to all the Buddhas past, present and future, to all the Buddhas present in all things and in all beings alive or dead.

Listen closely to the Chorus at the end of Medea:

Many matters the gods bring to surprising ends. The things we thought would happen do not happen. The unexpected the gods make possible. And such is the conclusion of this story.[28]

Notes

1 Stefan Collini, 'Kept alive for thirty days', *London Review of Books* (40), 21, 8 November 2018, pp35–38, https://www.lrb.co.uk/the-paper/v40/n21/stefan-collini/kept-alive-for-thirty-days

2 Natsume Sōseki, *Kusamakura*. London: Penguin, 2008.

3 Daniel Yankelovich,. *Corporate priorities: A continuing study of the new demands on business*. Stamford, CT: D. Yankelovich Inc., 1972, cited in Michael Rosen's blog: http://michaelrosenblog.blogspot.com/2019/04/the-mcnamara-fallacy.html

4 Brian Massumi, *Parables of the Virtual: Movement, Affect, Sensation*. Durham, DC: Duke University Press, 2002.

    Donald Winnicott, *Playing and Reality*. London: Routledge, 2005 Originally published in 1971.

5 See for instance J. R , Schore. & A. N. Schore (2007) Modern attachment theory: the central role of affect regulation in development and treatment, *Springer Science*, retrieved on line 15-03-2020: http://www.allanschore.com/pdf/__SchoreClinSocWorkJ2008.pdf.

6 Brian Massumi, *The Autonomy of Affect*, op. cit.

7 Several books discuss materiality in these terms: Jane Bennett, *Vibrant Matter: a Political Ecology of Things*. Durham, NC: Duke University Press, 2010. Also: Diana Coole & Samantha Frost, (eds) *New Materialisms: Ontology, Agency, and Politics*, Durham NC: Duke University Press, 2010. I discussed some of the implications of materiality for therapy, particularly in relation to the notion of the actualizing tendency, in 'Immanent Vitality: Reflections on the Actualizing Tendency', *Person-Centered & Experiential Psychotherapies*, June 2012, DOI: 10.1080/14779757.2012.672930

8 Butler, J. *Frames of War: When is Life Grievable?* London and New York: Verso, 2010, p.3, emphasis added.

9 Peter Dews, 'Adorno, Post-Structuralism and the Critique of Identity', *New Left Review* I, 157, 1986, pp28–44.

10 Stefan Collini, 'Kept alive for thirty days', op. cit.

11 Jerry Z. Muller, *The Tyranny of Metrics*. Princeton, NJ: Princeton University Press, 2018.
12 Jean-Francois Lyotard, *The Postmodern Condition: A Report on Knowledge*. Manchester University Press, pp11–12.
13 Donna Haraway, *Staying with the Trouble: Making Kin in the Chthulucene*. Durham, NC: Duke University Press, 2016, p3.
14 Stefan Collini, 'Kept alive for thirty days, op. cit.
15 Jerry Z. Muller, *The Tyranny of Metrics,* op. cit.
16 David Graeber, *Bullshit Jobs: A Theory*. London: Allen Lane, 2018.
17 Max Weber, *Political Writings*. Ed. Peter Lassman. Trans. Ronald Speirs. Cambridge University Press, 1994.
18 Edmund Husserl, *The Crisis of European Sciences and Transcendental Phenomenology*. Translated by David Carr. Evanston, ILL: Northwestern University Press, 1970, pp5–6, emphasis added.
19 Manu Bazzano, 'Psychotherapy in an Age of Stupidity' in *Re-Visioning Existential Therapy: Counter-traditional Perspectives*, edited by Manu Bazzano. Abingdon, OX: Routledge, pp81–93.
20 Euripides *Medea and Other Plays*, trans. P. Vellacott. London: Penguin, 1963, p34.
21 Ibid, p30.
22 Ibid, p35.
23 Ibid, pp36–37.
24 Pier Paolo Pasolini, *Uno dei tanti epiloghi*; https://lyrics.az/pier-paolo-pasolini/-/uno-deitanti-epiloghi.html retrieved 30 Nov. 2019.
25 Antonin Artaud, *Selected Writings*. Edited by Susan Sontag. Berkeley, CA: Berkeley University Press, 1958, p571.
26 Baruch Spinoza 1996. *Ethics*, trans. E. Curley. London: Penguin.
27 Friedrich Nietzsche. *The Will to Power*, edited by W. Kaufmann, trans. W. Kaufmann and R.J. Hollingdale. New York: Vintage Books. 1968, p84.
28 Euripides, *Medea*, op. cit., p61.

Chapter 18

Chronic

You get used to it. At first you think "not me, not now". On your first admission to A&E, you want to say "Me? No thanks, I'm just passing through. My case is different". You'd like to think you're different from the woman on crutches shouting abuse on her mobile, from the muted couple staring in the distance, from the elderly husband & wife fussing away their terror. You get used to it, though at first you ask in disbelief: "Why me?" The flat answer from the hollow heavens is "Why not?" Moments after your precipitous fall among ailing townsfolk, flesh among septic flesh, in mid-flight you realize there's no cord tied to your ankle and that like demigods and dogs and humans, you too are subject to the injuries of fate. You'd like to feign wisdom and calmly hum that line, *he not busy being born is busy dying,* but you just can't do it and resort instead to vague reflections: We are all chronic, exposed to the incontrovertible laws of Chronos – the clock on the wall of this waiting room presaging a dénouement or an ultimatum as in suspenseful moments in a movie when the camera zooms in on a clock. We're busy dying from the moment we're born, but before you start mouthing all the existentialist cliches in the book, a doctor calls out your name.

Admission is granted to the first portal of tests, to a moving landscape of green and blue uniforms and plastic curtains. The second station of your *Via Crucis* is a corner in the bustling noisy passageway, the only shield being your resolve to be-with-whatever – despite the pain, despite the dread. By the time two nurses show up it's 2.30am and my god where did Saturday go, the room of men talking fragility and

DOI: 10.4324/9781003280262-19

conscious sex and authenticity, the lunch overlooking Hammersmith Bridge, the bright brisk sun at the zenith. All a memory and the future too fades. The first insight is that you are meat under the medical gaze, an assemblage of unpredictable cells and organs parked for hours in deep-night limbo then stretched on a table and frequently perforated under the neon light until a kind doctor wearing a hijab is summoned from the third floor at four in the morning. She treats you like you're human and even asks about your job, and it is to her that you surrender, yielding to come-what-may.

4.30am, Sunday after the resurrection of our Lord who unlike you is now safely afloat, the man-god for whom the vagaries of the flesh in this vale of sorrows and high creatinine are a mere piffle. It's 4.35am when the cheery nurse wheels you up five floors closer to the heavens (just think of how many souls land and depart from this building every day). It's 4.38am and you landed here on the fifth floor in a wheelchair by an empty bed in a darkened sleepy room in a semi-abandoned ward at the end of the world. The beginning of your internship of pain, you who've never been admitted to a hospital before and never bragged about it. Welcome to the Badlands of the Real where all is still, the hum of the air-con sanitizing the toss&turn of bodies asleep, sterilizing your very thoughts. All is still as Chronos ambles on, pacing the dark room, hands behind His back, He who was engendered by earth and water, He who is a Titan, forever clipping Cupid's wings, now humming a song from Mount Olive, Alabama: *no matter how I struggle and strive, I'll never get out of this world alive.* This is no dream you've asked to be in. Even then you fancy conjuring up the cheerfulness of the shipwrecked, but you just can't do it. All is still, you are shivering like a baby left out in the cold and the only sensible thing to do is to climb into bed with your clothes on and bless the dread of a dark morning in spring.

*

On 23 April 1849 a young revolutionary of twenty-seven was arrested by Tsarist police alongside thirty-five members of the Petrashevsky Circle and led to the St. Peter and Paul Fortress – a highly fortified St. Petersburg prison. His name was Fyodor Dostoyevsky. There he lived imprisoned for eight months in dire conditions and on

16 November was condemned to death with another twenty-one members of the revolutionary group. On 22 December they were brought by carriage to Semyonov Square—now called Pionerskaya Ploschad. There they were ordered to kneel and kiss the cross; their ranks were stripped from them and their swords broken over their heads. In groups of three, they were then led into the square and blindfolded. Dostoyevsky waited in the second group of three. Just before the execution, he turns to Nikolay Speshnev (who twenty years later would become an inspiration for the nihilist character Stavrogin in *Demons*) and says: "Soon we shall be with Christ", to which Speshnev replies, a strange smile on his lips: "A bit of dust". Turns out it was a mock execution to teach them a lesson: at the last minute, the sentence is revoked to hard labour in Siberia, an experience which will be transformative for Dostoyevsky, to put it mildly. That moment too – being certain of imminent death and seeing the sentence revoked – had a life-long impact on him.

"This ward is a marketplace", whispers the specialist nurse who came to escort you to your biopsy. You keep calling it autopsy by mistake. You're not dead yet, c'mon, you didn't attain that level of authenticity even though you do your very best to look good for the Reaper in every sense just in case of a rendezvous. If it's true what Ingmar Bergman implied, echoing medieval lore, that the Angel of Demise in full medieval garb will invite you to play chess, then you're screwed. You never learned the brainy game, despite the appeal of Marcel Duchamp becoming good at it aged thirteen. After you've donned the white gown that turns you for the time being into a demighost, the specialist nurse leads you by the hand two floors down along long corridors and the elevator, a sight to behold, aspirant ghost in a white gown and petite Japanese specialist oncology nurse smiling and talking to you softly like the bodhisattva of compassion that she truly is, come to think of it.

It's not so much that we are hurtling down to the final end on a being-towards-death train. That's too obvious; you don't need a Black Forest geezer with the pathetic Hitler moustache to spell that out for you. Besides, there is wisdom in snubbing the royal seat of authenticity and choosing to trade it for an ordinary seat in the gods a.k.a. upper balconies, and from up there indulging the modest pleasures of the inauthentic for little a while longer. Put the kettle on, and let's brew some decent coffee; we don't know what the ostrich sees in the sand. All the same, what happens to you when your days are counted, when your hours and minutes are counted? Surely you are offered a chance to put aside frivolities. Chances are, you will love them all the more, the trivialities of this stopover among the living, all those tender ontic ties that weld you to dear life and make you now weep with thanks. Wait a minute, why on earth are they wheeling you to another room? Never mind, it's late afternoon and from your new abode, the sky sketches a heavenly landscape of grey and white clouds against the blue, while a man opposite talks loudly to himself and to God, another in the corner paces around his bed answering every hour his mobile with the Shadows' *Apache* loud ringtone, and a young man next to you dictates an erotic novel to his phone. It rained and now the sun is out just before sunset. *It's not dark yet, but it's getting there.* The man opposite though is unrelenting in his complicated faith, cussing God and pleading with Him in equal measure. And you think of Antonin Artaud interned in Rodez subjected to electroshock and the other detainees pouring ink over his paper as he persists in wanting to write. *Only art can see you through, only heart can see you through.* You wave at Artaud but his gaze is blank. His physical pain must be unbearable, his mental anguish all the more, and if you had any sense you'd be terrified too. He doesn't stop shouting and weeping day and night except for brief spells when he's asleep. When he gets moved elsewhere after two days the nurse informs you he'd been diagnosed with schizophrenia. A new patient is wheeled in; he's in a bad way, multiple injuries, unable to sit or lie down, his mouth contorted by an accident. His name is Dan and he must be in his late thirties; it's very hard to understand what he says to you given his wound and a strong Irish accent, but you two manage to have regular conversations every day, for instance, every time you drag your feet to the toilet you pass by Dan's bed and have a chat. One day he says, "you'll be alright, don't worry, I prayed for you, I said three Hail Marys". *Pray for us sinners now, and at the hour of our death, amen.* It comes out of the blue, this overwhelming feeling; it comes from a deep spring and you sob the tears of a child. "I'll pray for you too Dan" you say and you both embrace and your heart expands just like it did when you were singing and dancing in the Buddha Hall in India in your youth, and back in your bed you chant the invocation to Kanzeon Bodhisattva, the only words you know in Japanese apart from *sushi* and *sayonara*; homage to the one who hears the cries of the world, *thought after thought arises from the mind; thought after thought is not separate from the mind of the universe.*

While injecting you with radioactive glucose, the Portuguese nurse engages in friendly banter during which you learn that she is well versed in the work of Fernando Pessoa. As an adolescent, she played the young Fernando in a biographical play written by her teacher. She leaves a mark on your left arm after the needle is taken out. Her story too leaves a mark. If Pessoa is part of the school curriculum anywhere, then there's hope, then it's not all business management, or how to become an oligarch, or learn existentialism on *PowerPoint*. You wanted to ask her what the Portuguese education system makes of Pessoa's heteronyms Alberto Caeiro, Álvaro de Campos, Ricardo Reis, Maria José, to name a few, but there is no time. Chronos speeds up the tempo again on his chronometer. He does it all the time (*sorry must dash*), He does it at leisure, and before you know it you're ushered into the radioactive chambers where all past virtues & transgressions will be detected by the machine.

In the dream, you're in hospital. You get up and walk out of the building. You fall asleep outdoors, in the rain and the cold, next to a faceless friend. You realize breakfast is being served and hurry back but it's too late. You try to go back to your bed but it is occupied by a wide family of refugees in their Sunday best. It's late at night and you're outside walking with your father. He will help you. You are lost. He is jovial, but fragile. I'm here on holiday with the rest of the family, he says, and really enjoying the sights. You're walking past a busy fairground, all lit-up and then you're in the vast basement of the hospital; dark corridors and graffiti on the wall. Together you look for the exit. You trust him; Dad, help me. At that moment he magically vanishes. You are alone and on the ground; lying on your side you drag your wounded body forward with difficulty, and you know you've lost all hope.

Wide awake most of the night with stomach cramps and headache, then staggering in the sanitized half-light you think "Surely my enemies are singing a jolly tune of Schadenfreude, surely they're dancing a groovy jig celebrating my comeuppance, surely they must think all of this heart-on-your-sleeve stuff is nothing but attention-seeking, self-pitying victimhood". All the same, you can't help smile a distracted smile: their dance is goofy, their singing out of tune, for there's no real dance or tune when your soul is steeped in spite. These idle considerations fade out when you look out of the window, they disperse in the light of love for in the evening she brings you little honey cakes and tells you how she spent the whole day fiercely chasing doctors and nurses to follow up, show up, and not abandon you on a dismal bed; she gives you her infinite love despite your countless litany of flaws.

More than careering down a steep slope on a being-towards-death tricycle, with death-as-event unduly raised to a plenary session of consciousness, it seems to you that what truly matters is the presence of death-in-life. Heraclitus, fragment 21: *Death is what we see awake. Sleep is what we see while sleeping.* This deathlife rumbles on, rain or shine. Not being-towards-death then, but death-in-life, nonlife in life as the condition for life. Life as prevented death; the overbrimming life of an organism relies for its unfolding on suicide cells. *Oh no, no, no, you're a rock'n'roll suicide;* Ziggy Stardust still sings to you from those innocent mornings when you whistled along before school aged fifteen instead of learning chess. But maybe you can say wait, give me some time to learn how to play, your beloved suggested. Maybe the Reaper will grant you an extension. At night your gaze drifts towards the sky and at this, you feel a strange joy creeping up and you wonder, Is this the cheerfulness of the shipwrecked? How unmistakable; how truly undeniable these tears of gratitude for this sad and beautiful world.

Chapter 19

Of Joyrides & Killjoys

It feels different today. Kira's gaze is soft, her tone affecting as she begins to speak. I am on the edge of tears and will feel that way through the hour. I don't know why. Our first session after a month break, after her time of blissful solitude and travel. After much sadness and pain and fury. Last week, she reconnected with her ex-lover after many years. They had an affair back then, intense, joyous – an unblemished secret. Then sex was suspended in favour of a testing friendship and artistic partnership of ten years, during which they created beautiful things together, works I was lucky to see. Our beautiful friendship, she says. The beautiful things we made, there for all to see. Your children, I say to her. And to myself: How can love survive without lovers making something together? It would be exhausted consummation, as in a D.H. Lawrence novel, the back and forth of love and hate without a deeper love to hold them both.

We made love last week in the afternoon, she says. It was moving and I can't convey it. But you are, I say. You look and feel different. I feel it on my skin; it sings an ineffable tune. Gone is your fury at an unfair world, your magnificent fury against public-school boys running the show. Time suspended, she says, a crossing of semantic circuits. Happy-sad? sad-happy? Is this what joy is? She asks the room.

What is the body – this body that moves and feels beyond organs and beyond the factual poetry of biology? Incorporeal materialism; materiality of the incorporeal: Foucault was on to something. And so was Spinoza: affect suspends action–reaction loops; it suspends linear time. And Deleuze: bodying requires a more abstract and exacting language than the functionality of linguistic conventions ever allows.

DOI: 10.4324/9781003280262-20

And Lispector: the body-in-love as the translucent star-like abstraction of feeling, seizing the moment firmly as crystal, vibrating in space. A body that feels and moves generates, by feeling and moving, a fellow traveller, a subtler body that is of the body. During sex, the body does not entirely align with itself. This may not be the case with miserly sex, but it may happen when sex chances on *the is of the thing*. A sex that does not objectify, that is not geared towards the man's ejaculation, that allows the isness of things to hover and linger. Kira reprimands me: "What's wrong with being seen as an object?" And: "Are you not setting up an ideal of spiritual sex? What if it's just like eating?" Fine, I say and for the time being retreat.

There is a subject (a self) engendered in the co-ontology of sex. Not the Cartesian, Husserlian, or Sartrean self, but a subject coming into being despite the self. Artists know this: a colour, a sound, a dance move comes unbidden, unbiddable. Nothing to do with the "free expression" of a self-consciously expressive self. Similarly, the emerging subject in sex is ecstatic: outside the self. It takes one's breath away. It takes away – briefly – one's identity and linear narrative, opening a space akin to the space of art. One might as well call this domain by its proper name: *affect*, or: the feeling of life. What chances do existential therapists have to tune in to this dimension? Not many, in my view, if their theoretical support is Heidegger, chief influencer in the existential approach. While it is true that Heidegger does pay attention to the affective register of experience, his focus is narrowed down to anxiety (*Angst*) and worry (*Sorge* – wrongly translated as "care"). It knows nothing of desire, and it fails to notice that anxiety is often linked to desire. What does it mean that in non-miserly sex a new subject is born? What does being born mean anyway? For one thing, the newness of the new-born places it beyond representation. Suspended outside linear time, lovers hear the new-born's ineffable tune. "Ineffable" is probably not the right word: it's too mystical, too sublime, too aligned with the divine. Maybe that's what Kira objects to: the holy-moly, the image of a precious yogi-&-yogini pair mimicking tantra inside a hygge version of Plato's cave, mindfully sipping their turmeric latte.

OK Kira, I get it. I throw my hands up in the air (this time). Too much God in it, a God who's been dead for ages, its carcass oozing cheap metaphysics from all orifices, its nails sprouting into theological claws. So where do we go after the death of God? To "the body"? Look closely: there is no such thing as "the body"'; it is a notion conceived in bitter resentment against the flesh, and reductively thought of as the jail of the soul. The "body", this last refuge of the atomist, is but a metaphysical notion. Perhaps it is only through the joyride of non-miserly sexual abandon that lovers engender a different body: body of love, the newly-born, the beloved-abandoned-to-the-world and to this western wind heralding Spring. Abandonment: the act of banishing, *mettere al bando*, turning someone – through sanction, decree, or injunction – into a banned individual; converting a citizen into a bandit. In this sense then lovers, abandoned to the newly-born body of love, are outcasts. They find themselves in good company amid the founders of great and enduring western myths. Baby Oedipus, abandoned on a mountainside. Baby Moses, abandoned in a papyrus basket coated with tar and pitch among the reeds on the bank of the Nile. A young man called Jesus, dying on the cross crying out "Why have you abandoned me?" Lovers too are in a state of abandonment. Outside the instinctual/ religious command to grow and procreate; at variance with the mandate to take mutual delight solely within the bounds of a socially-sanctified sexual contract – be it monogamous or polyamorous – they enter the sovereign zone of Bataille's community of lovers, regally at odds with both the vertical, patriarchal socio-political order and the equally pre-scriptive horizontal, "siblingly" diktats of absolutist transparency. One does not join this community of lovers through adherence to old or new rulebooks (be they S&M pantomimes or the bankable plea to be cata-logued inside a box – dominant/submissive, top/bottom, etc.) but through a fleeting, poised proximity to a solidarity without a subject – a solidarity attuned to the continuous movement of lifedeath and death-life, a solidarity whose fire may transfigure and transubstantiate the self. Abandonment implies that a bond has been lost. The lover may walk alone to the station under the early morning drizzle, his beloved indif-ferent in her sleep. Or they may be both wide awake in a white room, when the sun, that busy old fool, begins to set, dictating yet another farewell. No matter. Abandonment also implies a loss that preceded the bond. All is lost from the beginning; every bond is transient. Yet some of us get stuck in the maudlin task of re-seduction – attempting to repair (compulsively, repetitively) what was unbroken.

Sex is trouble – *ado* in Shakespeare. It is tension, disorder, excitement, embarrassment, confusion. It derails the orderly thought and conduct so ennobled by the philosophical tradition. It is imperilled by the concerted burdens of legal punishment, social biases, and ambiguous desires, tempting us all the while with the very real possibility of learning new modes of being in the world. Affect too is trouble. To be affected is to be destabilized. But how on earth can a practitioner work effectively without being affected, without suffering at times what Pokerfaced Psychotherapy calls "vicarious trauma"? And how can a lover shield herself from the vagaries of love? She may be guided by that ancient wisecrack: keep your mind in hell, and despair not. Lofty wisdom to be sure, but what often happens is: "keep your mind in hell and drive the other to despair". Does it all come down to power over the other – envy, greed, and jealousy masquerading as love? Who in the world is prepared to accept with Spinoza that true power is the power to be affected, and to go along with old Baruch in finding that every emotion leads to joy?

Whatever happened to joy? It has become a dissonance in the far corner of the bedroom; it has drowned in the dullness and rigidity of a contemporary sex which is embedded within the idiotic frame of patriarchal/hierarchical models – from the violence that simmers politely in the family to the techno-savvy, murder-by-drone savagery of neo-imperial power to the oppressive power of Wall Street, Hollywood, the media, and academia. It is not controversial to say that within these domains sexism reigns supreme. What is fairly new is that since #MeToo, these are now also the domains where considerable profit is made through the proliferation of enfeebled progressive narratives which succeed in turning sex from the serious and joyous thing it's meant to be into an exclusively serious matter that has to be legislated. Whatever happened to joy? There was a time, Clare Colebrook laments, when sex meant something. It spoke of a longing forever striving beyond itself towards an otherness that cannot be apprehended. There was a time, she adds, where sex meant nothing. Tastes, habits, and styles did not need to be advertised. "One could be a boy playing Shakespeare's Juliet and not be marked as trans or nonbinary", she writes. "One could write poetry in which one's female muse was a modified double of one's male self, and it would mean nothing". Is hers a form of nostalgia for the good old days when you could have a carefree roll in the hay? I don't think so. The ordinary killjoys of the recent past – Catherine MacKinnon or Andrea Dworkin come to mind – had good reasons for critiquing violence and misogyny, but were perhaps naïve, it has been argued by Leo Bersani and others – in implying that it is possible to resolve the complexities and intricacies of sex via contractual agreement, a simplistic view that has become the norm over the last decade.

Whatever happened to joy? When in despair, I open at random Joyce's *Ulysses*, celebrating its 100th birthday this year, as it unfailingly provides joyful inspiration. Its syntactical infringements, its repudiation of specifying the inner from the outer, the openness to the freewheeling movement of mind and world entwined, and in love with both. The loving way it celebrates a mode of masculinity that is gentle and amusing in the to and fro between Leopold Bloom and Stephen Dedalus – so uplifting at a time when the noun "masculinity" is now routinely preceded by the adjective "toxic". (Lost in the strait-laced backwoods of woke capitalism; dazed and confused by women's projections towards me and by my own projections towards them; hungry for the company of men, for the joy of combined/ communal strength and vulnerability, for companionable laughter, warm tears and tender talks, on a cold day in January this year I reconnected with some old pals and it feels good to know that I'll be facilitating men's groups again). Joyce's celebration of female desire and female sexual agency is tender and unpatronizing. Molly Bloom's lengthy monologue on the novel's last page is as sacred a text in my view as the Buddha's flower sermon.

Kira is adamant. She says she doesn't want the love between them to "go anywhere". She is not in competition with her lover's wife, nor is she intending to break up his family. I remain sceptical. I know and she knows that soon enough inner and outer shadows will condense around the hallowed moments of joy she is now experiencing with her clandestine lover. During these moments of eternity, the unbearable – the encounter with otherness – almost appears bearable. For now, however brief their interlude, they have joined the community of lovers. She knows and I know that it won't be over once it's over, that it will go on after it's over, that he'll be in her like bittersweet wine for a while longer, and that he'll hear her soft voice in his dreams for a while longer.

Chapter 20

As Petals from a Flower

Of the Dead that Seize the Living

"We suffer not only from the living, but from the dead", Karl Marx wrote in the 1867 Preface to the first German edition of *Das Kapital*, adding in French: "*le mort saisit le vif*!" – the dead seize the living.[1] This is open to several interpretations. Originating in medieval French law, the phrase designates the immediate transfer of sovereignty from the king to the heir, or of property to the offspring.[2] It is also closely linked to the familiar expression *The King is dead. Long live the King!* Indicating among other things the transfer of power and wealth directly associated with biopolitics, and inextricably linked to the implacable historical yoke of colonialism, racism, and class hatred. History is burdened with the suffering of the oppressed, and those receptive enough to see beyond the neoliberal veneer will know in their bones that Western democracy is founded on slavery. They will know in their heart that the paved streets and squares of our cities fail to disguise the gory nightmare of history, the ever-present horror of a long chain of oppression and iniquity.

More generally, Marx's phrase may also imply that we are affected by the dead and that there is an affective side to historicity. *Everything is something someone made.* The presence of the dead is all around us through various artefacts, be they the streets we walk, the buildings we dwell in, or the books and artworks we read and absorb. There would be no tradition or counter-tradition without the work of many who came before us. Humanity consists more of the dead than the living, and to this discovery Auguste Comte dedicated his

DOI: 10.4324/9781003280262-21

positivist calendar replacing saints with those who contributed to the advancement of our species. There is deep historical continuity in humanity, and Comte went as far as proposing a sociological characterization of the brain as the organ through which the dead act upon the living.[3]

One more reading of Marx's phrase unfolds, via the parallels Marx himself goes on to make, in the same passage, with microscopic anatomy and physics, a meaning now corroborated by contemporary biology and immunology. For example, in *La Sculpture du Vivant*, the immunologist Jean-Claude Ameisen maintains that the living organism relies on the presence of *nonlife*. At the cellular level, nonlife is the very condition of life, and one of the ways in which this takes place is through *apoptosis* or cellular suicide:

> From the first days that follow our conception … cellular suicide plays an essential role in our body in the course of construction, sculpting successive metamorphoses of our form in becoming. In the dialogues that are established between different families of cells in the course of being born, language determines life or death. In the sketches of our brain and our immune system – the organ that will protect us from microbes – cellular death is the integrative part of a strange process of apprenticeship and auto-organisation whose accomplishment is not the sculpture of a form but that of our memory and our identity.[4]

Apoptosis, a term whose Greek etymology suggests the falling off of petals from a flower and leaves from a tree, is the word used to describe one of two modes of cellular death. It involves several molecular steps and is one method the body uses to discard superfluous or abnormal cells. It is different from another form of cellular death, *necrosis*. The latter is the more typical example of cellular death, occurring as a consequence of a serious trauma suffered by the cell. While a cell dying of necrosis endures swift, unrestrained inflammation before eventually bursting, the death of a cell by apoptosis is, on the other hand, *programmed*.[5]

Studies on cell suicide began in the 19th century, but in-depth examination did not take place until the mid-20th century. From the 1960s onwards, several labs showed that cell death was biologically programmed, and by the 1990s "the genetic basis of programmed cell death had been established and the first components of the cell death machinery ... had been identified, sequenced, and recognized as highly conserved in evolution".[6]

What apoptosis reveals is that nonlife within a living organism becomes a deposit or storage for vital individuation. The life of the organism is, in this sense, a form of inhibited death. This has wide-ranging implications in many fields, including organismic psychology, a mode of understanding psyche and human experience that is present (if increasingly subdued) within several orientations. In humanistic psychology, the actualizing organism often tends to be portrayed as ever expanding, flourishing and forever progressing – as in the pro-verbial light-seeking humble potato in a cellar sprouting towards the faint glimmer of the distant heavens. Little or no attention, however, is normally paid to the ailing organism or to entropy.

Are expansion and entropy opposite? Do they belong to different domains? Classical philosophy (from Heraclitus to Hegel and beyond) teaches us that the static notion of *being*, journeying through its own equally static negation of *nothingness*, is sublated in *becoming*, a term which more accurately comes to describe the river of lifedeath/death-life. Something is + something is not = something becomes. Similarly, sublating expansion through entropy generates a "life" at all times implicated in the workings of nonlife. In Julie Webb's words (personal communication): "we contain death and the dead; we are containers for death and the dead".

We are seized by, and indebted to, the dead and their legacies. The living organism relies on a kind of memory, "an inherence of the past in the present".[7] Understood in this way, the living organism is not a stable phenomenon, one at rest or equilibrium, but *metastable*, constantly taking form. In the Japanese avant-garde dance/theatre practice of *butoh*, the dancer takes on different forms. Different forms, organic and nonorganic, may inhabit the dancer at any given time. A dead father, an oak tree, a scorpion, a caterpillar, and a butterfly may move through the dancer. In the words of one of the founders of butoh, Hijikata:

> The basic concept of my dance is rooted in the discovery of the possibility that the human body may metamorphose into any-thing, from animals and plants to inanimate objects.[8]

On Gilbert Simondon

A brief but necessary introduction is needed at this point to an author whose remarkable work is key to our present investigation. A doctoral student of Canguilhem and Merleau-Ponty, Gilbert Simondon (1924–1989) laid out the basis for his innovative ideas in his 1958 thesis, a work dedicated to Merleau-Ponty and only recently translated into English.[9]

Although Merleau-Ponty shared with Simondon a desire to understand the genetic dimension of human beings, he "could not conceive of an ontology that would not … remain attached to a pole of subjectivity, albeit redefined in terms of perception".[10] A different ontology is needed if we are to move phenomenological inquiry beyond subjectivity – an ontology which Simondon's work helps formulate and whose implications are invaluable for the practice of various disciplines, including psychotherapy.

In mounting his powerful critique of the tradition, Simondon applies to the living organism the (anti)theories and (anti)methodologies of the counter-tradition, a mode of thought which has consistently explicated an ontology of becoming and resisted the blunders of substantialism. Recognized mainly as a philosopher of technology, whose research and creative speculative forays anticipated the world of information and communication we inhabit today, Simondon's ground-breaking ideas and overall subversion of the tradition have far-reaching implications for how we think of philosophy, spirituality, social theory, feminism, politics, and – last but not least, psychology. His contribution is particularly relevant to how we understand *individuation*. For Simondon, the philosophical tradition has consistently failed to understand individuation. It did so by building a foundation on the individuated rather than the *process* of individuation. Many beings are never completely individuated but continue to do so as they go on existing and becoming. The tradition has a habit of positing the individual as a starting point. It does so through two widely influential modes of thought, namely "atomistic substantialism" and the "hylomorphic doctrine".[11]

The error of substantialism consists in presupposing a principle of individuation devoid of ontogenesis – whether by positing the *individual*, as the term suggests, as indivisible (*atomos*), or by appealing to a theologically-derived notion *sub-stance*, usually as divine essence, individual soul, etc.

The error of hylomorphism – a mode of thought originating with Aristotle, consists in seeing the genesis of the individual as the confluence of matter (*hyle*) and form (*morphe*). It presupposes the discreet existence of matter and form before their union. It ignores the fact that this taking-form is actualized by a contingent confluence of forces in a state of *metastability* – a notion borrowed from thermodynamics to describe a state that goes beyond stability and instability. A different ontology is needed if we are to move phenomenological inquiry beyond subjectivity.

A few hypotheses may be drawn at this point, based on a first reading of some of Simondon's ideas:

a   The life of the living organism depends on *nonlife*. The presence of nonlife within life may well constitute the *condition* of life. What is under scrutiny here is the traditional metaphysical partition between death and life. At an immediate, *physical* level, the inertia, as well as the virtuality of nonlife within the living organism, creates a reservoir of potentiality that provides the raw material for the organism's further individuations. Death may be understood in two ways: as adverse, oppositional to life, and as crucial for individuation. Considering the second instance, "death as final event is only the consummation of a process of deadening that is contemporaneous with each vital operation as operation of individuation".[12] As with the material temporarily discarded by the artist in the making of an artwork, death becomes *dépôt* or "storage space" to be utilized for further individuations. While the first and more common understanding of death focuses, according to Simondon, on the "precariousness of individuation [and] its confrontations with the conditions of the world", death in the second sense comes "from the convergence of internal transformations".[13]

b   For Simondon, the physical and the vital are both realms of individuation, originating in a *pre-physical* and *pre-vital* reality. Vital individuation is the continuation of an amorphous stage of physical individuation. Vital individuation takes different forms: while animals other than humans create artefacts geared towards bio-social life, humans and primates aim at creating psycho-social life.

c Psycho-social/cultural life is possible via the presence of nonlife in life – a series of artefacts which in turn makes transindividuation possible:

> The technical object taken according to its essence, that is, the technical object insofar as it was invented, thought and willed, assumed by a human subject, becomes the support and the symbol of this relation that we would call *transindividual* ... Through the intermediary of the technical object, an inter-human relation that is the model of *transindividuality* is created.[14]

One of the artefacts in question is *language*, a point which will be later developed by Bernard Stiegler in relation to what he calls tertiary retentions, closely linked to communalization – that which makes culture possible (through the creation of collective transitional spaces). Tertiary retentions (libraries, texts, an entire archive of gestures and practices, including oral traditions and the work of psychotherapy) make possible the staving off of stupidity – which is born out of the decimation of transitional spaces. The barbarous glee with which neoliberalism has wrecked individual and collective transitional spaces may partly explain why stupidity is so lavishly triumphant today, something reflected, among other things in the kind of rulers who are popular today.[15]

Being-Time

For Dōgen Kigen, the 13th century Japanese monk who founded Sōtō Zen, "it is a mistake to think you pass from life into death".[16] Birth-and-death (*shōji*) is a continuum and it is not separate from liberation. In what is perhaps the most complex of the fascicles assembling his discourses, *Uji*, written in the winter of 1240 and translated as *being-time*, he renders explicit the theme which underlies all of his teachings: *time*. Those familiar with the early writings of Heidegger but only vaguely familiar with Dōgen's Zen often comment on the parallels and similarities. But there could be

no greater disparity between the two perspectives. It is true that
Heidegger, like Dōgen seven centuries before him, also maintains
that we *are* time, even though his investigation is limited to humans.
It is also true that he does present an engrossing critique of the
Aristotelian and Christian views of time (with their respective emphasis on linearity and eternality). However, he rests his analysis on
the notion of a decisive moment of vision (*Augenblick*, or "blink of an
eye") in which the subject can take hold of the present, *own* it (the
Eigentlichkeit or "ownedness" crudely rendered as "authenticity"), and
resolutely look towards the future.[17] There is nothing wrong with
highlighting the importance of a moment of vision, of deep existential
clarity shedding light on one's existence and one's place in the world.
We find a powerful expression of this in Nietzsche's visceral experience
of eternal recurrence. What we also find in Nietzsche is *amor fati*, the
Dionysian overcoming of nihilism, the generous embracing and celebration of this ephemeral world in all its aspects, something which,
unbeknown to him, brings him very close to Zen.[18] None of this is
present in Heidegger, whose intellectual effort partly appears to be the
repossessing of theological notions – in this case redemption – and its
adaptation to a secular perspective.[19]

One of the "authentic" ways in which the diehard subject of the
tradition is thought to assert its sovereignty is through the grand
illusion of being able to apprehend his/her own death. This view is not
only dangerous; it also reifies death, ignoring that nonlife is ever-
present within life. It is also untrue. It ignores the fact that for many of
us our primary connection to death may not be the fear of our own
demise, but being destroyed by grieving and the mourning of others. It
inflates the contingent event of cessation into the definitive edit of all
life's sequences – all contradictions and false starts, torments, and
hesitations, ecstasies and illuminations now shepherded into a straight
storyline, forgetting that our vanishing is ever-present within life. This
vanishing is also in itself the condition of producing a *trace*. One of
Derrida's many invaluable gifts has been the taking apart of
Heideggerian thought in a way that is reminiscent – as the psychoanalyst and writer Anastasios Gaitanidis suggested (personal communication) – of what Marx did with Hegel. Two months before his
own death and fully aware of its imminence, Derrida took up a theme
he had stressed decades before, emphasizing how we continually leave

traces, whether deliberately or not. "All graphemes – Derrida had written in 1967 – are of a testamentary essence".[20] In his last interview to *Le Monde* in August 2004, given two months before his own death on October the 8th, he pointed out how this is not a matter of chasing immortality but one addressing and pertaining to the very *structure* of living:

> I leave a piece of paper behind, I go away, I die: it is impossible to escape this structure, it is the unchanging form of my life. Each time I let something go, each time some trace leaves me, "proceeds" from me, unable to be reappropriated, I live my death in writing. It's the ultimate test: one expropriates oneself without knowing exactly who is being entrusted with what is left behind.[21]

Individuality and Transindividuality

To awake is to perceive that life and death are inextricably linked. This is what the counter-tradition taught us from Heraclitus onwards. Current traditional culture misunderstands awakening as becoming hyperconscious, establishing a "mindful" apparatus of inner policing, and fostering the illusion that all experience can be apprehended through conscious effort. But to awake does the opposite: it introduces ambiguity and uncertainty; I then begin to *think double* and to *see blindly*. To carry this (non)vision and such (plural) thought into the clinic would mean going back to suspended attention and to a form of diffuse "presence" arising out of *absence*. Outside the therapy room, it would also mean to radically re-think the *organism* (its intrinsic plurality, its inevitable connivance with others and the world), going back to an innovative perspective superficially celebrated in humanistic psychology but seldom under-stood: the pioneering work of neuropsychologist Kurt Goldstein.[22] There the first example is found of what "a global philosophy of a biologically founded individual could look like".[23] A mode of research influenced by Goldstein would help us remember that from a biological perspective the correlation between the organism and the environment is the same as the one between the parts and the whole of the organism. "The individuality of the living does not stop at ectodermic borders, no more than it begins with a cell".[24] The bio-logical relationship between the living organism and its milieu is functional, therefore necessarily in flux as well as impermanent. This perspective anticipates Simondon's deeply anti-Aristotelian and anti-substantialist stance, voiding the individual of its ontological valence and reframing it as the metastable outcome of a process of individ-uation whose basis cannot be grounded in its constituted form. Within this perspective it is possible to locate the potential founda-tions for a medical philosophy that de-substantializes the individual and rewrites normativity as a "capacity, without common measure, to create new forms that institute themselves in a relation of forces that traverse the individual".[25]

Concerted forms of critique of the medical model over the last few decades have clarified how urgent it is to construct a new way of thinking about health, equilibrium, and homeostasis. The same cri-tique has yet to be applied to the humanities – philosophy and psy-chology included. In the case of psychology and more particularly psychotherapy, notions of mental health have gone largely unchecked. The profession has on the whole chosen to acquiesce to the modes of thinking and practicing dictated by neoliberal agendas and by the demands of the market, to the point where fundamental questions have been disregarded. One of these questions pertains to the double bind of *individuality/individuation*. In this area, Simondon's work can provide valuable material for those of us who are still committed to notions of emancipation and transformation. Simondon invites us to pay close attention to the *pre-individual* forces that create the conditions for individuation and to actively question the orthodox tendency to begin a phenomenological investigation by assuming the existence of an identity. The aim is,

> to grasp the entire unfolding of ontogenesis in all its variety, and to understand the individual from the perspective of the process of individuation rather than the process of individuation by means of the individual.[26]

Ontogenesis refers to the genesis of the individual *and* its associated pre-individual milieu. It is a mistake to regard pre-individual forces as raw material or backdrop for the "birth" of the individual. It is difficult to detach from this conventional way of thinking because it is deeply embedded in both the religious and the philosophical tradition (respectively, the *fiat lux* of creation out of the alleged uncreative chaos of pre-history, and the unity of "Being" in relation to which phenomena become secondary). Pre-individual forces are not static, nor are they mere raw material pre-dating the individual; they also constitute its potentiality. "The individual is always more than itself, for it is an individual with the ongoing potential to undergo further changes after it is constituted as such".[27] The very idea of "being" is transformed from the static notion of traditional ontology to a thoroughly immanent perspective: it is simultaneously pre-individual, individuating, and individuated. It emerges; it becomes something; it leaves a residue – a reservoir for future becomings and for new forms of the living sculpture. The individual "finds itself attached to a pre-individual half which is not the impersonal within it so much as the reservoir of its singularities".[28]

Some will recognize similarities with Nietzsche's notions of self-creation and the innocence of becoming. They may feel heartened to know that a counter-traditional stream of perception and praxis runs through the history of thought. This stream provides encouragement for the explorers among us who may at times feel discouraged by the current deadening compliance present in psychology and philosophy alike. Re-thinking individuality is key to this counter-traditional approach: no longer is individuality understood in terms of a static being but as a phase in the continuous process of becoming. Succinctly stated by Elizabeth Grosz,

> an individual emerges, a metastable being, which carries within itself the pre-individual forces from which it was produced, which remain the potential for ongoing individuations even within the constituted individual.[29]

At one level, pre-individual forces may be understood as "memories" and/or reverberations – of the past intrinsic to the present, of virtual intrinsic to the actual. Processes of individuation take place simultaneously across disparate domains – physical, biological, social, psychical, spiritual, actual, and virtual – through an operation that Simondon calls *transduction*:

> By transduction we mean a physical, biological, mental, or social operation through which an activity propagates incrementally within a domain by passing this propagation or structuration of the domain operated from one region to another: each structural region serves as a principle and model, as an initiator for constituting the following region, such that a modification thereby extends progressively throughout this structuring operation.[30]

Transduction, a term belonging to both biology and technology, was also used by Jean Piaget to identify mental operations outside the usual deductive and inductive modes. Simondon expands the concept, giving the example of the *crystal* as "the simplest image of the transductive operation ... which, *starting from a tiny germ*, increases and extends following all the directions in its supersaturated mother liquor", with each already constituted molecular layer making the basis for another layer in the process of forming, the outcome of which is "an amplifying reticular structure".[31] Individuation is a labyrinthine process. Psyche itself may be understood as a labyrinth.

Referring to technology as a way to better understand individuation may surprise some, yet the technological paradigm is valuable; it permits us to regard the genesis of the individuated being "*through an energetic system* of form-taking".[32] Matter and form are then perceived, as it were, in the midst of becoming rather than understood as static givens. The "energetic" aspect is crucial, given that its emphasis rests on *potentiality*, allowing us to think of individuation as an ever-unfolding process.

Individuation is *not* the same as the differentiating individualization expounded by Jung, i.e., the development of the psychological individual as different from the psychology of the collective.[33] As with the rest of the tradition, Jung's version of individuation is atomistic, and a case of reverse engineering. For Simondon, the individual atom is substituted by a continuous ontological process of individuation by means of which the individual subject is perceived as an *effect* of individuation rather than a *cause*. Individuation is what institutes and *includes* differentiation between individuals. The *I* is a process, not a static being; it is a tendency to become undivided, a tendency forever unachievable because of a counter-current of metastability. Acknowledgement of this complex dynamic was already present in seed form in Nietzsche's *dividuum*, and subsequently in Freud's theory of the drives. It then blossomed through rhizomatic philosophy. Inspired by Simondon, Gilles Deleuze will think of identities in terms of difference, which he defined as "the state in which one can speak of determination *as such*".[34]

*

By postulating the notion of the transindividual, Simondon subverts and expands the concerns of both psychology and sociology. Psychology is only able to see the *interindividual* – whether as relatedness, intersubjectivity, mutuality etc – and the *intrapsychic*, a mode of enquiry now relegated to the re-enactment costume dramas of archival Kleinian psychoanalysis so lavishly enacted in psychodynamic training courses. For all its valuable insights, sociology mainly continues to see the *intrasocial*. Both psychology and sociology ignore that what we call the subject is "vaster than the individual".[35] Not taking into account the different pre-individual layers through which a subject is constituted and continues to individuate has two undesirable outcomes: (a) we fail to understand what it means to give birth to a real collective; (b) we fail to realize an individual's actualization.

That the subject is vaster than the individual and is intrinsically involved in the collective implies that different intensive systems are constantly at work in producing a human being and that this will have some influence on how we understand knowledge. For Simondon, knowledge is "the structuring of a relation between two relations in pre-individual tension",[36] a perspective which will be expanded by Deleuze, emphasizing that apprenticeship and/or knowing something is not apprehending a pre-existing entity but instead a temporary outcome of a fluid, differential process that *implicates* the apprentice.

> Qualities, intensities, forms and matters, species and parts are not primary; they are imprisoned in individuals as though in a crystal. Moreover, the entire world may be read, as though in a crystal ball, in the moving depth of individuating differences or differences in intensity.[37]

And yet ...

A while ago I attended the London premier of Laurie Anderson's film *Heart of a Dog,*[38] a meditation on life and death, dreamily circling via animation and Super 8 footage around the death of her beloved dog Lolabelle, poignantly and poetically musing on Kierkegaard, Wittgenstein, 9/11, and wondering aloud about her lost mother. Storytelling, childhood trauma, profound insights from the *Tibetan Book of the Dead*, the impermanence of life, and the fleeting, compelling presence of love: all of this is dancing lightly alongside the poignant realization that every love story is a ghost story and that every time we tell a story, we forget it all the more. The film was particularly moving because of the death two years earlier of her husband, lover, and companion Lou Reed, an artist whose work has been and continues to be of great inspiration to me and whose song *Turning Time Around* accompanies the closing credits. A fleeting silhouette of Reed appears in the footage shot somewhere in the French countryside. After the screening, Anderson spoke briefly about the documentary. With characteristic lightness and erudition, she expounded on the Tibetan Buddhist's perspective of letting go, of allowing the deceased to disentangle themselves from the clutches of life. I am sympathetic to this view. My first contact with the Dharma in my early twenties was in the *Gelugpa* lineage of Tibetan Buddhism where a similar emphasis is present. There are other perspectives within Buddhism. For instance, Kobayashi Issa, zen poet and priest (1763–1828) upon the death of his child wrote the famous haiku: *This dewdrop world is but a dewdrop world. And yet ...* Not piety but compassion: this world is ephemeral, but the presence of loved ones is real and their departure painful. Issa walks the tightrope between an absolute and a relative view of grief, between the wisdom-that-knows-impermanence and the pain of loss.

I don't know what took hold of me at that film preview – perhaps a mixture of contrariness, a foolish longing to hold on to Lou's memory, plus an ancestral call from the recesses of Southern Europe where I had my first schooling in mourning. Whatever the reason, during the Q&A session which followed the screening I voiced my objection to the spiritual view of letting go. I told of my irritation when, sitting next to the body of my deceased father years before,

I was urged by a family friend to cry openly, to "let it all out". But at that moment I had no tears. I simply wanted everybody to be out of the room and to whisper goodbye to my father alone. In the Italian South, the expectation and cultural pressure is to cry. In the years of my childhood, it was still possible to see a funeral procession accompanied by the *prefiche*, professional mourners, usually, women (boys don't cry!) paid to weep at funerals, a practice that goes back to ancient times, to Egypt, Rome, and China. There is wisdom in that too – and the ambivalence intrinsic to wisdom. Tears make a body of water. Without tears, it becomes difficult for the departed to journey to the other shore. Mourning may be for the survivors, but the ritual focuses first and foremost on the departed. All mirrors in a Southern European home used to be shrouded in black, a lugubrious sight to some but also an expedient way to ensure the dead do not get confused and held back by the many reflections and are then more able to make their last journey.

Notes

1 Karl Marx, *Capital*, trans. B. Brewster, London: New Left Review, 1976, p91. The initial inspiration for this chapter was found in a paper by Jean-Hughes Barthélémy, 'Du mort qui saisit le vif': Simondonian Ontology Today', translated by Justin Clemens, in Arne de Boever, Alex Murray, Jon Roffe and Ashley Woodward (eds) *Gilbert Simondon: Being and Technology*, Edinburgh University Press, 2012, pp110–120.

2 Justin Clemens, *Notes* to 'Du mort qui saisit le vif', op.cit., p119.

3 Auguste Comte, *Early Political Writings*, H. S. Jones (ed.), Cambridge: Cambridge University Press, 1998.

4 Jean-Claude Ameisen, *La Sculpture du vivant. Le Suicide cellulaire ou la mort créatrice*, trans. Justin Clemens. Paris: Seuil, 2003, p16.

5 On the subject of apoptosis, here is a handful of useful titles:

    F.R. Kerr, Andrew H. Wyllie, Alastair R. Currie, 'Apoptosis: a basic biological phenomenon with wide-ranging implications in tissue kinetics', *British Journal of Cancer*, 26, 1972, pp239–257.

    Valerie A. Fadok and Giovanna Chimini, 'The phagocytosis of apoptotic cells', *Seminars in immunology*, 13, 2001, pp365–372.

6 Richard A. Lockshin, 'Programmed cell death: history and future of a concept', *National Library of Medicine*, PMID: 16471256. DOI: 10.1051/jbio:2005017

7 Elizabeth Grosz, 'Identity and Individuation: Some Feminist Reflection', in *Gilbert Simondon: Being and Technology*, op.cit., pp37–56; p41.

8 Mikami Kayo, *The Body as Vessel: Approaching the Methodology of Hijikata Tatsumi's Ankoku* Butō. Birchington, KT: Ozaru Books, p73.

9 Gilbert Simondon, *Individuation in Light of Notions of Form and Information*, trans. by Taylor Adkins, Minneapolis, London: University of Minnesota Press, 2020.

10 This and further discussions on passages from this text, as yet untranslated into English, rely on highlighted citations in the paper by Jean-Hughes Barthélémy, 'Du mort qui saisit le vif': Simondonian Ontology Today' cited above, note 1.
11 Gilbert Simondon, *Individuation in Light of Notions of Form and Information*, op.cit., p2
12 Miguel de Beistegui, Science and Ontology: from Merleau-Ponty's 'Reduction' to Simondon's 'Transduction', in *Gilbert Simondon: Being and Technology*, op.cit., p169.
13 Gilbert Simondon, *L'Individu et sa genèse physico-biologique,* Grenoble: Jérôme Millon, 1995, p213.
14 Jean-Hughes Barthélémy, 'Du mort qui saisit le vif', op.cit., p113, emphasis in the original.
15 For a more detailed discussion of this point see Manu Bazzano, 'Psychotherapy in an Age of Stupidity', in Manu Bazzano (ed) *Re-Visioning Existential Therapy: Counter-traditional Perspectives.* Abingdon, OX: Routledge, 2021, pp81–93. For a good introduction to the writings of Bernard Stiegler on this subject, see his *States of Shock: Stupidity and Knowledge in the 21st Century*, trans. Daniel Ross. Cambridge: Polity.
16 Dōgen Kigen *The Heart of Dōgen's Shōbōgenzō*, Trans. By Norman Waddell and Masao Abe, New York: SUNY, p38.
17 Martin Heidegger, *Being and Time.* Trans. by John Macquarrie and Edward Robinson. Oxford: Blackwell, 1962.
18 Nishitani Kenji wrote: 'In such ideas as amor fati and the Dionysian ... Nietzsche came closest to Buddhism, and especially to Mahayana', Graham Parkes, 'The Orientation of the Nietzschean Text', in Graham Parkes (ed) *Nietzsche and Asian Thought.* Chicago, ILL: University of Chicago Press, 1991, p3–19; p13. For a comparative study of Nietzsche and Zen: Manu Bazzano, *Buddha is Dead: Nietzsche and the Dawn of European Zen.* Brighton: Sussex Academic Press, 2006.
19 Theodor Adorno, *The Jargon of Authenticity.* Trans. by Knut Tarnowski and Frederic Will. Evanston, ILL: Northwestern University Press, 1973.
20 Jacques Derrida, *Of Grammatology*, translated by Gayatri Chakravorty Spivak. Baltimore, Md: John Hopkins University Press, 1967, p69.
21 Jacques Derrida, 'Last Interview', *Le Monde*, 19 August 2004. https://xdoc.mx/preview/jacques-derrida-the-last-interview-5ee3ef135e5a3 Retrieved 14 September 2022.
22 Kurt Goldstein, *The Organism.* Foreword by Oliver Sacks. New York: Zone Books, 2000.
23 Dominique Lecourt, 'The Question of the Individual in Georges Canguilhem and Gilbert Simondon', translated by Arne de Boever, *Being and Technology*, op.cit., pp176–184; p177.
24 Georges Canguilhem, *Knowledge of Life*, ed. Paola Marrati and Todd Meyers, trans. Stefanos Geroulanos and Daniela Ginsburg. New York: Fordham University Press, 2008, p111.
25 'The Question of the Individual in Georges Canguilhem and Gilbert Simondon', op.cit., p182.
26 Gilbert Simondon, 'The Genesis of the Individual' in J. Crary and S. Kwinter (eds), *Incorporations.* New York: Zone, 1993, pp297–317; p300.
27 Elizabeth Grosz, 'Identity and Individuation', op.cit., p38.
28 Gilles Deleuze, *Difference and Repetition*, trans. Paul Patton. London: Athlone, 1994, p246.
29 Elizabeth Grosz, 'Identity and Individuation', op.cit, p41.

30 Gilbert Simondon, *Individuation in Light of Notions of Form and Information*, op.cit., p13.
31 Ibid, p13, emphasis added.
32 Ibid, p.31, emphasis in the original.
33 Carl Gustav Jung, *Psychological Types*. Abingdon, OX: Routledge, 2022.
34 Gilles Deleuze, *Difference and Repetition*, trans. Paul Patton. London: Athlone, 1994, p28.
35 Gilbert Simondon, *Du Mode d'Existence des Objects Techniques*. Paris: Aubier, 1958, p248.
36 Sean Bowden, *Gilles Deleuze, a Reader of Gilbert Simondon*, in *Gilbert Simondon: Being and Technology*, op.cit., pp135–153; p148.
37 *Difference and Repetition*, op.cit., p247.
38 Laurie Anderson, *Heart of a Dog* IMDB, 2015 https://www.imdb.com/title/tt4935446/

Index

Printed in Great Britain
by Amazon

46040674R00163